Understanding
Death of a Salesman

A scene from the first daydream sequence of *Death of a Salesman*. The actors in the 1958 *CBC Folio* production are Leslie Nielsen as Biff, Albert Dekker as Willy, and George Carron as Happy. Courtesy of the Canadian Broadcasting Corporation.

UNDERSTANDING
Death of a Salesman

A STUDENT CASEBOOK TO ISSUES, SOURCES, AND HISTORICAL DOCUMENTS

Brenda Murphy and Susan C. W. Abbotson

The Greenwood Press
"Literature in Context" Series
Claudia Durst Johnson, Series Editor

GREENWOOD PRESS
Westport, Connecticut • London

Library of Congress Cataloging-in-Publication Data

Murphy, Brenda.
     Understanding Death of a salesman : a student casebook to issues,
sources, and historical documents / Brenda Murphy and Susan C.W.
Abbotson.
       p.   cm.—(Greenwood Press "Literature in context" series,
ISSN 1074–598X)
     Includes bibliographical references and index.
     ISBN 0–313–30402–5 (alk. paper)
     1. Miller, Arthur, 1915– Death of a salesman. 2. Literature and
society—United States—History—20th century—Sources. 3. United
States—Social conditions—20th century. 4. Miller, Arthur, 1915–
—Sources. 5. Sales personnel—United States. 6. Success—United
States. I. Abbotson, Susan C. W., 1961– . II. Title.
III. Series.
PS3525.I5156D4358   1999
812'.52—dc21   98–26437

British Library Cataloguing in Publication Data is available.

Library of Congress Catalog Card Number: 98–26437
ISBN: 0–313–30402–5
ISSN: 1074–598X

First published in 1999

Greenwood Press, 88 Post Road West, Westport, CT 06881
An imprint of Greenwood Publishing Group, Inc.

Printed in the United States of America

The paper used in this book complies with the
Permanent Paper Standard issued by the National
Information Standards Organization (Z39.48–1984).

10 9 8 7 6 5 4 3 2 1

Contents

Introduction

The premiere of *Death of a Salesman* on February 10, 1949, was a significant event in the history of the American theatre. Recognized from its opening night as one of the greatest achievements by an American playwright, *Salesman* ran for an extraordinary 742 performances on Broadway, winning the Pulitzer Prize, the Donaldson Award, and the New York Drama Critics Circle Award for best play of the season. In July it opened in London, beginning a stage life that has gone on continuously ever since. The play's immense popularity through the years has demonstrated that it has something to say to audiences across several generations and in diverse cultures throughout the world. Landmark productions have been staged in France, Germany, England, Australia, Russia, and China, where it was directed by Miller himself.

Death of a Salesman has had even wider influence in its film and television versions. It was first filmed in 1951. It has been televised in England by the BBC and in Canada by the CBC. In the United States, a 1966 CBS television production with the original stars, Lee J. Cobb and Mildred Dunnock, reached an audience of 17 million viewers. In 1985 a new CBS television version based on the 1984 Broadway revival, with Dustin Hoffman, Kate Reid, and John Malkovich, reached an audience of 25 million. In book form, *Death of a Salesman* was the first play to be included as a Book-of-the-Month Club selection. By 1968, a million copies had been sold. Universally recognized as the greatest of American plays, it has been included in academic courses and reading lists throughout the world. Willy Loman's tragedy has become a central element of America's vision of itself and of the world's vision of America.

One of the play's important contributions to world theatre was its theatrical style, which is closely linked to its new conception of dramatic form. Arthur Miller's collaboration with director Elia Kazan, designer Jo Mielziner, composer Alex North, and producer Kermit Bloomgarden, as well as the actors of the first Broadway production—Lee J. Cobb as Willy, Mildred Dunnock as Linda, Arthur Kennedy as Biff, and Cameron Mitchell as Hap—fully realized a new theatrical style that had been evolving on the postwar American stage. The new, fluid dramatic form that Miller developed in the process of collaboration made possible what he called his "mobile concurrency of past and present" in the play. This approach to dramatic form exploded the traditional distinction between realism, which represents the events on stage as actually taking place within the "reality" of the world on stage, and expressionism, which represents the events on stage as taking place within the mind of a single character. Miller's approach to dramatic structure enables the audience of *Death of a Salesman* to experience the disintegration of Willy Loman's mind as Willy experiences it. While the play is firmly anchored in the mundane events of the Loman family's present reality, the past, in the form of Willy's memories, intrudes ever more insistently upon the audience's consciousness as well as Willy's until, in the restaurant scene, where Biff's discovery of Willy with The Woman is also staged, Willy's subjective experience of the past is more intensely real on stage than the action that is taking place outwardly in the social "reality" of the final day of his life.

This new dramatic style, called subjective realism, was made possible only when designer Jo Mielziner conceived of a way to make the physical changes from present to past as instantaneous on the set as the time changes in Willy's mind. Mielziner achieved the change in time almost entirely through the use of light rather than through traditional set changes, flooding the stage with amber light and projections of green leaves during the memory scenes and surrounding the darkened Loman house with the threatening shapes of towering apartment houses during the scenes in the present. Together with the technique that Mielziner called "abstract realism"—a minimal use of furniture and props that were real in themselves combined with structures, like the Lomans' house, that became merely skeletal as the eye traveled upward—this experimentation with light was the cornerstone of what became known as the "American style" in the modern theatre. Juxtaposed with director Elia Kazan's intense and visual version of The Method, an American theory of acting and directing derived from the Russian director Konstantin Stanislavsky's system, the new staging created a tense energy on the stage that emphasized the inherent conflicts in Miller's play between past and present, the objective and the subjective, the realistic and the expressionistic.

Death of a Salesman has been no less important as dramatic literature than as a production. From the time of its premiere, the play has been the subject of a spirited critical debate, centering on some of the most significant issues in the discussion of modern drama. The issue that received the earliest and the most sustained attention was the play's status as a tragedy. To the opening-night newspaper critics, there was no question that what they were seeing was, as Howard Barnes called it, "a soaring tragedy." Robert Coleman wrote that " 'Death of a Salesman' is a play written along the lines of the finest classical tragedy. It is the revelation of a man's downfall, a destruction whose roots are entirely in his own soul. The play builds to an immutable conflict where there is no resolution for this man in this life." In the years since the premiere, whether the play is a tragedy, and whether writing a tragedy about a modern life like Willy Loman's is either appropriate or possible, have become perennial issues for debate by critics and scholars. Can *Death of a Salesman* be a tragedy if its hero does not fall from a high position and undergoes no fundamental process of learning and transcendence as a result of his experience?

One aspect of the debate was raised by critic John Mason Brown, who called Willy "a little man sentenced to discover his smallness rather than a big man undone by his greatness" (*Saturday Review* 32 [26 February 1949]: 31). In "Tragedy and the Common Man" (*New York Times*, 27 February 1949: Sec. 2, 1), published a few days later, Arthur Miller set forth an important definition of tragedy in the twentieth century: "I believe that the common man is as apt a subject for tragedy in its highest sense as kings were" and that "the thrust for freedom is the quality in tragedy which exalts." Classical tragedy emphasizes the hero's guilt for his violation of a higher, divinely willed order and the necessity of sacrificing him in order to restore that order. Rejecting this concept, Miller insisted on the individual's right to self-actualization and to personal freedom, rights he assumed were inherently human. Miller's notions of good and evil and of the individual's relation to society were entirely in keeping with the values of the post–World War II United States in which the play was written.

Recognizing the difference in Miller's new tragedy, some critics saw a contradiction between Miller's criticism of American society and its values in the play and his use of the tragic form. Eric Bentley said that Miller was either "a Marxist who, consciously or unconsciously, lacks the courage of his convictions" or "a 'tragic' artist who without knowing it has been confused by Marxism." The question of *Salesman*'s social statement has been a major issue in the debate over the play for fifty years. Miller has been criticized for presenting Willy's failure as the inevitable end of a man who has finally broken under the pressures of an economic system that he is fatally incapable of understanding.

In 1957, in the introduction to his *Collected Plays*, Miller responded to this kind of criticism by saying that "a play cannot be equated with a political philosophy." But he also made it clear that he sees Willy's tragedy in the fact that "Willy Loman has broken a law without whose protection life is insupportable if not incomprehensible to him and to many others; it is the law which says that a failure in society and in business has no right to live." While Miller refused to allow his play to be reduced to its political implications, he made those implications clear whenever he had the opportunity.

Although Miller provides a great deal of information about the myths, beliefs, and mores of the United States in the 1940s, it enhances one's understanding of the play to learn about the issues of the time in more detail. This detail is provided by a number of the selections in the following chapters. Considering *Death of a Salesman* through social documents from a wide range of sources not only better elucidates the ideas and feelings prevalent at a time long before most of the play's newer students were born, it also assists such students in better determining the play's continued relevance and importance.

A working knowledge of the play is a necessary prerequisite to eliciting the full potential benefit from the following chapters, as they ask for responses that demand a degree of familiarity with the characters, events, and general concerns of *Death of a Salesman*. The first chapter offers a basic literary analysis of the play that serves as both background and starting point for further considerations. It outlines the essential structure of the play, which, through Miller's use of dissonant theatrical idioms and a complex time scheme, reflects the numerous conflicts contained within the minds and actions of the characters. Subsequent chapters highlight the most interesting of these conflicts by presenting documents pertinent to American culture during the years Willy and Linda would have grown up, through the events of the play itself, and beyond.

These selections have been chosen to illustrate thoughts, moods, and ideas covering the span of the twentieth century, all of which are relevant to any discussion of the play. While a number of the central characters in *Death of a Salesman* were born in the nineteenth century and spent their formative years absorbing the ways of thinking of that era, others, like Biff, Hap, and Bernard, formed their ideas about life in the 1920s. The play actually takes place in 1948 but has continued to have an impact up to the present day, due both to its universal themes and to the continuance of certain beliefs and mores it illustrates, as is evident from a number of the more recent documents included in this volume.

The materials provided here come from a variety of disciplines: history, sociology, psychology, popular culture, business, and literature. They help to build a social and historical background for the play that offers students interesting and useful issues to explore. They help students to gain a better understanding of both the full impact of the play when it was first produced and the ways in which its themes have remained relevant to current audiences.

A number of broad questions about the play are raised:

- How does a grasp of the commonly held cultural beliefs about American destiny and its convoluted value systems lead us to an understanding of the conflicts families like the Lomans continually face?

- How does information about economic interests and forces of the era shed light on the lives and decisions of the characters in the play?

- How does knowledge about the history of traveling salesmen in America help us to better understand Willy Loman's conflicting senses of unreasonable optimism and failure and the problems faced by his children?
- How do commentaries on male and female roles bring into focus questions raised by the play over family and gender expectations?
- How does information about the role of sports and leisure in American society deepen our appreciation of the relationship among sports, business, and American cultural values?
- How can a play influence a culture, and what does that say about both the play and the wider culture that has been affected?

A variety of different cultural records and sources are excerpted here as material for our study of *Death of a Salesman*:

- juvenile and adult fiction
- advertisements
- song lyrics
- magazine articles
- newspaper articles
- a memoir
- historical and sociological studies
- how-to books
- an editorial
- an obituary
- a survey
- a self-test
- essays
- interviews
- a speech
- a diary

These materials have been selected to work with *Death of a Salesman* to bring the issues the play raises into sharper focus. In addition to the documents, each chapter also contains an introductory essay, study questions, topics for writing and discussion, and a list of suggested readings.

1 ───────────────────────────────

The Significance of *Death of a Salesman*

THE NATURE OF THE PLAY

Death of a Salesman is a unique achievement as a play. It is a compelling drama about an American family whose members are unable to communicate the love that they feel for each other or the existential despair that each of them experiences. It is a modern tragedy, moving relentlessly and inevitably from its opening scene to Willy Loman's death. It is an experimental piece of drama and theatre, a melding of the two styles that were prevalent on the stage at the time it was written and produced, realism and expressionism, into a unique theatrical idiom. It is also a pointed critique of the society it depicts and a rejection of some of the basic values that its author saw being lived out in the United States of the 1940s.

The plot is built on a double time scheme. The main "stage time" is the "today" of Willy Loman's world, 1948, when Arthur Miller wrote the play. As the play opens, Willy returns home in the middle of the night from a sales trip that was supposed to take him from his home in Brooklyn to New England, which is his sales territory. He has cut the trip short because he cannot concentrate on his driving and has nearly hit a child in Yonkers, just north of New York City. He talks to his wife, Linda, who tries to soothe him, and then he goes to the kitchen to get a glass of milk. Talking to himself about the past, Willy wakes his sons, Hap, thirty-two, who is staying with his parents rather than in his own apartment to spend time with his brother Biff, thirty-four, who is home for a visit from Texas, where he has been working on a ranch. The brothers talk briefly about their lives and ambitions and go back to sleep.

The scene then shifts to Willy in the kitchen, who gradually enters into a daydream about the past, fixing on a time seventeen years earlier, when his boys were in high school. The younger boys appear as characters, and the world of 1931 is realized on the stage as Willy talks with his sons about his hopes for their future and about Biff's career as a high school football hero. Willy then talks with Linda, offering her a number of justifications for not having sold more on his recent trip. Then a third level of reality appears, as Willy succumbs within his daydream to an image of a character who is called simply The Woman, a buyer's secretary with whom he has been having an affair on the road. As he comes out of that daydream, he is remorseful toward Linda, telling her he will make it up to her. Then he becomes increasingly agitated as she and the neighbor boy, Bernard, warn him that Biff is getting into trouble, shouting back at them that he never taught Biff anything but decent things. The scene then shifts back to 1948, as Hap, awakened by Willy's shouting, comes downstairs to quiet him, and his neighbor and friend, Bernard's father, Charley, comes over to engage him in a card game to help him get to sleep.

The play continues on the dual time scheme, with two plot lines. The 1948 action proceeds through a series of scenes that culminate in Willy's suicide; the 1931 action proceeds through a series of scenes that culminate in Biff's discovery of Willy's affair and his disillusionment with his father. The 1948 plot includes the following scenes:

- a scene with Linda and the sons, in which she tells them that Willy is breaking down and has been trying to kill himself;
- a scene in which Biff promises Willy that he will try to get his old boss, Bill Oliver, who fired him when he stole merchandise, to lend him money to start a sporting goods business;
- a scene with Willy and his boss, Howard Wagner, in which Willy tries to get a job in New York so he won't have to travel anymore

and is fired instead because he loses control of himself and attacks
Wagner;

- a scene in which Willy goes to borrow money from Charley and
  encounters Bernard, now a successful lawyer, who questions him
  about Biff's failure to go to college seventeen years earlier;

- a scene in which Biff and Hap go off with two women and leave
  Willy in a restaurant after Biff tells Willy he has stolen Bill Oliver's
  pen and has no appointment to see him about the sporting goods
  business;

- a scene in which Linda confronts the boys with their irresponsibility toward their father, and Biff says that he will leave in order
  not to upset Willy anymore;

- a scene in which Biff confronts Willy with the truth, that the Lomans are not special beings, but "a dime a dozen," and begs Willy
  to drop his inflated dreams for him;

- a scene in which Willy, realizing that Biff loves him, and still thinking that his son could be "magnificent" with the help of his
  $20,000 life insurance policy, goes off to kill himself;

- a "Requiem" scene in which the family stands at Willy's graveside,
  trying to understand him.

The meaning of these events in the present is provided largely
by the events that take place in the daydream scenes of 1931. In
these scenes:

- Willy passes up the chance to work for his brother Ben in Alaska
  because he feels he is building a future with the Wagner firm, and
  Ben appears several times as an embodiment of the success myth
  that Willy is trying to live up to, Ben supposedly having walked
  into the jungle at age seventeen and emerged at twenty-one a
  wealthy man;

- the family leaves to see Biff play in a championship football game
  at Ebbets Field;

- Biff flunks math, goes to Boston to see Willy, finds him with The
  Woman, and, completely disillusioned with Willy, refuses to consider going to summer school so that he can go to the University
  of Virginia as planned.

In a conventional realistic play, the events that take place in 1931
would be treated as exposition, probably related by one character

to another in an early scene in order to provide the motivation that drives Willy's actions in 1948. By creating a dual time frame for the play, Miller enables the audience to experience these events just as Willy does, simultaneously with the "objective reality" of the events in 1948. In doing this, he gives the audience's empathy with Willy a greater immediacy and a greater depth. He also provides a second plot line that creates interest and suspense. If the audience were simply watching Willy plod inevitably on to his suicide, the experience of watching the play would be relentlessly bleak and somber. Miller uses the events of 1931 to create another source of suspense with the question, What happened between Willy and Biff? By treating the scenes in the past as they are colored in Willy's mind, with an idyllic hopefulness, Miller is also able to change the mood of the play in these scenes to an upbeat and even humorous one that contrasts with the hopelessness of the Lomans' current reality.

THEMES AND ISSUES

Death of a Salesman takes place a few years after World War II has ended. America is enjoying a postwar economic boom, but the war has caused a shake-up in American society, changing the way people view business, leisure, themselves, and others. Not everyone can keep up with the times. The Lomans live in Brooklyn, a busy suburb of New York City. In the years they have lived there they have watched their house being gradually surrounded by new apartment construction.

The set of *Death of a Salesman* presents Willy as living in a claustrophobic urban setting indicative of the harsh life he has chosen. His home is surrounded by apartment houses that emanate a threatening orange glow. When memory takes over, this glow gives way to a more dreamlike background with shadowy leaves and music, evoking a happier pastoral era. At the close of the play, however, we see the looming "hard towers of the apartment buildings" dominating the setting once more. Without Willy's memories, the dream of a happier, Edenic life cannot exist in this city.

Many of Willy's activities can be seen as highly symbolic. He plants seeds just as he plants false hopes: both will die and never come to fruition, largely because the house has become too hemmed in by the city. The front porch, constructed from stolen lumber, is indicative of how the Lomans' live, as well as their house, have been built on something false. Willy does not fit into the modern world of machinery. The values he espouses, where deals are made with a smile and a handshake, are clearly those of a bygone age. To illustrate this point, Miller frequently depicts Willy's uneasy relationship with machinery such as his car, his refrigerator, and Howard's tape recorder.

Analysis of the play's social statement has centered mostly on its treatment of the "American Dream" or "success myth," the notion that any American can achieve material success and a comfortable life through hard work and devotion to business. While there has been some effort to defend Miller as an upholder of the American Dream, most critics who have written on this subject have attempted to explain Willy's demise as a failure on his, and often Miller's, part to comprehend American history and values. Willy's failure to achieve the American Dream is a personal one, this line of reasoning goes, not an inevitable result of the American economic system. Willy fails because he never understands what is really needed to succeed in business, insisting to the end that "personality wins the day," when, as Charley says, he ought to know from experience that "all you have is what you can sell."

Willy has convinced himself that the way to succeed is to be well liked, and he passes this belief on to his two sons. However, Miller makes it clear by his assortment of characters that being well liked has little to do with success. In the world of *Death of a Salesman*, people get ahead through hard work (Charley and Bernard), inheritance (Howard), or sheer luck (Ben). Neither Howard nor Ben wastes any time trying to be liked, and both are depicted as selfish, brusque, and rude. Howard represents an uncaring and exploitative business world in which being well liked holds no relevance. Ben is a hard man who survives the jungle by plundering it. Charley, on the other hand, is successful, content, and a nice guy. He is satisfied with moderate success without feeling compelled to be the best. He doesn't take any shortcuts but relies on steady, hard work, and he has taught these lessons to his son Bernard.

As children, Biff and Happy idolized their father and looked down on Bernard for his more cautious lifestyle and belief in work. But Willy neglects to instill in his sons the moral values a parent should teach a child. Biff appears successful in high school as a football player, but he reaps no benefit from this because he never goes to college. Away from his father, Biff gains self-knowledge and begins to recognize his own true nature, replacing his father's dream with one of his own. Whether or not Biff can achieve his dream of working on the land is not as important as the fact that it is more suited to his nature. Happy does not reach the same level of awareness as his brother, and lives a shallow life which he pretends is a lot more glamorous than it really is. Bereft of even the few decencies Willy retains, such as a conscience and a sense of responsibility, Happy cuts an entirely disreputable figure, taking bribes from manufacturers and sleeping with the fiancées and wives of men higher in the firm than he.

Linda Loman's central importance seems to be as a voice of protest and outrage against what is happening to her husband. While dreams, illusions, and self-deceptions feed the action of this play, Linda, in contrast, seems very much planted in reality with her concerns over house payments, mending, insurance premiums, and her husband's care. Yet despite Linda's clear sight she allows her family's dreams to flourish; she even encourages them.

One of the most hotly debated issues in recent years has been the depiction of women in the play, particularly Linda. Early critics generally saw Linda as a positive representation, and sometimes an ideal, of the loyal, nurturing wife and mother. This view was disputed during the sixties and seventies, however, as critics informed by the new feminist movement questioned the basic assumptions about marriage and the role of women in society that this view implied. At this time, some critics began blaming Linda for collaborating in Willy's unrealistic fantasies and for remaining passive as her family was being destroyed around her. Linda has even been described by Charlotte Epstein as prodding Willy to his doom.

In the eighties and nineties, critics have suggested that Miller creates a world in the play where the most important thing for men is to bond successfully with other men, and women appear as either sex objects or idealized, selfless wives and mothers. In *Death of a Salesman* one finds The Woman and Miss Forsythe on the one hand, and Linda on the other. This view of women is articulated by Hap, who compares his sexual relationships with women to bowling: "I just keep knockin' them over and it doesn't mean anything." Nevertheless, he longs to "find a girl—steady, somebody with substance. . . . Somebody with character, with resistance! Like Mom, y'know?'' While there is a temptation to confuse the Lomans' view of women with Miller's, however, it is important to note that the play exposes the inadequacy of the cultural stereotypes that Willy and Hap apply to women, including Linda. The character of Linda in the daydream scenes, viewed through Willy's remorseful idealization of her, is quite different from the Linda in the scenes of the present, who is, as director Elia Kazan perceived, like a tiger protecting her young when she defends Willy from the boys.

Death of a Salesman, from the first night of its realization on the stage, has been recognized as a significant and controversial play. Throughout the second half of the twentieth century, it has occasioned searching and sometimes heated debate about fundamental literary, cultural, and moral issues. It has served as a site for examining some of the most complex and difficult questions about the relationships among human beings, and between human beings and social institutions, in a democratic society. This volume is intended to provide a broad cultural and literary context in which to continue this exploration and debate.

STUDY QUESTIONS

1. Look at the play's opening stage directions, which are a description of the set that was designed by Jo Mielziner for the original production. Analyze the set as if it were a visual work of art. What meaning does Mielziner convey through the background, the light, the objects on the stage?

2. Biff Loman steals a football from the locker room, a carton of basketballs from Bill Oliver, a suit in Kansas City (in an earlier draft of the play, he says that the suit was Willy's size), and Bill Oliver's pen in the course of the play. What motivations does the play suggest for his stealing? What part does stealing play in his character as a whole?

3. Hap Loman says he suffers from an "overdeveloped sense of competition or something." What are the aspects of Hap's family life that have contributed to this characteristic?

4. Arthur Miller has said that Biff Loman represents "the system of love which is the opposite of the law of success" to which Willy has devoted his life, and which eventually kills him. Discuss the nature of Biff's love for Willy. Why does it fail to save Willy from destruction?

5. The only roles that seem to be open to women in the world of *Death of a Salesman* are those of Linda, the at-home wife and mother, and The Woman, the single working woman who makes do with casual love affairs for her emotional life (Miss Forsythe and Letta seem to be following the path of The Woman). Discuss the advantages and disadvantages that Miller ascribes to each of these roles for women.

6. What purpose do Charley and Bernard serve in the play? What part do they play in developing the characters of the Loman family?

7. Analyze Miller's use of the card game that Willy and Charley play. What is being conveyed about each of the characters and about their relationship in this scene?

8. What purpose does Ben Loman serve in the play? How is he related to Willy's character and to his actions? What is the significance of his appearing only in Willy's mind?

9. Why does Willy kill himself? What is your response to this act as a reader or audience member?

10. What function does the "Requiem" scene play in terms of the plot and in terms of the emotional experience of the audience? Traditional tragedy involves a "katharsis" or "purgation" of the feelings of pity and fear for the hero, in which the audience leaves at peace, feeling that justice has been done. Does this happen with *Death of a Salesman*?

11. At the end of the play, Linda says, "We're free and clear . . . We're free . . . We're free." Discuss Linda's financial situation at the end of the play, assuming that Biff leaves and the insurance company does not pay off on Willy's suicide. What does Miller imply with these lines?

TOPICS FOR WRITTEN OR ORAL EXPLORATION

1. You have the assignment of stage designer for a new production of *Death of a Salesman*. As a group or individually, consider the possibilities for staging the shifts between past and present that are crucial to the play's rhythm and flow, as well as the shifts from room to room in the Loman house and the scenes in Howard's and Charley's offices and the Boston hotel room. Then write your own opening stage directions, describing the set that you would use for the Loman house.

2. You are the merchandise manager of Hap Loman's department store. Write a memo to your boss explaining why you do or do not think Hap should be promoted to Assistant Buyer. Discuss his aptitude for and attention to business as well as his character.

3. Write a character sketch of Biff, explaining his stealing from a psychological point of view.

4. Biff Loman is a deeply divided character who seems to enjoy working on a ranch but is still drawn back to the city periodically to try a business career. He tells Hap that he is "mixed up very bad." As a group or individually, consider the conflicting feelings that are working on Biff at the beginning of the play. Then write an essay explaining why you do or do not think Biff makes the right decision at the end of the play.

5. Write an essay explaining your agreement or disagreement with Hap's statement at the end of the play that Willy had "the only dream you can have—to come out number-one man" and Hap's determination to stay in the city and "win it for him."

6. Choose one of the characters who appears in both the scenes of the present and the scenes of the past—Linda, Biff, Hap, Charley, or Bernard—and analyze the differences between the character as he or she appears in the "reality" of the present and the character as he or she appears in the past, filtered through Willy's memories and emotions.

7. Write Hap Loman's résumé, and Bernard's, presenting their accomplishments as you think each of these characters would present them.

8. Compare and contrast Howard Wagner and Charley as successful

businessmen. How do their characters and their attitudes toward human relationships affect the way they do business?

9. Compare and contrast Biff and Bernard as high school students, and then as young men, concentrating on the qualities that Miller suggests will lead to success.

10. Write an essay on "How to Succeed in Business, According to Ben Loman." Try to extract Ben's business principles from his actions and his advice throughout the play.

11. In traditional tragedy, the hero violates a divine or social order and is destroyed for this violation, but achieves some kind of enlightenment or deeper understanding as a result of his destruction. In some modern tragedies, this enlightenment may occur for the audience or another character instead of the hero. Write an essay in which you defend your opinion on whether or not *Death of a Salesman* is a tragedy.

12. Some critics have seen *Death of a Salesman* as a criticism of the basic American economic system, blaming capitalism for Willy's destruction. Arthur Miller has pointed out that the most decent person in the play, Charley, is a businessman and a capitalist. Discuss the treatment of American business values in the play. Is it the system, or individual characters who abuse the system, or Willy's own failure that makes for Willy's destruction?

13. Evaluate Linda Loman as a wife and mother.

14. Write an essay in which you explain whether you would rather be in the position of Linda Loman or the position of The Woman, comparing and contrasting the advantages and disadvantages of each. Remember the time period in which the play is set.

15. Some critics see Linda Loman as partially, or even mostly, responsible for Willy's suicide. Write an essay in which you develop both sides of the argument on this question, explaining which argument you find to be stronger.

16. Taking on the role of Biff as he was at seventeen, write Biff's personal statement for his application to the University of Virginia.

17. Ralph Waldo Emerson wrote, "Things are in the saddle, and ride mankind." Write an essay in which you explain how his statement applies to the Loman family.

SUGGESTED READINGS

This is a selection of criticism related to the discussion of *Death of a Salesman* in the Introduction and Chapter 1. It includes the articles and reviews cited there as well as several discussions of the critical issues that are raised. Although it represents only a small portion of the substantial body of criticism that exists on the play, it offers a suggestion of the variety of viewpoints on the major critical issues.

Aarnes, William. "Tragic Form and the Possibility of Meaning in *Death of a Salesman.*" *Furman Studies* 29 (1983): 57–80.

Austin, Gayle. "The Exchange of Women and Male Homosocial Desire in Arthur Miller's *Death of a Salesman* and Lillian Hellman's *Another Part of the Forest.*" In *Feminist Rereadings of Modern American Drama.* Ed. June Schlueter. Rutherford, NJ: Fairleigh Dickinson University Press, 1989. 59–67.

Barnes, Howard. "A Great Play Is Born." New York *Herald Tribune*, 11 February 1949: 14.

Bentley, Eric. "Back to Broadway." *Theatre Arts* 33 (November 1949): 12–15.

Bigsby, C.W.E. *A Critical Introduction to Twentieth-Century American Drama.* Vol. 2: *Tennessee Williams, Arthur Miller, Edward Albee.* New York: Cambridge University Press, 1984.

Bliquez, Guerin. "Linda's Role in *Death of a Salesman.*" *Modern Drama* 10 (February 1968): 383–86.

Clurman, Harold. "The Success Dream on the American Stage." *Tomorrow* 8 (May 1949): 48–51.

——. "Theatre: Attention!" *New Republic* 120 (28 February 1949): 26–28.

Coleman, Robert. " 'Death of a Salesman' Is Emotional Dynamite." New York *Daily Mirror*, 11 February 1949.

Epstein, Charlotte. "Was Linda Loman Willy's Downfall?" *New York Times*, 20 July 1975, section 2:5.

Graybill, Robert V. "Why Does Biff Boff Bimbos? Innocence as Evil in *Death of a Salesman.*" *Publications of the Arkansas Philological Society* 13 (Fall 1987): 46–53.

Jackson, Esther Merle. "*Death of a Salesman*: Tragic Myth in the Modern Theatre." *CLA Journal* 7 (September 1963): 63–76.

Kazan, Elia. *Elia Kazan: A Life.* New York: Knopf, 1988.

Martin, Robert A. "Arthur Miller: Tragedy and Commitment." *Michigan Quarterly Review* 8 (Summer 1969): 176–78.

McMahon, Helen. "Arthur Miller's Common Man: The Problem of the Realistic and the Mythic." *Drama and Theatre* 10 (1972): 128–33.

Mielziner, Jo. *Designing for the Theatre: A Memoir and a Portfolio.* New York: Bramhall House, 1965.

Miller, Arthur. *Arthur Miller's Collected Plays.* New York: Viking, 1957.

——. *Death of a Salesman.* New York: Viking, 1949.

————. *Timebends: A Life*. New York: Grove, 1987.

————. "Tragedy and the Common Man." *New York Times*, 27 February 1949, section 2: 1, 3.

Murphy, Brenda. *Miller: Death of a Salesman*. Plays in Production Series. New York: Cambridge University Press, 1995.

Stanton, Kay. "Women and the American Dream of *Death of a Salesman*." In *Feminist Rereadings of Modern American Drama*. Ed. June Schlueter. Rutherford, NJ: Fairleigh Dickinson University Press, 1989. 67–103.

Steinberg, M. W. "Arthur Miller and the Idea of Modern Tragedy." *Dalhousie Review* 40 (1961): 329–40.

Trowbridge, Clinton W. "Arthur Miller: Between Pathos and Tragedy." *Modern Drama* 9 (December 1967): 221–32.

Williams, Raymond. "The Realism of Arthur Miller." *Critical Quarterly* 1 (1959): 140–49.

2

Cultural Myths and Values

Miller tells us that *Death of a Salesman* was written to reflect the contemporary scene of the late 1940s. Born toward the end of the nineteenth century, by the 1940s Willy Loman is "past sixty years of age" and reaching the end of his life. For more than forty years he has striven to be a success and has tried to pass on his beliefs to his sons. However, his struggles have not been influenced entirely by the mores and beliefs of the 1940s, although they have certainly been affected by them. Willy's direction in life has been determined by beliefs to which he has been exposed throughout his life, from the end of the last century up until this moment. Therefore, we need to consider not only the state of society in the late 1940s, but American social values from the turn of the century, especially those prevalent during Willy's most formative years of adolescence. To this end, some of the documents included here were written long before the 1940s.

The Declaration of Independence promised every American citizen the right to life, liberty, and the pursuit of happiness. While the first two rights are relatively unproblematic when it comes to deciphering what they mean, the third lies at the heart of numerous dilemmas as people strive to determine exactly what might bring them happiness. In the 1840s John L. O'Sullivan summed up a popular American belief of the time by speaking of a "mani-

fest destiny" by which all Americans are born to potential greatness. Many Americans do have great expectations of life, and any
failure in achievement leads to keen disappointment. In his own
search for happiness, Willy can be viewed as an everyman figure
whose personal dilemmas speak to all times and to all people, but
to Americans in particular. The documents in this chapter, taken
from magazines, advertisements, and essays or speeches by notable figures, cover an array of opinions regarding popular American myths. We need to determine which of these beliefs may have
been influential in the lives of the Loman family and their friends.

It is evident that Willy Loman's family experience has been influential in his development. Both Willy's father and his older
brother, Ben, are portrayed as archetypal pioneers—men who
have successfully tamed the West—whom Willy has often been
tempted to emulate, despite their evident self-absorption and lack
of compassion. However, their sense of freedom and adventure
clashes with Willy's more humane sense of responsibility as well
as his caution, for Willy is the product not only of his family upbringing, but of a far wider array of cultural myths and values. It
is little wonder that Willy is unable to find happiness, for he is
continuously being influenced by conflicting ideologies that never
allow him to feel any satisfaction. This chapter explores some of
those conflicts.

American society, since its inception, has simultaneously embraced a number of beliefs and myths that often seem to conflict
when closely considered. These varied beliefs have led to many
internal divisions and dissensions among the American populace.
This chapter examines the essential differences between the Protestant work ethic and a variety of success myths, the clash between
the lure of the pastoral and the lure of the big city, and the different ways American culture views the young as opposed to the old.
Tracing how far Willy and his family are affected by each of these
conflicts allows for insights into both the characters and the society
they inhabit. With the cast of *Death of a Salesman*, Miller explores
and confronts each of these divisions, showing the audience the
dangers and advantages of living in a divided society such as that
of the United States.

THE PROTESTANT WORK ETHIC VS. MYTHS OF SUCCESS

The Protestant work ethic was brought to America by the Puritans, who believed that the way to contentment lies through hard, honest labor, thrift, and a pride of craftsmanship. Indolence was seen as sinful and as an inevitable source of misery. It was on such beliefs that America was largely founded, and all Americans owe a debt to this viewpoint. However, in time the desire for success began to overshadow belief in hard work. A variety of "get rich quick" myths of success sprang up from the late nineteenth century onwards, many of which stressed finding the speediest road to riches with the least amount of effort.

However, not every vision of success privileges the accumulation of money. The Lomans may benefit from uncovering goals more suited to their own particular strengths and talents by which to measure success and find contentment. The following selections offer a number of views on success and how to attain it. We need to weigh the merits of these different assertions and decide for ourselves if any are realistic. We should also consider the effect such varied views might have on the consciousnesses and belief systems of the characters in *Death of a Salesman*.

Americans have a tendency to idolize success, paying homage to artists who get rave reviews, businessmen who make the largest profits, or politicians who win by a landslide. In *Death of a Salesman*, Miller tries to show a clear moral distinction between the success of callous people like Ben Loman and Howard Wagner, whose greed and selfishness win them fortunes at the cost of others, and people like Charley and Bernard, whose success is tempered with a concern for others. Willy foolishly admires the Bens of his world more than the Charleys. However, in America, being successful brings prestige, respect, and the envy of others, virtually regardless of how that success was achieved; while those who are unsuccessful lose prestige, respect, and support from their fellow citizens. In a culture that places so much emphasis on success, failure of any kind becomes disastrous. It is in such a climate that the Lomans fruitlessly struggle to rise to the top, with their own natures, ironically, working against them at every step.

Willy Loman's era saw numerous Americans live the rags to riches story that writers such as Horatio Alger Jr. and Oliver Optic popularized. Many wondered, If men like Edison, B. F. Goodrich, Red Grange, and J. P. Morgan can be rich and successful, then why can't I? Although some have claimed that there are ways to guarantee success, there are no hard and fast rules by which one person definitely will be more successful than the next. Indeed, becoming rich is only one narrow definition of success. Unfortunately, one truth of which we can be sure is that any economy will support only so many rich people—the rest must learn to be satisfied with less.

Benjamin Franklin (1706–1790) is a figure whose life and writing sum up all that was essential to eighteenth century belief and thought. The youngest of ten sons, he began working for his father, a tallow chandler and soap maker, at the age of ten, and began to learn the profession of printing two years later. Having made enough money from printing to retire at forty-two, he began to pursue his interest in inventions, science, and politics. He lived his whole life in accordance with what he preached, working hard at whatever he set his mind to. From 1732 to 1757 he published annually the popular *Poor Richard's Almanack*, filled with proverbs and advice; this contributed largely to his reputation as a man of morality and common sense.

In his "Preface" to *Poor Richard Improved*, Franklin gives a clear explanation of the Protestant work ethic, which was still an accepted code by which many Americans lived more than a century later, when Willy Loman came into the world. Franklin recounts a speech he supposedly overheard an old man, called Father Abraham, giving to his friends and neighbors when asked to comment on the nature of the times and the heavy taxes imposed upon them by their government. We should consider to what extent any of the characters in *Death of a Salesman* subscribe to this work ethic, and whether those that do have gained either contentment or success from their efforts.

FROM BENJAMIN FRANKLIN, "PREFACE" TO *POOR RICHARD
IMPROVED: BEING AN ALMANACK AND EPHEMERIS OF THE
MOTIONS OF THE SUN AND MOON; THE TRUE PLACES AND
ASPECTS OF THE PLANETS; THE RISING AND SETTING OF THE
SUN; AND THE RISING, SETTING, AND SOUTHING OF THE MOON,
FOR THE YEAR OF OUR LORD 1758.*
(Philadelphia: B. Franklin and D. Hall, 1758, n.p.)

"Friends," says he, "and neighbors, the taxes are indeed very heavy, and if those laid on by the government were the only ones we had to pay, we might more easily discharge them; but we have many others, and much more grievous to some of us. We are taxed twice as much by our idleness, three times as much by our pride, and four times as much by our folly; and from these taxes the commissioners cannot ease or deliver us by allowing an abatement. However, let us hearken to good advice, and something may be done for us; *God helps them that help themselves*, as Poor Richard says, in his almanac of 1733.

"It would be thought a hard government that should tax its people one-tenth part of their time, to be employed in its service. But idleness taxes many of us much more, if we reckon all that is spent in absolute sloth, or doing of nothing, with that which is spent in idle employments or amusements, that amount to nothing. Sloth, by bringing on diseases, absolutely shortens life. *Sloth, like rust, consumes faster than labor wears, while the used key is always bright*, as Poor Richard says. But *dost thou love life, then do not squander time, for that's the stuff life is made of*, as Poor Richard says. How much more than is necessary do we spend in sleep, forgetting that *The sleeping fox catches no poultry* and that *There will be sleeping enough in the grave*, as Poor Richard says. If time be of all things the most precious, *wasting time* must be, as Poor Richard says, *the greatest prodigality*; since, as he elsewhere tells us, *Lost time is never found again*; and what we call *Time enough, always proves little enough*: let us then be up and be doing, and doing to the purpose; so by diligence shall we do more with less perplexity. *Sloth makes all things difficult, but industry all easy*, as Poor Richard says; and *He that riseth late must trot all day, and shall scarce overtake his business at night*; while *Laziness travels so slowly, that poverty soon overtakes him*, as we read in Poor Richard, who adds, *Drive thy business, let not that drive thee*, and *Early to bed, and early to rise, makes a man healthy, wealthy, and wise*.

"So what signifies wishing and hoping for better times. We may make these times better, if we bestir ourselves. *Industry need not wish*, as Poor Richard says, and *He that lives upon hope will die fasting. There are no gains without pains*; then *Help hands, for I have no lands*, or if I have, they are smartly taxed. And, as Poor Richard likewise observes, *He that hath a trade hath an estate*, and *He that hath a calling, hath an office of profit and honor*; but then the trade must be worked at, and the calling well followed, or neither the estate nor the office will enable us to pay our taxes. If we are industrious, we shall never starve; for, as Poor Richard says, *At the working-man's house hunger looks in, but dares not enter.*"

• • •

"Methinks I hear some of you say, 'must a man afford himself no leisure?' I will tell thee, my friend, what Poor Richard says, *Employ thy time well if thou meanest to gain leisure*; and, *since thou art not sure of a minute, throw not away an hour*. Leisure is time for doing something useful; this leisure the diligent man will obtain, but the lazy man never; so that, as Poor Richard says *a life of leisure and a life of laziness are two things*. Do you imagine that sloth will afford you more comfort than labor? No, for as Poor Richard says, *Trouble springs from idleness, and grievous toil from needless ease. Many without labor, would live by their wits only, but they break for want of stock*. Whereas industry gives comfort, and plenty, and respect: *Fly pleasures, and they'll follow you. The diligent spinner has a large shift*, and *now I have a sheep and a cow, everybody bids me good morrow*; all which is well said by Poor Richard."

Horatio Alger Jr. (1832–1899) was the oldest child of a Massachusetts Unitarian minister. Alger started out following in his father's footsteps by attending Harvard Divinity School, but found the life too restrictive. He discontinued his studies to go abroad and indulge in a more Bohemian life. Returning to America a few years later, he decided to try his hand at writing books for boys and was incredibly successful in this new enterprise. He was one of the most popular authors during the years Willy Loman was growing up, and it is interesting to speculate about how much Alger's stories may have influenced someone like Willy. Alger wrote over a hundred books. Most followed the same formulaic plot: a lowly hero such as a janitor, bootblack, or newsboy becomes rich and successful through hard work and good luck. People liked the possibilities that his books suggested, hoping that they too might fall so easily upon such rewards. His heroes all display a smug goodness that presumably justifies the amazing fortune they never fail to achieve.

Bound to Rise: The Story of a Country Boy tells the story of

Harry Walton, born into a poor farming family made the poorer by his father's inefficiency. The first two excerpts reprinted here describe Hiram Walton and his son, Harry. The third excerpt recounts Harry's reaction to *The Life of Benjamin Franklin*, a book he has won at school. The plot involves Harry's efforts to earn forty dollars to buy a new cow for his family after the old one dies. Inspired by Franklin's example, Harry gets permission from his parents to leave home to earn money. The final excerpt shows how he copes with various setbacks he faces. His enterprise and goodness, for he is always ready to help other people along the way, are eventually rewarded, and he finds a job that pays better than his initial employment. Harry works hard and succeeds, and by the end of the book is able to buy his family a cow and more. We should ask ourselves how credible a character like Harry Walton is and what might happen to those, like Willy, who believe too readily that success is so easily granted.

FROM HORATIO ALGER JR., *BOUND TO RISE: THE STORY OF A COUNTRY BOY*
(New York: A. L. Burt, 1873, 4, 8–9, 47, 190–91)

Hiram Walton was a man of good natural abilities, though of not much education, and after half an hour's conversation with him one would say, unhesitatingly, that he deserved a better fate than this hand-to-hand struggle with poverty. But he was one of those men who, for some unaccountable reason, never get on in the world. They can do a great many things creditably, but do not have the knack of conquering fortune. So Hiram had always been a poor man, and probably always would be poor. He was discontented at times, and often felt the disadvantages of his lot, but he was lacking in energy and ambition, and perhaps this was the chief reason why he did not succeed better.

• • •

Harry would have liked to remain and watch the steps which were being taken for the recovery of the cow; but he knew he had barely time to do the "chores" referred to before school, and he was far from wishing to be late there. He had an ardent thirst for learning, and, young as he was, ranked first in the district school which he attended. I am not about to present my young hero as a marvel of learning, for he was not so. He had improved what opportunities he had enjoyed, but these were very limited. Since he was nine years of age, his schooling had been for the most part limited to eleven weeks in the year. There was a summer as well as a winter school; but in the summer he only attended irregularly, being needed to work at home. His father could not afford to hire help, and there were many ways in which Harry, though young, could help him. So it happened that Harry, though a tolerably good scholar, was deficient in many respects, on account of the limited nature of his opportunities.

He set to work at once at the chores. First he went to the woodpile and sawed and split a quantity of wood, enough to keep the kitchen stove supplied till he came home again from school in the afternoon. This duty was regularly required of him. His father never touched the saw or the ax, but placed upon Harry the general charge of the fuel department.

After sawing and splitting what he thought to be sufficient, he carried it into the house by armfuls, and piled it up near the kitchen stove. He next drew several buckets of water from the well, for it was washing day, brought up some vegetables from the cellar to boil for dinner, and then got ready for school.

• • •

So he began the story [of Franklin's life], and the more he read the more interesting he found it. Great as he afterward became, he was surprised to find that Franklin was a poor boy, and had to work for a living. He started out in life on his own account, and through industry, frugality, perseverance and a fixed determination to rise in life, he became a distinguished man in the end, and a wise man also, though his early opportunities were very limited. It seemed to Harry that there was a great similarity between his own circumstances and position in life and those of the great man about whom he was reading, and this made the biography the more fascinating. The hope came to him that, by following Franklin's example, he, too, might become a successful man.

His mother, looking up at intervals from the stockings which had been so repeatedly darned that the original texture was almost wholly lost sight of, noticed how absorbed he was.

"Is your book interesting, Harry?" she asked.

"It's the most interesting book I ever read."

• • •

"It seems as if all my money must go," thought Harry, looking despondently at his little hoard. "First the ten dollars Luke Harrison stole. Then work stopped. I don't know but it would be better for me to go home."

But the more Harry thought of this, the less he liked it. It would be an inglorious ending to his campaign. Besides, he feared that he would not again obtain permission to start out for himself. Again, dark as the prospect looked just at present, something might turn up. Probably now he would not be able to carry out his plan of paying for the cow; but if his father should lose it, he might be able, if he found work, to buy him another. Squire Green's cow was not the only cow in the world, and all would not be lost if he could not buy her.

"I won't give up yet," said Harry, pluckily. "I must expect to meet with some bad luck. I suppose everybody does, first or last. Something'll turn up for me, if I try to make it."

This was good philosophy. Waiting passively for something to turn up is bad policy, and likely to lead to disappointment; but waiting actively, ready to seize any chance that may offer, is quite different. The world is full of chances for those who are waiting thus, and from such chances so seized has been based many a prosperous career.

Dale Carnegie (1888–1955) won fame during the 1920s and after for his courses and books of advice aimed at helping insecure people who lacked confidence and poise. In his 1936 book, *How to Win Friends and Influence People*, Carnegie legitimized the popular notion that anyone can be successful if he or she is well known and liked. The similarity between this idea and Willy's views on Dave Singleman should be obvious. Carnegie's book sold millions of copies, was translated into dozens of languages, and made him a household name. Carnegie asserted that his "Six Ways to Make People Like You" will guarantee a person, especially anyone in sales, great success.

FROM DALE CARNEGIE, *HOW TO WIN FRIENDS AND INFLUENCE PEOPLE*
(New York: Simon and Schuster, 1936, 102, 30)

RULE 1: Become genuinely interested in other people.

RULE 2: Smile.

RULE 3: Remember that a man's name is to him the sweetest and most important sound in any language.

RULE 4: Be a good listener. Encourage others to talk about themselves.

RULE 5: Talk in terms of the other man's interest.

RULE 6: Make the other person feel important—and do it sincerely.

• • •

[Carnegie believed in a basic human need to be important. He explained it this way:]

The desire for a feeling of importance is one of the chief distinguishing differences between mankind and the animals. To illustrate: When I was a farm boy out in Missouri, my father bred fine Duroc-Jersey hogs and pedigreed white-faced cattle. We used to exhibit our hogs and white-faced cattle at the county fairs and livestock shows throughout the Middle West. We won first prizes by the score. My father pinned his blue ribbons on a sheet of white muslin, and when friends or visitors came to the house, he would get out the long sheet of muslin. He would hold one end and I would hold the other while he exhibited the blue ribbons.

The hogs didn't care about the ribbons they had won. But Father did. These prizes gave him a feeling of importance.

If our ancestors hadn't had this flaming urge for a feeling of importance, civilization would have been impossible. Without it, we should have been just about like the animals.

It was this desire for a feeling of importance that led an uneducated, poverty-stricken grocery clerk to study some law books that he found in the bottom of a barrel of household plunder that he had bought for fifty cents. You have probably heard of this grocery clerk. His name was Lincoln.

Many, many people, particularly Americans, have been influenced by Carnegie's ideas and have used his rules as a guide for success. However, is this realistic? We need to consider if the characters in *Death of a Salesman* might be following Carnegie's rules.

Elbert Hubbard (1856–1915) was a well-known businessman, printer, and writer. He could have become a millionaire through his first business venture, selling soap, but he preferred the business of selling ideas, in which he was equally accomplished. Unfortunately, his was one of the lives lost when the Germans sank the *Lusitania* during World War I, but he left the legacy of his thoughts in a number of books of homily and advice. Dale Carnegie, one of his admirers, believed in Hubbard's advice about the importance of positive thinking. However, although thinking positively may seem like a good way to live, it may cause unnecessary problems if it is perceived to be an infallible means to success. This seems to be a central mistake in Willy's philosophy; and he is clearly a man who has been influenced by the type of belief Hubbard advances.

ADVICE FROM ELBERT HUBBARD
(Source unknown, 1911?)

Whenever you go out of doors, draw the chin in, carry the crown of the head high, and fill the lungs to the utmost; drink in the sunshine; greet your friends with a smile, and put soul into every handclasp. Do not fear being misunderstood and do not waste a minute thinking about your enemies. Try to fix firmly in your mind what you would like to do; and then, without veering of direction, you will move straight to the goal. Keep your mind on the great and splendid things you would like to do, and then, as the days go gliding by, you will find yourself unconsciously seizing upon the opportunities that are required for the fulfillment of your desire, just as the coral insect takes from the running tide the element it needs. Picture in your mind the able, earnest, useful person you desire to be, and the thought you hold is hourly transforming you into that particular individual. . . . Thought is supreme. Preserve a right mental attitude—the attitude of courage, frankness, and good cheer. To think rightly is to create. All things come through desire and every sincere prayer is answered. We become like that on which our hearts are fixed. Carry your chin in and the crown of your head high. We are gods in the chrysalis.

By the start of the twentieth century it was becoming a commonly accepted belief that success was to be measured in terms of how much money one was capable of making. In the prosperous 1920s, prior to the Wall Street crash of 1929, making money seemed to be easy, and many people saw themselves as authorities on how to be a success. M. T. Horwich was the president of the Process Corporation, a Chicago stationery company. The following item appeared in a booklet he sent out to people to encourage them to become agents and salespeople for his company's products. The assurance of great rewards to all who follow his "simple rules" is as persuasive as it is potentially insidious, and it lies at the heart of Willy's failure. It may be useful to speculate about whether or not Willy could have been a successful salesperson for the Process Corporation, and why.

FROM M. T. HORWICH, "SUCCESS IS EASY *AND* SURE IF YOU
KNOW THE SIMPLE RULES FOR ACHIEVING IT"
(Chicago: Process Corporation, 1929)

Here I Give You Five Sure Rules of Testing Money-Making Possibilities

Most people spend a lifetime groping for success and financial independence, and never find them. Others waste years looking before they
finally stumble on the simple road that is open to every one. Why do
most people fail, even though they work hard? Because they devote their
efforts to a business or a proposition that does not possess the elements
that every successful business or proposition must have. Months and
years fly by before they discover that they have not picked a winner, and
often this discovery is made too late in life. If you pick a real proposition,
the battle of life is more than half won at the beginning. Many men and
women with only ordinary ability have made good by selecting the right
line of work; and many a genius has remained poor because he did not
devote himself to a proposition that could go over.

It took me many years to discover the rules that test a money-making
proposition. As soon as I discovered them, fortune began to favor me
generously. And for years I have been telling others how to do the same
thing, and they, too, have prospered. And now I am about to reveal these
rules to you—I am going to tell you how to measure any proposition
that is offered you. Apply these rules, arrive at a sane and studied decision, and you cannot fail. You will succeed. I built my own business with
these rules, and I will show you how to build your business with them.
They are the very same rules that have guided all famous and financially
successful men. They are the rules that have made my thousands of representatives big money-makers. You will apply these rules to the proposition I have for you, and find that it has all the makings of success—that
with the Process Corporation you cannot fail if you but put your mind
and your heart into the work. Read my proposition in this book. Keep
these rules ever before you while you do this and see how perfectly they
fit my offer.

Then, as soon as you are ready, I will make you my partner, trust you
with expensive materials, invest real money in your success—if you will
give me your hand and tell me that you will help me to help you. You
will want to fill out and rush the enclosed application for equipment to
me at once in the addressed envelope which requires no stamp. Read—
then ACT. I am waiting to welcome you.

Here Are the Five Rules That Guarantee Success

Before you put your time into any proposition, measure it by the five following rules:

1. Is it a REPEAT business? Will orders keep on coming to me in the future, without too much work on my part, once I have established my business?

2. Is it a RESPONSIBLE and PERMANENT business of which I can be proud? Is there a real and justified demand and need for this merchandise?

3. Is the work PLEASANT? Does it put me in touch with refined and prosperous people whom I will be glad to call my friends?

4. Is the company WELL ESTABLISHED? Has it been in business a long time and does it have a reputation for manufacturing merchandise of genuine quality and value? Will I get a square deal from them?

5. Can I do this work SUCCESSFULLY? Will the company show me how to do it, and will it back me up with the kind of co-operation that insures success?

THE PROCESS CORPORATION offers you a business opportunity that measures up fully to every one of the requirements named above. Read on, and you will see why your success is practically assured when you become a Process Partner.

Theodore Roosevelt (1858–1919) was a soldier, writer, and, beginning in 1901, the twenty-sixth president of the United States. A popular public speaker, he was a man to whom people would listen, although he was often considered a little unorthodox. He led a very active life despite poor health and won a lot of respect while succeeding in a number of careers. He believed very strongly in the Declaration of Independence's insistence on equal rights, but he was wise enough to realize that this did not necessarily make everyone equal. In this speech he discusses what he regards as misleading ideas about the nature of success in vogue at the time. Roosevelt knew from personal experience that success was not easily won, and he suggests that a person needs to possess a number of qualities to succeed. Roosevelt also realizes that success need not be measured in monetary terms, a notion that has bypassed several of the characters in *Death of a Salesman*. Roosevelt's opinions on what makes a person successful may help explain some of the reasons why neither Willy nor his sons can attain the success they desire.

FROM THEODORE ROOSEVELT, "THE CONDITIONS OF
SUCCESS: AN ADDRESS AT THE CARNEGIE UNION, MAY 26,
1910, MR. ROOSEVELT'S ESTIMATE OF HIMSELF"
(*Outlook*, 22 January 1919: 142–44)

There are two kinds of success. One is the very rare kind that comes to the man who has the power to do what no one else has the power to do. That is genius. I am not discussing what form that genius takes; whether it is the genius of a man who can write a poem that no one else can write ("The Ode on a Grecian Urn," for example, or "Helen, thy beauty is to me") or of a man who can do 100 yards in nine and three-fifth seconds. Such a man does what no one else can do. Only a very limited amount of the success of life comes to persons possessing genius. The average man who is successful—the average statesman, the average public servant, the average soldier, who wins what we call great success— is not a genius. He is a man who has merely the ordinary qualities that he shares with his fellows, but who has developed those ordinary qualities to a more than ordinary degree.

Take such a thing as hunting or any form of vigorous bodily exercise. Most men can ride hard if they choose. Almost any man can kill a lion if he will exercise a little resolution in training the qualities that will enable him to do it. [Taking a tumbler from the table, Mr. Roosevelt held it up.] Now it is a pretty easy thing to aim straight at an object about that size. Almost any one, if he practices with the rifle at all, can learn to hit that tumbler; and he can hit the lion all right if he learns to shoot as straight at its brain or heart as at the tumbler. He does not have to possess any extraordinary capacity, not a bit; all he has to do is to develop certain rather ordinary qualities, but develop them to such a degree that he will not get flustered, so that he will press the trigger steadily instead of jerking it, and then he will shoot at the lion as well as he will at that tumbler. It is a perfectly simple quality to develop. You don't need any remarkable skill; all you need is to possess ordinary qualities, but to develop them to a more than ordinary degree.

• • •

It is just so in public life. It is not genius, it is not extraordinary subtlety or acuteness of intellect, that is important. The things that are important are the rather commonplace, the rather humdrum, virtues that in their sum are designated as character. If you have in public life men of good ability, not geniuses, but men of good abilities, with character—and, gentlemen, you must include as one of the most important elements of character common sense—if you possess such men, the Government will go on very well.

I have spoken only of the great successes; but what I have said applies just as much to the success that is within the reach of almost every one of us. I think that any man who has had what is regarded in the world as a great success must realize that the element of chance has played a great part in it. Of course a man has to take advantage of his opportunities; but the opportunities have to come. If there is not the war, you don't get the great general; if there is not a great occasion, you don't get the great statesman; if Lincoln had lived in times of peace, no one would have known his name now. The great crisis must come, or no man has the chance to develop great qualities.

There are exceptional cases, of course, where there is a man who can do just one thing, such as a man who can play a dozen games of chess or juggle with four rows of figures at once—and, as a rule, he can do nothing else. A man of this type can do nothing unless in the one crisis for which his powers fit him. But normally the man who makes the great success when the emergency arises is the man who would have made a fair success in any event. I believe that the man who is really happy in a great position—in what we call a career—is the man who would also be happy and regard his life as successful if he had never been thrown into that position. If a man lives a decent life and does his work fairly and squarely so that those dependent on him and attached to him are better for his having lived, then he is a success, and he deserves to feel that he has done his duty and he deserves to be treated by those who have had greater success as nevertheless having shown the fundamental qualities that entitle him to respect. We have in the United States an organization composed of the men who forty-five years ago fought to a finish the great Civil War. One thing that has always appealed to me in that organization is that all of the men admitted are on a perfect equality provided the records show that their duty was well done. Whether a man served as a lieutenant-general or an eighteen-year-old recruit, so long as he was able to serve for six months and did his duty in his appointed place, then he is called Comrade and stands on an exact equality with the other men. The same principle should shape our associations in ordinary civil life.

Albert W. Atwood was a regular contributor to the *Saturday Evening Post*, a popular general interest magazine. In the following article Atwood explores the potential realities behind common dreams of success and polls a variety of social leaders as to their opinions on the matter. As American essayist and philosopher Ralph Waldo Emerson once stated:

> There is a time in every man's education when he arrives at the conviction that envy is ignorance; that imitation is suicide; that he must take himself for better, worse, as his portion; that though the wide universe is full of good, no kernel of nourishing corn can come to him but through his toil bestowed on that plot of ground which is given to him to till. The power which resides in him is new in nature, and none but he knows what that is which he can do, nor does he know until he has tried. ("Nature" 1836)

Emerson is insisting that people need to understand and accept their own natures in order to be content. It follows that if one does not have the type of nature suited to worldly success, then trying to be a success could be very disruptive. Willy and his sons are all guilty of pursuing courses in life that are not particularly suited to their natures, although Biff does begin to learn the mistake he has made and try to rectify it. We need to consider what Atwood is saying that the chances for success actually are, and what he believes a person needs in order to be successful.

FROM ALBERT W. ATWOOD, "WHAT ARE THE CHANCES OF
SUCCESS TODAY?"
(*Saturday Evening Post*, 12 June 1920: 14–15, 77–78)

The title of this article propounds a question that goes to the very root of modern life. If the people as a whole in this country have very little or no chance or opportunity to rise or get ahead, if they are doomed to a bare existence without hope of betterment, then perhaps it is time to make exceedingly radical changes.

It is a question of intense interest, of far-reaching ramifications, of direct bearing upon most of the vexed questions of the day, whether the door of opportunity is being closed or not by large-scale modern methods of doing business. We know, of course, that men like Rockefeller, Schwab and thousands upon thousands of other millionaires and multi-millionaires have risen from humble beginnings. It is a commonplace, everyday matter of observation to anyone with even half-open eyes that other thousands of office boys, clerks and manual workers are now engaged in the same process of rising. But how many young men out of the total population are destined to rise? To put it bluntly, just what is the importance, the meaning and significance of the many notable cases that can be cited?

• • •

[Atwood interviewed a number of people for this article. Here, he quizzes a successful assistant to the president of a large New York City corporation:]

To him I put my question of the extent of business opportunity and its real significance.

"I can best answer your question," he replied, "by telling you about the bench outside. These young men keep coming to me for advice and encouragement, just why I do not know. When they are blue and think they are not getting ahead fast enough they come to me for suggestions, and this is what I say to them.

" 'You can't all be presidents, you know. Any one of you may be president, but all of you can't and won't be.'

"Of course I have to be careful not to discourage them, but I believe in telling them the truth. What is the use of kidding ourselves on this subject? We know perfectly well that everyone cannot and does not rise to the top. Let us do away with all this bunk about short cuts to the presidency. Perhaps I should not talk this way if I were not over fifty. If I were twenty-five perhaps the world would seem empty unless I could be president of the company. But I do not feel that way at all now, and that is the beauty of my viewpoint. Why not admit frankly that not every soldier carries a marshal's baton in his knapsack?"

• • •

The great underlying truth is that most men have not the physical, nervous, mental and moral qualities and endowments to lead or manage. This may seem an obvious truth, but very few people fully realize its meaning. Most persons fall into the easy habit of grouping their fellow men into a few easily recognized types or classes. Those who have not been very successful in life are well aware of the existence of a Morgan or a Rockefeller, and they have an even more keen appreciation that millions of men like themselves are poor. So they think of the rich and the poor, and fail to recognize that Nature has created thousands upon thousands of different types. Indeed, hardly any two men are alike. Only the trained scientist appreciates to the full how much men do vary in their native abilities or in their capacity to develop these abilities.

That most men have not the physical, nervous, mental and moral qualities to attain what we call success does not really need scientific demonstration. Every now and then the papers tell of some poor chap who has happened upon a rich deposit of ore or oil, only to blow in the money in the course of a few weeks or months. Most of us believe that if all the wealth in the country were divided up equally it would not be long before the shrewd, thrifty, strong and able members of society would again have more than their share. They might not be the same persons who were rich in a previous state, for the older plutocracy might be killed off or banished, as in Russia, but wealth in all probability would gravitate to those able to seize and hold it. Stated somewhat differently, the failure of so many to manage and lead or acquire large wealth is due not so much to the social and industrial system under which we live as to their own individual qualities or lack of qualities.

• • •

[The head of a large commercial training school tells Atwood:]

"The reason why many young men stand still—and, of course, standing still between twenty and thirty becomes equivalent to retrogression—is because they neglect self-development. They seem quite satisfied with life if only they have a job which yields them what they consider a decent livelihood. After school days are over they strive for no further mental development, but are content to devote what leisure they have to social pleasures, sports and amusements of various kinds. They may grumble now and then because their salary is not raised, but they give no thought to self-improvement or to plans for bettering their lot. Such men lack ambition. They bear a very close resemblance to animals of the field."

STUDY QUESTIONS

1. What is the meaning behind the additional "taxes" about which Father Abraham speaks in the excerpt by Franklin? How can people avoid having to "pay" them? And according to Father Abraham, what happens to idle or slothful people?

2. According to Franklin, what is the difference between a life of laziness and a life of leisure? Also, what does he suggest are the precise rewards of an industrious life?

3. Why is Alger's Hiram Walton fated never to be successful?

4. How would you describe Harry Walton? How does he respond to events in his life? What are the main differences between Harry and his father?

5. What kind of things does Carnegie suggest that the "desire to be important" drives people to do? Do any of these apply to Willy Loman and his family? What do the Lomans do to feel important?

6. What is the tone of Carnegie's writing, and what does this suggest?

7. Do any characters in *Death of a Salesman* appear to be following Hubbard's advice? If so, do they attain the rewards Hubbard implies will follow?

8. How do Horwich's ideas differ from those of Carnegie and Hubbard?

9. What type of people does Horwich seem to be addressing? What are the key words he uses, and what is he promising his salespeople?

10. What are the two kinds of success Roosevelt describes? How are they achieved?

11. Is Roosevelt saying that anyone can be successful? Does he offer any guarantees to people who are pursuing success?

12. Roosevelt describes the perfect equality of an organization formed by men who fought in the Civil War. Are people in ordinary civil life generally afforded the same equality? Is Willy Loman?

13. What does Atwood imply is the social impact of men like Rockefeller and Schwab becoming millionaires from humble beginnings?

14. What is meant by "Not every soldier carries a marshal's baton in his knapsack"? How far do the comments of the head of the commercial training school in Atwood's article apply to the young men in *Death of a Salesman*?

15. Which character in *Death of a Salesman* seems to fit most closely the description of the typical young man given in Atwood's article by the head of the commercial training school?

16. What would Atwood think about people like Carnegie and Horwich who claim to know the secrets of success?

17. To what extent does the Protestant work ethic survive, become adulterated, or become entirely lost in the various rules for success offered in this section?

PASTORAL MYTH OF THE GOLDEN WEST VS.
THE URBAN MYTH

In its earlier days especially, with its abundance of land and resources, the frontier presented people with many opportunities for
advancement and the accumulation of wealth. However, the cities,
with their subsequent development of industry and big business,
often fueled by the resources they had extracted from the West,
offered equal opportunities to many aspiring young men and
women. As David Potter states, "The urban migration is almost as
great a factor in American development as the Westward migration" (*People of Plenty*, p. 93). The question quickly becomes,
Which will offer an enterprising young person better opportunities, the Golden West or the big city? The following selections attempt to answer this question and to show the various advantages
and pitfalls of idealizing either place.

In a September 1, 1996, interview in the *Anchorage Daily News*,
Arthur Miller told Mike Dunham: "The Alaskan metaphor was
based on the dream of the eternal West as a place where the individual could determine his destiny more than in the crowded
city, where he's simply one more digit in the economic calculus.
A place where character mattered" (p. 3H). But Miller also points
out that not everyone who went to Alaska did well. Ben succeeded
largely because he is a good manipulator. The other Lomans are
very different types. We need to consider whether or not Willy's
family is more suited to life in the city or in the country, and what
has made them want the lifestyles that they appear to have chosen.

American development has witnessed a clash between the lure
of the pastoral Golden West and that of the big city. While the idea
of the American frontier suggests great opportunity and potential,
its offerings are finite. Once the West Coast was reached and its
resources plundered, people were forced to turn back on themselves and reconsider what lay behind. Numerous metropolises
rose up during this period, and their urban communities offered
new possibilities, challenges, and dangers. While some tried to
maintain a belief in the fading Western dream, others, though
faced by a possible reality of urban overcrowding, crime, and ho-
mogenization, recognized the tarnished reduction of the once

Golden West and transferred their faith to the modern, shining cities. Willy puts all of his faith into the potential of the city, even though his father and brother both preferred to strike out toward the frontier. But has the city rewarded Willy for his allegiance? While Hap seems content to follow in his father's footsteps, Biff dreams of a life lived closer to the land. We should consider whether or not Biff's dream was still viable by the late 1940s.

Born in Wisconsin, Frederick Jackson Turner (1861–1932) was a historian. In 1893 he read a short essay, "The Significance of the Frontier in American History," to an annual meeting of the American Historical Association in Philadelphia. His essay advocated the view that the frontier experience had played the greatest role in forming the American character. His ideas, which suggested that the American experience was as full of promise as it was unique, were enthusiastically received by his American audience, and his career was made. He published a number of studies on this subject, including *The Rise of the West* (1906) and *The Frontier in American History* (1920). The following excerpts, from an essay Turner wrote shortly after delivering his ground-breaking speech, discuss the new American society's close relationship to the land. Turner goes on to explain how the Western image has evolved in the American psyche. We see this image manifested most clearly in characters such as Willy's father, Ben, and Biff, although there are also vestiges of it in Willy's worldview despite his city bias.

FROM FREDERICK JACKSON TURNER, "THE PROBLEM OF THE
WEST," IN *THE FRONTIER IN AMERICAN HISTORY*
(New York: Holt, 1920, 290–96)

The fundamental fact in regard to this new society was its relation to land. Professor Boutmy has said of the United States, "Their one primary and prodominant [*sic*] object is to cultivate and settle these prairies, forests, and vast waste lands. The striking and peculiar characteristic of American society is that it is not so much a democracy as a huge commercial company for the discovery, cultivation, and capitalization of its enormous territory. The United States are primarily a commercial society, and only secondarily a nation." Of course, this involves a serious misapprehension. By the very fact of the task here set forth, far-reaching ideals of the state and of society have been evolved in the West, accompanied by loyalty to the nation representative of these ideals. But M. Boutmy's description hits the substantial fact, that the fundamental traits of the man of the interior were due to the free lands of the West. These turned his attention to the great task of subduing them to the purposes of civilization, and to the task of advancing his economic and social status in the new democracy which he was helping to create.

· · ·

It followed from the lack of organized political life, from the atomic conditions of the backwoods society, that the individual was exalted and given free play. The West was another name for opportunity. Here were mines to be seized, fertile valleys to be preempted, all the natural resources open to the shrewdest and the boldest. The United States is unique in the extent to which the individual has been given an open field, unchecked by restraints of an old social order, or of scientific administration of government. The self-made man was the Western man's ideal, was the kind of man that all men might become. Out of his wilderness experience, out of the freedom of his opportunities, he fashioned a formula for social regeneration,—the freedom of the individual to seek his own. He did not consider that his conditions were exceptional and temporary.

· · ·

. . . [T]he frontiersman's dream was prophetic. In spite of his rude, gross nature, this early Western man was an idealist withal. He dreamed dreams and beheld visions. He had faith in man, hope for democracy, belief in America's destiny, unbounded confidence in his ability to make his dreams come true. Said Harriet Martineau in 1834, "I regard the American people as a great embryo poet, now moody, now wild, but bringing out results of absolute good sense: restless and wayward in action, but with deep peace at his heart; exulting that he has caught the true aspect of things past, and the depth of futurity which lies before him, wherein to create something so magnificent as the world has scarcely begun to dream of. There is the strongest hope of a nation that is capable of being possessed with an idea."

It is important to bear this idealism of the West in mind. The very materialism that has been urged against the West was accompanied by ideals of equality, of the exaltation of the common man, of national expansion, that makes it a profound mistake to write of the West as though it were engrossed in mere material ends. It has been, and is, preeminently a region of ideals, mistaken or not.

Dissatisfied with his indoor life in the East, Edward Townsend Booth decided to see for himself what the West was like, with the expectation of permanently moving out there as a farmer if the life agreed with him. After spending ten weeks working on various farms, he happened upon an article by William T. Foster, "The Spirit of the West," which clearly promoted the West as a kind of paradise. In view of his recent experiences as an ordinary field hand, Booth felt compelled to respond. He begins by discussing Foster's article and goes on to show a darker, more problematic side to the Western dream, one that Foster has ignored. Booth's brief experience has convinced him that not everyone who heads west is guaranteed success. This should help us to assess how successful Willy might have been had he taken the chance Ben once gave him to head west, and also how realistic Biff's dreams for the future might be.

FROM EDWARD TOWNSEND BOOTH, "THE WILD WEST"
(*Atlantic Monthly*, December 1920: 785–87)

Yes, here were the stride and clamor and the extravagant good humor of the Pacific Slope, distilled into such telling advertisement of all that is fine in the region that I seemed to be reading the work of a first-rate literary man turned publicity agent. The goods were displayed for the Eastern buyer in a way that would prove irresistible to many a young man of Atlantic seaboard traditions who had returned from service in France with a flux of impatient energy that the older communities could not contain. It occurred to me that the Chambers of Commerce of the Far West might well reprint in circular form, with suitable fine-screen electrotypes, this latest version of the post-war commandment, "Go West, young man!"

• • •

. . . [I]t seemed to me that this Spirit of the West that Mr. Foster celebrated was merely the sparkling, rarified atmosphere that may be breathed at the upper levels of Western society. Who can withhold admiration from the initiative of Seattle business men who have moved mountains and made real estate of them on the floor of Puget Sound? And who can move with the tide that floods Market Street, San Francisco, on a May morning, without abandoning himself to the flush of vigor and power that sweeps up from the Oakland Ferry like a strong, clean wind off the sea? But this is the Spirit of the West that flows in free channels for the young business men and the gentlemen of the boards of trade.

What of the noisome and dangerous concentration of this freely flowing energy, the baulked, convulsive power of the lower levels where dwell the long logger and the short logger, the miner and mucker, the railroad boomer, the fruit glummer, the roustabout, the longshoreman, and the great armies of the migratory agricultural laborer? Surely, these are the vast majority. What is their spirit?

During the first cutting of alfalfa, as a shocker and spike-pitcher, I had had my first contact with the casual laborer of the Far West. Swinging down the windrows of freshly cut hay behind a giant "pacer," who was paid double the wages of the "stiffs"; wretched with fatigue that became grievous pain before the end of the day, I heard for the first time the heavy undertone of a will to revolution that growls in the underpinning of Western society. If I had not offered my services from the same "slave-market" in Wapato, while the filthy lodging-house and "hash-house" consumed the wages I had well earned at hand-mixing concrete; if I had not slept in the same haystacks or verminous bunkhouses, and seen the same look of contempt for the "working stiff" in the eyes of the *haute et petite bourgeoisie*; if I had been a detached observer and listener, in short, I might well have been horrified by the thunder and lightning of blasphemy and hatred that sounded and played over the shockers as they stumbled along the windrows of the bonanza hay-ranch.

It was the same in the second cutting and in the barley and wheat harvest. One found one's self working with men whose single hope of rehabilitation and human dignity lay in the revolutionary programme of the I.W.W. Out of the heavy fatigue, the fetid torpor of the bunkhouse, at the end of the day's labor, the only influence that could stir the sullen hulks who lounged in the bunks was the zeal of the agitator tirelessly and astutely instructing the "working stiff" in the strategy of class warfare.

Lewis Mumford (1895–1990) was a writer, philosopher, and historian whose works explored the relation of modern humans to their natural and self-created surroundings. Mumford did a lot of work in regional and city planning. He saw cities as an expression of the growth of civilization; if planned correctly, they could in turn influence that growth. This selection discusses the potential attraction of the city vis-à-vis the countryside and suggests ways in which cities, if properly developed, can offer people tremendous benefits. How far might such views have been influential in persuading Willy to stick it out in the city?

FROM LEWIS MUMFORD, "THE CITY"
(1922; Reprinted in *City Development.*
New York: Harcourt, 1945, 22–23)

Metropolitanism in America represents, from the cultural angle, a re-action against the uncouth and barren countryside that was skinned, rather than cultivated, by the restless, individualistic, self-assertive Amer-ican pioneer. The perpetual drag to New York, and the endeavor of less favorably situated cities to imitate the virtues and defects of New York, is explicable as nothing other than the desire to participate in some meas-ure in the benefits of city life. Since we have failed up to the present to develop genuine regional cultures, those who do not wish to remain barbarians must become metropolitans. That means they must come to New York, or ape the ways that are fashionable in New York. Here opens the breach that has begun to widen between the metropolis and the countryside in America. The countryman, who cannot enjoy the advan-tages of the metropolis, who has no center of his own to which he can point with pride, resents the privileges that the metropolitan enjoys. Hence the periodical crusades of our State Legislatures, largely packed with rural representatives, against the vices, corruptions, and follies which the countryman enviously looks upon as the peculiar property of the big city. Perhaps the envy and resentment of the farming population is due to a genuine economic grievance against the big cities—especially against their banks, insurance companies, and speculative middlemen. Should the concentration of power, glory, and privilege in the metropolis continue, it is possible that the city will find itself subject to an economic siege. If our cities cannot justify their existence by their creative achieve-ments, by their demonstration of the efficacy and grace of corporate life, it is doubtful whether they will be able to persuade the country to sup-port them, once the purely conventional arrangements by means of which the city browbeats the countryside are upset.

Paeans to the city, telling of its allure, are quite common in American literature, especially in that of the 1920s. Take for ex-ample F. Scott Fitzgerald's evocation of New York as a city of pos-sibility in *The Great Gatsby* (New York: Scribner, 1925). He describes it "rising up across the river in white heaps and sugar lumps all built with a wish out of non-olfactory money. The city seen from the Queensboro Bridge is always the city seen for the first time, in its first wild promise of all the mystery and the beauty in the world" (pp. 74–75). Sinclair Lewis also saw this attraction and conveys it in the opening pages of his novel *Babbitt*, where he describes the fictional city of Zenith. Compare his description to Willy's and Ben's views of the city.

FROM SINCLAIR LEWIS, *BABBITT*
(New York: Harcourt, 1922, 5–6)

The towers of Zenith aspired above the morning mist; austere towers of steel and cement and limestone, sturdy as cliffs and delicate as silver rods. They were neither citadels nor churches, but frankly and beautifully office-buildings.

The mist took pity on the fretted structures of earlier generations: the Post Office with its shingle-tortured mansard, the red brick minarets of hulking old houses, factories with stingy and sooted windows, wooden tenements colored like mud. The city was full of such grotesqueries, but the clean towers were thrusting them from the business center, and on the farther hills were shining new houses, homes—they seemed—for laughter and tranquillity.

Over a concrete bridge fled a limousine of long sleek hood and noise-less engine. These people in evening clothes were returning from an all-night rehearsal of a Little Theater play, an artistic adventure considerably illuminated by champagne. Below the bridge curved a railroad, a maze of green and crimson lights. The New York Flyer boomed past, and twenty lines of polished steel leaped into the glare.

In one of the skyscrapers the wires of the Associated Press were closing down. The telegraph operators wearily raised their celluloid eye-shades after a night of talking with Paris and Peking. Through the building crawled the scrubwomen, yawning, their old shoes slapping. The dawn mist spun away. Cues of men with lunch-boxes clumped toward the immensity of new factories, sheets of glass and hollow tile, glittering shops where five thousand men worked beneath one roof, pouring out the honest wares that would be sold up the Euphrates and across the veldt. The whistles rolled out in greeting a chorus cheerful as the April dawn; the song of labor in a city built—it seemed—for giants.

The following selection was written a number of years after Lewis Mumford's speculative 1922 essay, "The City," in which he suggested the potential of cities to play a glorious and beneficial role in American development. Here, Mumford considers how far cities have lived up to his hopeful expectations, and whether or not they have fallen into any of the traps he foresaw. As an emblem of what he sees cities as having become, Mumford describes "The

Paper Dream City" and outlines the impact that such a place might have on those who live in it. In the light of this we should assess how far the city has fed and/or betrayed Willy's hopes and dreams. Many questions need to be raised. For example, What are the realities of the "Paper Dream City"? What is Mumford saying is the fate of those who live in such "Paper Dream Cities"? Is this the fate suffered by the Loman family, or have any of them managed to escape such consequences?

FROM LEWIS MUMFORD, "THE PAPER DREAM CITY," IN *THE CULTURE OF CITIES*
(New York: Harcourt, 1938, 255–58)

When one examines the state of the metropolis one discovers a curious hallucination: the notion that its size, power, mechanical equipment and riches have effected a corresponding improvement in the life of its inhabitants. What is the mechanism of this error? We shall find it in the pseudo-environment of paper.

To believe that civilization has reached a culmination in the modern metropolis one must avert one's eyes from the concrete facts of metropolitan routine. And that is precisely what the metropolitan schools himself to do: he lives, not in the real world, but in a shadow world projected around him at every moment by means of paper and celluloid: a world in which he is insulated by glass, rubber, and cellophane, from the mortifications of living.

• • •

The swish and crackle of paper is the underlying sound of the metropolis: more important to the inner content of its existence than the whining rhythm of its machines. What is visible and real in this world is only what has been transferred to paper. The essential gossip of the metropolis is no longer that of people meeting face to face on the crossroads, at the dinner table, in the market-place: a few dozen people writing in the newspapers, a dozen more broadcasting over the radio, provide the daily interpretation of movements and happenings. The principle of concentrated propaganda and irresponsible dictatorship is written over the popular intellectual activities of the metropolis: in its evaluations, no less than in its deliberate suppressions. It is a short step from a yellow journal proprietor, skillfully manufacturing the day's news, to a propaganda ministry in a war government or a fascist dictatorship. Was it not from the commercial advertisers that political governments perhaps learned not to argue about the merits of their actions, but to keep on asserting with forceful insolence whatever they wanted the public to believe?

• • •

The words and actions of men are more and more framed for their effect on paper: or they are posed, with a view to historical reproduction, in the photograph and the motion picture. That life is an occasion for living, and not a pretext for supplying items to newspapers or spectacles for crowds of otherwise vacant bystanders—these notions do not occur to the metropolitan mind. For the denizens of this world are at home only in the ghost city of paper: they live in a world of "knowledge about," as William James would have said, and they daily drift farther away from the healthy discipline of first-hand "acquaintance with."

Hence the importance of statistics. The principal achievements that quicken the metropolitan mind are quantitative ones: record-breaking in some fashion or another. Size competition is indeed the very mode of metropolitan expansion: a forty-story building is *ipso facto* a more important building than a two-story one, and a university teaching ten thousand students is similarly more important than one teaching ten hundred. If these were not axioms in the metropolitan mind it might be a prey to occasional doubts about its own importance. To lop a quarter of a second off the running of a mile, to sit on a flagpole three days longer than a rival, to graduate so many hundred more bachelors of art a year, to build a building ten stories higher than the nearest rival—these are typical metropolitan records—important only on paper. Metropolitans flout the wise Biblical story of the king who insisted on counting his army.

This metropolitan world, then, is a world where flesh and blood is less real than paper and ink and celluloid. It is a world where the great masses of people, unable to have direct contact with more satisfying means of living, take life vicariously, as readers, spectators, passive observers: a world where people watch shadow-heroes and heroines in order to forget their own clumsiness or coldness in love, where they behold brutal men crushing out life in a strike riot, a wrestling ring or a military assault, while they lack the nerve even to resist the petty tyranny of their immediate boss: where they hysterically cheer the flag of their political state, and in their neighborhood, their trades union, their church, fail to perform the most elementary duties of citizenship.

Living thus, year in and year out, at second hand, remote from the nature that is outside them and no less remote from the nature within, handicapped as lovers and as parents by the routine of the metropolis and by the constant specter of insecurity and death that hovers over its bold towers and shadowed streets—living thus the mass of inhabitants remain in a state bordering on the pathological. They become the victims of phantasms, fears, obsessions, which bind them to ancestral patterns of behavior.

David Potter wrote his sociological study *People of Plenty* about the time *Death of a Salesman* is set. Here Potter compares cities to the frontier and considers how city living has impacted upon the average family. Is this an accurate assessment of what has happened to the Lomans? How is it that their fellow city-dwellers, Charley and Bernard, have achieved so much more than the Lomans from living in the city?

FROM DAVID M. POTTER, "ABUNDANCE, MOBILITY, AND STATUS," IN *PEOPLE OF PLENTY*
(Chicago: University of Chicago Press, 1954, 93–95, 107)

Today our somewhat disillusioned intellectuals tend to emphasize the fact that the American dream of absolute equality and of universal opportunity was never fulfilled in the literal sense, and they often play up the discrepancy between the realities of American life and the beliefs of the American creed. Discrepancy there is, was, and perhaps ever shall be, and it must be confronted in any analysis; but the recognition of it should not obscure another primary fact, namely, that American conditions, in addition to encouraging a belief in mobility, actually brought about a condition of mobility far more widespread and pervasive than any previous society or previous era of history had ever witnessed.

The classic illustration, always cited in this connection, is the frontier, and it is indeed true that the existence of the frontier presented people with a unique opportunity to put behind them the economic and social status which they held in their native communities and to acquire property and standing in the newly forming communities of the West. But, while we constantly remind ourselves that the West offered abundance in the form of free land and provided the frontier as a locus for the transformation of this abundance into mobility, we often forget that the country as a whole offered abundance in the form of fuel resources, mineral resources, bumper crops, industrial capacity, and the like, and provided the city as a locus for the transformation of this abundance into mobility. More Americans have changed their status by moving to the city than have done so by moving to the frontier. The urban migration is almost as great a factor in American development as the westward migration, and more young men have probably followed Horace Greeley's example in moving from a rural birthplace to a metropolis than have followed his precept to go west and grow up with the country.

• • •

There is a real question how much of the rapid transformation of America has been marked by actual mobility in the sense of advancement by the individual through the ranks of society from one status to another and how much has been a mere change in the manner of life and standard of living of classes which retain pretty much the same relative position. The middle-class city dweller of today has a money income that would have connoted wealth to his frugal, landowning, farm-dwelling forebear of the nineteenth century, and his facilities for living make his forebear's life seem Spartan by comparison; but his standing in the community is no higher and is, in fact, considerably less independent. Improvements in the standard of living of society at large should not be confused with the achievement of separate social advancement by individuals.

• • •

In this connection, however, one should take the precaution of noting that the mobility drive and the doctrine of equality were not the only factors in the destruction of status, although they caused it to be repudiated morally. A fully articulated status system rested, technologically and socially, upon two bases which have now been very seriously impaired. One of these was the workman's satisfaction in and identification with his work. However humble his position, the craftsman knew that his community, with its economy of scarcity, needed his work, and, since it was his own work in the craft sense, he could regard his product as an extension of himself. The age of abundance, however, requiring a greater volume of processed goods, utilized machinery to meet the demand and made the former craftsman a more productive but less creative and less essential attendant upon the machine. The other basis was the position of the family as a matrix within which status was contained. Biologically and psychologically the family was a unit, and, so long as its members worked together, cultivating the crops, tending the animals, preparing the food and clothing, and practicing the handicrafts of early America, it was socially and economically a unit as well. The completeness of its integration assured to each member strong ties of relationship with the group. But again the age of abundance, arising from industrial growth and in turn stimulating further industrialization, caused a transformation. By compelling the individual to work outside the family, it divorced the family from the economy. For instance, it even took children, who had previously worked within the family, and made them work in the factory.

STUDY QUESTIONS

1. What does Turner suggest are the defining qualities of the West? How have they influenced the American psyche?

2. To what extent do Turner's suggestions account for, or agree with, the ways Biff and Willy view the West?

3. How would you describe Booth's reaction to Foster's article? Does he agree with the picture of the West that Foster paints?

4. Why does Booth feel that laborers in the West are so ripe for revolution?

5. In his essay "The City," what does Mumford say are the advantages of a city over the country? Do any of these advantages explain why Willy and his family chose to remain in New York?

6. What is the effect of Lewis' description of Zenith? What kind of city does Zenith appear to be?

7. What are the implications of what life is like for people who live in Lewis' Zenith? Which of these aspects seem evident in the Lomans' city existence?

8. In the second excerpt from Mumford's work, is he saying that life in the city has improved or worsened over the years of its development? How does his "Paper Dream City" compare to "The City" he pictures in his earlier article?

9. What does Mumford feel is the difference between a world of "knowledge about" and a world of "first-hand 'acquaintance with' "?

10. What does Potter see as the main differences between living in a city as opposed to the country? Does he show any favor toward one way of life over the other?

11. Are the Loman family happy in the city, or would they prefer to live in the countryside?

CULTURE OF YOUTH VS. CULTURE OF AGE

One of the problems Willy faces is that of becoming old in a culture that tends to idolize the young and reject the elderly. It is partly his advanced age that causes him to lose his job. Ever since Ponce de Leon came searching for that fountain of youth, American culture has reflected a similar desire to stay young forever. Despite the association of wisdom and valuable experience that inevitably attaches itself to old age, America has tended to embrace more readily a culture of youth. In America, the aged are rarely venerated, for to be old is to have outlived one's usefulness. It becomes hard to grow old gracefully, for the elderly feel compelled to compete in this youthful world in order to survive and keep their self-esteem intact. This is an error that Willy makes, though we should consider whether or not society has offered him any choice in this matter. The following documents explore ways in which the young and old tend to be viewed and treated in America.

In the following selection Ashley Montagu describes what he sees as a particularly American phenomenon, "the cult of youthfulness." Members of this "cult" tend to admire and worship youth while they reject anything that cannot be considered young. Montagu clearly sees such behavior as damaging to society as a whole. We need to consider how big a role it has played in Willy's downfall.

FROM ASHLEY MONTAGU, "THE CULT OF YOUTHFULNESS," IN
THE AMERICAN WAY OF LIFE
(New York: Putnam's, 1967, 218–20)

To be over forty in the United States is a sin against both the flesh and the spirit. It represents a fall from grace. There is no profit in it; the profits are all to the industries that cater to the young or would-be young. To be young, to be beautiful, to be handsome—what else matters?

• • •

The emphasis on youthfulness is an evidence of insecurity, a fear of aging, of not being in the swing, of becoming superfluous, and ultimately an unwillingness to face the fact of human mortality. These are immature attitudes and reflect the failure of a culture to prepare its members to be their age and to define for them, and enable them to play, the roles appropriate to their age.

In a culture in which men place so high a premium on youthfulness in women and in which the workaday world of that culture places an equally high premium on youthfulness, youthfulness will understandably come to be regarded as a quality of the highest value. Hence, if the cult of youthfulness is ever to be relegated to the museum of false values, its damaging consequences will first have to be recognized, and healthier attitudes toward the various age phases will have to be cultivated. Since the whole of America is geared to youth—education, industry, advertising, the movies, the theater, TV, the magazines, the novel all are oriented toward the support and aggrandizement of youth—an implicit disrespect for and undervaluation of the older age grades become endemic. This is, of course, reflected in the manner in which Americans brush the problems of the aging, its so-called senior citizens, under the rug. For all practical purposes the aging do not exist, and if they do, then they do not matter. The disregard for the aging is one of the worst of the damaging effects of the cult of youthfulness. It is dehumanizing, and that is another of the detrimental effects of this cult. But most of all, it is damaging to the individuals who suffer from it, for what it does in effect is to focus their energies on remaining young so that they neglect attending to the process of growing old. Hence, when age finally catches up with them, they often experience it as a trauma, instead of what it could have been—an enriching and rewarding enlargement of one's life and horizons and, in many ways, a much happier period than that of the *Sturm und Drang* of youth.

The title of the following article refers to men who have reached the age of fifty. Sprague describes a speech given by an eminent business expert at an annual sales convention of a big manufacturing organization. The speaker insists that anyone over fifty is past his prime in the business world. Sprague describes the effect of this speech on one of the assembled group, "Old Bill," and then he relates the inspiring story of Mr. Henderson. It is useful to compare Willy to both of these men.

FROM J. R. SPRAGUE, "THE DANGEROUS AGE"
(*Saturday Evening Post*, 20 August 1921: 6–7, 56)

His closing words were direct, incisive.

"Remember this, gentlemen," he said: "your real producing years are between the ages of twenty-five and fifty. You must get yourself fixed during that time if you do not want to have a dependent old age.

"I do not mean to say that a man cannot be a producer after he is fifty; some of the most active men in this organization are beyond that. But I do want to impress upon you that it is dangerous to make a business change after you are fifty. You can carry along something you have already got going, but you can't safely engage in anything new. Get safe before you are fifty!"

There was a thoughtful hush among the men grouped about the banquet tables as the speaker bowed and sat down. He had meant only to say something which would stimulate them to work harder in the interests of their company, but he had struck deeper than that. Some of the salesmen and branch managers were already past fifty. From the abstracted looks on their faces anyone could see that they had not all got themselves safe.

I noticed one man at a table near me who seemed particularly preoccupied. He was a pleasant-looking man of fifty-five, perhaps, with grayish hair and some crow's-feet about his eyes. His companions were calling him Bill. He shifted uneasily in his chair during the expert's remarks, looking intently at the tablecloth and moving his glass of water from one place to another. When the banquet was over he did not stick round with his fellow workers, but went directly to the check room, where he got his hat and coat, and left the hotel by himself.

The gray-haired man's actions did not escape the notice of the young branch manager whose guest I had been during the banquet. "I am afraid that business expert's talk hit Old Bill pretty hard," he said as we walked out of the ballroom; "I mean the remarks he made about a man's getting safe by the time he is fifty."

"Bill isn't safe, then?" I queried.

"No, he isn't," answered the young branch manager, "and I know he worries a lot about it. . . .

"Old Bill is up against it. He is in charge of one of our smaller offices, because he hasn't been with the company as long as a lot of the younger fellows. He is past fifty-five years old, and I don't believe he could scare up five thousand dollars to save his life."

"Does he seem to be slipping?" I asked. "Isn't he making good with the company?"

"Oh, I guess the company is well enough satisfied with his work," the branch manager replied; "but that isn't the question. You heard what the business expert said. Everyone knows that a man ought to have himself safely fixed by the time he is fifty. Bill is older than that, and he hasn't got himself safely fixed by a long shot. All in the world he has got to depend on is his job with this company, and he can't possibly save enough out of his salary to have enough to quit on when he has to stop work. Poor Old Bill is surely up against it.''

"Maybe he could go into something else," I suggested. "He might start a business of his own and build up."

The young branch manager looked at me quickly to see if I meant it. When he answered it was with a faint breath of sarcasm.

"A man of Bill's age go into business for himself!" he exclaimed. "It can't be done. The best he can hope to do is to plug along at what he is doing and save what little he is able. But to break into something new— not a chance!"

• • •

From the time he was twenty-five years old until he became fifty-three Mr. Henderson was connected with an importing house in Lower Manhattan. When he started with the concern it was a rather small affair. He was assistant bookkeeper at first, then head bookkeeper. This gave him some knowledge of credits, and as the concern grew to the point where it needed a regular credit man Mr. Henderson graduated into the job. By the time he was thirty-five he was drawing a salary of six thousand dollars a year.

The head of the firm was Mr. Henderson's friend as well as employer. It was understood that he would be taken into the firm some day, but before that day arrived the owner died and the management came into the hands of his two sons, who felt that they did not want any part of the ownership to get out of the family. But Mr. Henderson seemed an indispensable part of the business, and so instead of making him a member of the firm they offered him an increased salary. By the time he was forty he was earning ten thousand dollars a year, which salary was continued as long as he was connected with the house.

• • •

[Four years later the sons decided to sell the business.]

Mr. Henderson had supposed he was an indispensable part of the business, inasmuch as he had helped so largely to build it up; but he learned differently. The new owner had bought a going business, not traditions or sentiment. Almost his first act was to lop off the expense of Mr. Henderson's ten-thousand-dollar salary. He figured that he could act as credit man himself. It was, in fact, no time for a credit man to regard himself as indispensable anywhere. . . . With his long record of success, Mr. Henderson thought he would be able to connect up with some other concern, but there was little chance. No one needed a credit man.

• • •

[Unable to find work and near despair, Henderson met an old friend, now working as a traveling salesman. He gave Henderson advice and spelled out his personal theory about salesmanship, which encouraged Henderson to embark upon a similar career.]

"I hope you haven't got the idea about salesmanship that a lot of people have," he said. "There really isn't anything mysterious about selling things. You don't have to pull off any wonderful stunts or use applied psychology on prospective customers. If you did it wouldn't get you anywhere. There isn't any short cut to successful salesmanship any more than anywhere else.

"I have found," he continued, "that the main thing about selling goods on the road is being willing to do hard work and not lie down on the job when things are dull. There are lots of fair-weather salesmen who are cracker-jacks as long as business is good, but let a depression come along and they lose their courage about as quick as a barnyard rooster that is matched against a thoroughbred gamecock. A man like that gets into a town in the morning and calls on about four people. All four turn him down. He comes to the conclusion that business in the town is rotten, and so takes the noon train out for the next place, hoping things will be better there. Maybe things were rotten in the first town; but like as not there was some concern right round the corner which had put off buying so long that its stock was low and it really needed goods. If the salesman had waited until the evening train and called on every prospect he would have got some business."

The traveling man changed from his consideration of salesmanship in general to the individual case of his friend, Mr. Henderson.

"Perhaps you think," he said, "that because you have been an office man all your life it will be impossible to change into a salesman, now that you are well past fifty years old. I can't see why you should worry about that. You know how to approach people in an agreeable way, neither truckling nor overbold. That, as I understand it, is about the only thing in salesmanship which might be called a trick of the trade. Almost any man will listen to your story if you don't rub him the wrong way at the start.

"For the rest, your age is in your favor instead of being against you. When you yourself go into a retail store to buy something, don't you feel a little more confidence in the article if a middle-aged salesman tells you it is guaranteed instead of being obliged to take the word of a young fellow of twenty-two or twenty-three? Of course you do. And it will be the same way when you take a line of merchandise out on the road. You will gain a hearing from buyers many times when a younger man couldn't, and your sales talk will have more weight than his."

• • •

Mr. Henderson accepted his friend's advice, and at fifty-four became a traveling man. He says he likes it. He is his own boss, because he sells entirely on commission and pays his own expenses. The worst feature is that he is away from home so much, but even that isn't so bad when figured out accurately. He and his wife have calculated that they actually spend more time together now, counting the periods when he is at home between trips, than in the old days when he left for the office at half past seven every morning and didn't get home until after six in the evening. Last fall she went out with him on a four weeks' trip, and they covered his whole territory together, having a great time. All his customers were glad to meet her. At several places they were invited out to dinner, and at other places they would have the customer and his wife to dinner with them at the hotel. It was like a regular wedding trip, his wife had said.

STUDY QUESTIONS

1. In what ways is Montagu saying that American society is biased toward the young? How has this affected the way America views the elderly?

2. Does American society today seem to be biased toward a particular age group? If so, which one, and how?

3. Montagu describes his "cult of youthfulness" as a failure of culture to deal with age properly. What does he suggest should be done to rectify this problem? Do you think his suggestions will work? Can you think of any additional suggestions?

4. In what ways is this "cult of youthfulness" evident in *Death of a Salesman*?

5. Why is Old Bill in Sprague's article so worried? Does Old Bill remind you of Willy Loman in any way?

6. How far is age a handicap or an advantage to Mr. Henderson's career?

TOPICS FOR WRITTEN OR ORAL EXPLORATION

1. Poor Richard evidently has a lot of sayings. List them all and, by explaining what each means, consider what essential messages they hold in common. Which of these sayings are followed by any of the characters in *Death of a Salesman*?

2. Write a comparison between the Walton family and the Lomans. Consider whether or not anyone in the Loman family shares Harry Walton's outlook on life.

3. Write the outline for what you feel might be a typical Horatio Alger Jr. story for today.

4. Write an account of how Harry Walton might fare in today's society.

5. Write a letter in which Dale Carnegie describes the Lomans to a friend.

6. Write down what you feel are the six most important rules for success.

7. Consider how accurately Carnegie is describing Willy when he considers what it is that people want. In what ways does Willy's outlook on life appear to have been influenced by men such as Carnegie?

8. Write a report M. T. Horwich might have written about Willy if the latter had been one of his salesmen.

9. Which of the characters in *Death of a Salesman* (if any) do you feel

are able to develop what Roosevelt calls "ordinary qualities to a more than ordinary degree"?

10. What "individual qualities" do the Loman men possess that prevent them from becoming brilliant successes? What qualities do they lack that hinder their advancement? Explain how the Loman men choose the jobs they pursue, and to what jobs they actually seem best suited.

11. Outline which of the various attitudes toward success in this chapter appear to be the most realistic, and pick the person to whom it seems that Willy Loman has listened the most.

12. Would you prefer to live in a city or in the countryside, and why?

13. What does the "West" mean to you today?

14. Compare Booth's vision of the West first to that of Turner and then to the views of Biff and Willy Loman. Who seems to have the most balanced view?

15. Write a diary for a week in the life of a typical Zenith resident.

16. How might Lewis Mumford describe one of today's cities?

17. How do you think today's society treats the elderly?

18. Create a dialogue that might take place between a young person and an old person in which each one explains how they feel they are treated by others. You may set it in the 1940s or in the present, but you need to indicate in their conversation when it takes place.

19. Write about how the life of Sprague's Mr. Henderson compares and contrasts to the life of Willy Loman.

20. Imagine Sprague's Old Bill or Henderson bumping into Willy Loman on the road. Write a conversation they might have on meeting.

SUGGESTED READINGS

The Protestant Work Ethic vs. Myths of Success

Alger, Horatio Jr. *Risen from the Ranks, or Harry Walton's Success*. Philadelphia: John C. Winston, 1874.

Emerson, Ralph Waldo. "Self Reliance." *Essays*. Boston: Houghton Mifflin, 1841.

Jones, Howard Mumford. *The Pursuit of Happiness*. Cambridge: Harvard University Press, 1953.

Lerner, Max. "Life Goals and the Pursuit of Happiness." In *America as a Civilization*. New York: Simon and Schuster, 1957. 688–99.

Pastoral Myth of the Golden West vs. the Urban Myth

Emerson, Ralph Waldo. "Nature." Boston: J. Mawol, 1836.

Forbes, B. C. "Give Me the West! Story and Ideas of Harry W. Child." *American Magazine* 89 (May 1920): 16–17.

Lerner, Max. "City Lights and Shadows." In *America as a Civilization.* New York: Simon and Schuster, 1957. 155–72.

Turner, Frederick Jackson. "The Significance of the Frontier in American History." American History Association, *Annual Report for the Year 1893.* Washington, DC, 1894. 199–227.

Culture of Youth vs. Culture of Age

Atwood, Albert W. "Do Opportunities Still Exist?" *Saturday Evening Post* 192 (3 July 1920): 29, 90, 92, 97–98, 100.

Patterson, C. W. "Business Is a Young Man's Game." *American Magazine* 89 (June 1920): 34–35.

Walsh, J. J. "Don't Coddle and Boss the Old Folks!" *American Magazine* 87 (April 1919): 44–46.

3

Economic Interests and Forces

Death of a Salesman can be read as an illustration of the economic interests and forces operating on American society during the period of Willy Loman's life. Willy has lived through many major changes in the economic structure of his country. He witnessed the sense of hope and possibility at the beginning of the new millennium, a time when his father and brother both left home to embrace these possibilities to the full. He lived through the wild prosperity of the 1920s, a period when he felt he could become successful in the big city, and through to the 1929 Wall Street crash that marked the start of the Great Depression. The Depression lasted throughout the 1930s, and Willy would have found his products increasingly hard to sell, as few people had money to buy anything but necessities. With the economy being jump-started for the 1940s by the increased market demands and industrial advances of World War II, Willy has seen the renewed sense of vigor in the American economy, and this creates much of the hope he places in the prospects of his two sons. If they cannot make it in such a booming market, then surely there must be something wrong with them.

In addition to asking to what extent the Lomans might be trying to maintain an unrealistically high standard of living, we must also consider whether they are failing because of their own inadequacies or due to the unrealistic nature of such standards. In Miller's opinion, the blame for failure should not be attached to insignificant cogs in the social machine like the Lomans, but attributed to the larger social forces operating in these people's lives. Economics plays an important part in the creation of such forces. The selections in this chapter explore ways in which business matters seem at odds with conventional morality, how humanity is being threatened by the onset of technology, and the growing pressure to acquire material possessions. All these issues are reflected in the dilemmas of the Loman family and the other characters to whom they are economically linked.

Miller sees the constant American quest to be successful, especially in terms of wealth, as a potentially destructive and harmful one. Competition itself often creates negative values that may lead to success, but at what Miller sees as too heavy a price. Such people often place their very humanity in serious danger. Miller is keenly aware that those in power have a responsibility to those who are not—a responsibility toward which they all too often blind themselves. In some ways, Willy's inability to be really successful is tied to his intrinsic humanity. He cannot quite let go of his basic humanity and sense of responsibility to others.

BUSINESS VS. MORALITY

Willy Loman is living in a time when the nature of business itself is undergoing intrinsic changes, partly due to capitalist pressures to make more money and become more efficient, disregarding the kinds of ethical and honor systems that had guided many American "gentlemen" of business in the past. Systems designed to share wealth were shunned as containing the dangerous seeds of communism, and it was considered respectable to strive all out to make as much money as possible for oneself, regardless of who got left behind or trampled upon. A number of the characters in *Death of a Salesman* underline a definite clash between business and morality.

Since the nineteenth century, individualists like Henry David Thoreau have warned that business is in danger of taking over people's lives if they become too concerned with profit margins and becoming wealthier than necessary. "Life Without Principle" bemoans what Thoreau sees as a dangerous scramble for wealth inspired by the 1849 gold rush. He asks his readers to consider the difference between laboring to acquire material possessions and laboring toward cultural or spiritual growth. Thoreau is concerned with the way Americans perceive work, taking the viewpoint that people should work to live rather than live to work. It is useful to try to assess the importance of work to the various characters in *Death of a Salesman* and to consider whether or not work takes priority over everything else in their lives.

While some cultures have eschewed the acquisition of wealth as rapacious and unseemly, in American culture, the desire for wealth and status has become an almost virtuous pursuit. This is the point argued by Alexis de Tocqueville. However, there is a rather unpleasant side to living by such beliefs, as Tocqueville suggests when he discusses what he sees as the moral incongruities of many Americans. We need to consider just how far Willy's desire for wealth has led him into morally lax situations, such as his dalliance with a secretary in order to ensure that he gets in to see her boss. We should also consider the moral rectitude of other characters, especially Ben, Howard, and Hap. It seems that the best way to survive in a capitalist system is to become a better and more ruthless capitalist than your fellow workers; the road to wealth is only re-alized by treading on the backs of others. As Max Lerner points out, once the business spirit permeates the whole of American culture and making money becomes everyone's priority, morality itself becomes endangered. However, a character such as Charley seems to have found a way to survive with his morality intact; we should look closely at what he says and does in the play that en-ables him to do this. Using *Death of a Salesman* as evidence, assess whether Miller agrees or disagrees with the views of Thoreau, Tocqueville, and Lerner.

FROM HENRY DAVID THOREAU, "LIFE WITHOUT PRINCIPLE"
(Atlantic Monthly 12 [October 1863]: 484–88)

This world is a place of business. What an infinite bustle! I am awaked almost every night by the panting of the locomotive. It interrupts my dreams. There is no sabbath. It would be glorious to see mankind at leisure for once. It is nothing but work, work, work. I cannot easily buy a blank-book to write thoughts in; they are commonly ruled for dollars and cents. An Irishman, seeing me making a minute in the fields, took it for granted that I was calculating my wages. If a man was tossed out of a window when an infant, and so made a cripple for life, or scared out of his wits by the Indians, it is regretted chiefly because he was thus incapacitated for—business! I think that there is nothing, not even crime, more opposed to poetry, to philosophy, ay, to life itself, than this inces-sant business.

There is a coarse and boisterous money-making fellow in the outskirts of our town, who is going to build a bank-wall under the hill along the edge of his meadow. The powers have put this into his head to keep him out of mischief, and he wishes me to spend three weeks digging there with him. The result will be that he will perhaps get some more money to hoard, and leave for his heirs to spend foolishly. If I do this, most will commend me as an industrious and hardworking man: but if I choose to devote myself to certain labors which yield more real profit, though but little money, they may be inclined to look on me as an idler. Nev-ertheless, as I do not need the police of meaningless labor to regulate me, and do not see anything absolutely praiseworthy in this fellow's un-dertaking, any more than in many an enterprise of our own or foreign governments, however amusing it may be to him or them, I prefer to finish my education at a different school.

If a man walk in the woods for love of them half of each day, he is in danger of being regarded as a loafer; but if he spends his whole day as a speculator, shearing off those woods and making earth bald before her time, he is esteemed an industrious and enterprising citizen. As if a town had no interest in its forests but to cut them down!

• • •

Perhaps I am more than usually jealous with respect to my freedom. I feel that my connection with and obligation to society are still very slight and transient. Those slight labors which afford me a livelihood, and by which it is allowed that I am to some extent serviceable to my contemporaries, are as yet commonly a pleasure to me, and I am not often reminded that they are a necessity. So far I am successful. But I foresee, that, if my wants should be much increased, the labor required to supply them would become a drudgery. If I should sell both my forenoons and afternoons to society, as most appear to do, I am sure, that, for me there would be nothing left worth living for. I trust that I shall never thus sell my birthright for a mess of a pottage. I wish to suggest that a man may be very industrious, and yet not spend his time well. There is no more fatal blunderer than he who consumes the greater part of his life getting his living. All great enterprises are self-supporting. The poet, for instance, must sustain his body by his poetry, as a steam planning-mill feeds its boilers with the shavings it makes. You must get your living by loving. But as it is said of the merchants that ninety-seven in a hundred fail, so the life of men generally, tried by this standard, is a failure, and bankruptcy may be surely prophesied.

• • •

The rush to California, for instance, and the attitude, not merely of merchants, but of philosophers and prophets, so called, in relation to it, reflect the greatest disgrace on mankind. That so many are ready to live by luck, and so get the means of commanding the labor of others less lucky, without contributing any value to society! And that is called enterprise! I know of no more startling development of the immorality of trade, and all the common modes of getting a living. The philosophy and poetry and religion of such a mankind are not worth the dust of a puff-ball. The hog that gets his living by rooting, stirring up the soil so, would be ashamed of such company. If I could command the wealth of all the worlds by lifting my finger, I would not pay *such* a price for it. Even Mahomet knew that God did not make this world in jest. It makes God to be a moneyed gentleman who scatters a handful of pennies in order to see mankind scramble for them. The world's raffle! A subsistence in the domains of Nature a thing to be raffled for! What a comment, what a satire on our institutions! The conclusion will be, that mankind will hang itself upon a tree. And have all the precepts in all the Bibles taught men only this? and is the last and most admirable invention of the human race only an improved muck-rake? Is this the ground on which Orientals and Occidentals meet? Did God direct us so to get our living, digging where we never planted,—and He would, perchance, reward us with lumps of gold?

God gave the righteous man a certificate entitling him to food and raiment, but the unrighteous man found a *facsimile* of the same in God's coffers, and appropriated it, and obtained food and raiment like the former. It is one of the most extensive systems of counterfeiting that the world has seen. I did not know that mankind were suffering for want of gold. I have seen a little of it. I know that it is very malleable, but not so malleable as wit. A grain of gold will gild a great surface, but not so much as a grain of wisdom.

The gold-digger in the ravines of the mountains is as much a gambler as his fellow in the saloons of San Francisco. What difference does it make, whether you shake dirt or shake dice? If you win, society is the loser. The gold-digger is the enemy of the honest laborer, whatever checks and compensations there may be. It is not enough to tell me that you worked hard to get your gold. So does the Devil work hard. The way of transgressors may be hard in many respects. The humblest observer who goes to the mines sees and says that gold-digging is of the character of a lottery; the gold thus obtained is not the same thing with the wages of honest toil. But, practically, he forgets what he has seen, for he has seen only the fact, not the principle, and goes into trade there, that is, buys a ticket in what commonly proves another lottery, where the fact is not so obvious.

FROM ALEXIS DE TOCQUEVILLE, "OF HONOR IN THE UNITED STATES," IN *DEMOCRACY IN AMERICA*
(Trans. Henry Reeve. New York: Adlard and Saunders, 1838, Vol. 2, Book 3, Chapter 18, 248–49)

The Americans make a no less arbitrary classification of men's vices. There are certain propensities which appear censurable to the general reason and the universal conscience of mankind, but which happen to agree with the peculiar and temporary wants of the American community: these propensities are lightly reproved, sometimes even encouraged; for instance, the love of wealth and the secondary propensities connected with it may be more particularly cited. To clear, to till, and to transform the vast uninhabited continent which is his domain, the American requires the daily support of an energetic passion; that passion can only be the love of wealth; the passion for wealth is therefore not reprobated in America, and, provided it does not go beyond the bounds assigned to it for public security, it is held in honor. The American lauds as a noble and praiseworthy ambition what our own forefathers in the Middle Ages stigmatized as severe cupidity, just as he treats as a blind and barbarous frenzy that ardor of conquest and martial temper which bore them to battle.

In the United States fortunes are lost and regained without difficulty; the country is boundless and its resources inexhaustible. The people have all the wants and cravings of a growing creature; and, whatever be their efforts, they are always surrounded by more than they can appropriate. It is not the ruin of a few individuals, which may be soon repaired, but the inactivity and sloth of the community at large that would be fatal to such a people. Boldness of enterprise is the foremost cause of its rapid progress, its strength, and its greatness. Commercial business is there like a vast lottery, by which a small number of men continually lose, but the state is always a gainer; such a people ought therefore to encourage and do honor to boldness in commercial speculations. But any bold speculation risks the fortune of the speculator and of all those who put their trust in him. The Americans, who make a virtue of commercial temerity, have no right in any case to brand with disgrace those who practice it. Hence arises the strange indulgence that is shown to bankrupts in the United States; their honor does not suffer by such an accident. In this respect the Americans differ, not only from the nations of Europe, but from all the commercial nations of our time; and accordingly they resemble none of them in their position or their wants.

In America all those vices that tend to impair the purity of morals and to destroy the conjugal tie are treated with a degree of severity unknown in the rest of the world. At first sight this seems strangely at variance with the tolerance shown there on other subjects, and one is surprised to meet with a morality so relaxed and also so austere among the selfsame people. But these things are less incoherent than they seem to be. Public opinion in the United States very gently represses that love of wealth which promotes the commercial greatness and the prosperity of the nation, and it especially condemns that laxity of morals which diverts the human mind from the pursuit of well-being and disturbs the internal order of domestic life which is so necessary to success in business. To earn the esteem of their countrymen, the Americans are therefore forced to adapt themselves to orderly habits; and it may be said in this sense that they make it a matter of honor to live chastely.

FROM MAX LERNER, "THE REACH OF THE BUSINESS SPIRIT,"
IN *AMERICA AS A CIVILIZATION*
(New York: Simon and Schuster, 1957, 311–13)

Beyond these central and satellite activities of business the reach of the commercial spirit penetrates into every area of American culture. The business principle has sometimes been confused with the machine principle. The latter is used to dispense with human labor and make possible standardized and large-scale production, while the business principle focuses on market sale for profit. It puts the making of money ahead of other craft and civilization values, gives primacy to the cultural and personal traits which lead to that end, and tends to apply money values even to the human personality.

America has often been called a business civilization, but the term is too sweeping. One cannot say that the business principle is the only one operating in American culture. In some areas—religion, education, the arts, the family—it exerts only an incipient influence. But even where it has not become decisive, there has been a creeping imperialism of business over the other domains of life.

The business principle has given a synthetic cohesion to the far-flung diversity of American life. Before the Civil War it could genuinely be said that American culture was a loose collection of principalities—those of politics, of farming and industry, of religion, of literature and art and the press—tied together mainly by a pride of pioneering and a sense of the emerging national strength, and some belief in the democratic idea. The advance of business power and values weakened the hold of the democratic idea, while translating both the pioneering sense and the nationalist pride into the boom terms of growing industrial power and profit.

• • •

Yet the business spirit, which directly carries along in its torrential course so many of the talents and energies of men into money-making, also breaks down some of the moral barriers that had been built into the conscience for generations. The big temptation in the era of the expanding frontier was land speculation. In the era of an expanding capitalism the temptations lie less in speculation than in the sale of political influence to businessmen intent on getting some of the Big Money, by crucially placed governmental subalterns who don't see why they too should not get their cut. As in the post–Civil War days of Grant and Conkling, or the post–World War days of Harding and Daugherty, the torrents of fresh business energy which open new opportunities for big profits also carry away with them much of the terrain of social conscience. In this sense it is not the periods of business decay but the periods of business expansion and vitality which play havoc with moral principles, because they fix men's aims at the attainable goals of the Big Money.

STUDY QUESTIONS

1. What is it about business that truly bothers Thoreau? Why does he describe people making money out of the gold rush as "immoral" What does he see as the danger in thinking about nothing but work?

2. What does Thoreau see as the difference between "real profit" and "money," or "spending time well" as opposed to being "industrious"? What does Willy get from his job?

3. Who are the "police of meaningless labor"? What does Thoreau mean when he talks of selling one's "birthright for a mess of pottage"?

4. Is Thoreau an idle loafer or an enterprising citizen? Who makes such judgments, and on what do they base their assessments? Would Thoreau approve of Willy Loman?

5. How does Tocqueville think Americans see wealth as opposed to the rest of the world? In what ways does he believe Americans are different?

6. Why does Tocqueville insist that the love of wealth is essential to American progress? What does he suggest is the reason why so many Americans have been able to make such large fortunes?

7. What is the difference between ambition and cupidity? Does Willy possess either one?

8. What does Tocqueville see as the end results of American commercial business? Does Willy lose or gain by such business?

9. In what moral areas does Tocqueville see Americans as generally most lax and most strict? What does he believe "honor" means to Americans?

10. According to Lerner, what is the difference between the "business principle" and the "machine principle"? Which of these principles appears to be operating in *Death of a Salesman*?

11. How far does the "business principle" operate within the Loman family? In what ways do we see Willy's moral principles weakened by his desire to do business?

HUMANITY VS. TECHNOLOGY

The business boom that followed World War II saw a growth in mass production due to the increased development and understanding of technology. In 1928 Henry Ford declared machinery to be the "New Messiah," which could lead all Americans to their land of promise, as long as they embrace it without compunction. As the selections in this section show, many feared the idea of the subordination of man to the machine and worried over the effect this technological revolution would have on society as a whole. Willy certainly has very uneasy relationships with machinery in the play. Some people, like Ford, freely embraced mechanization as a way of becoming more efficient and increasing profits. But efficiency exacts certain costs, as Willy is to discover when he goes to see Howard Wagner, a man who is clearly captivated by technology.

Why does Willy Loman lose his job? We need to consider whether or not mass production necessarily requires that society itself become structured along mechanical principles. This is the fear expressed by such skillful social commentators as Charlie Chaplin in his movie, *Modern Times* (1936), or Aldous Huxley in his futuristic novel *Brave New World* (1932). They fear that in an entirely industrialized modern society people will become mere cogs in the machinery of production—Chaplin illustrates this quite literally by having his worker get caught up in the gears of a huge machine—and so lose all individuality and eventually their sense of self. Mass production seems to demand complete integration for it to run smoothly and efficiently. Workers become part of a larger pattern and lose their uniqueness. Once workers become so dehumanized, it becomes easier for management—swiftly becoming one of the new ruling classes by the 1950s—to treat those under them as things without feeling rather than as people, just as Howard treats Willy.

Miller recognizes that dangers lurk within technological advances and that in the pursuit of mechanical efficiency society may lose sight of a concern for actual people. Human beings need a sense of themselves as somehow unique to be content—both a sense of their place in society and a separate sense of themselves as important individuals. Technology can endanger both. Henry Adams' autobiography, *The Education of Henry Adams*, reflects on the changes that took place in America during his lifetime. In "The Dynamo and the Virgin" Adams examines the sensational growth of industry and its effect on Americans such as himself, who begin to worship technology. We need to consider how technology has changed the way both Adams and Willy perceive their worlds. Along with Adams, Willy recognizes and admires the power of technology, but both men are ultimately alienated by the new technologies that tend to destroy the worlds on which they had previously depended. Frederick Allen points out that technological advances have changed American society very swiftly and that everyone now seems to desire technological items. We see this in Willy's desire for things like new cars and refrigerators. However, Howard's obsession with his tape recorder becomes a potentially more dangerous pursuit in the way it seems to overtake all human considerations.

Joseph Schumpeter explains how business exploits rapid new inventions, leading to a depersonalized work environment in which the individual is increasing marginalized. Melvin Rader discusses the tendency of technology to move very fast, causing disorientation among families and people in general. We need to consider if any of the Lomans' lives are well organized, and whether any of them besides Willy show signs of disorientation. Rader's explanation of what might cause disorganization and disorientation in people's lives, and his description of the effect on society of the rapid spread of technological inventions in the 1940s, are depicted through the lives of the Lomans. Reading Rader encourages us to speculate why it might be uncomfortable to live in a constantly changing society. There is a tendency for technology to make people callous, and it becomes increasingly hard to be happy in a mechanized society that is intrinsically inhuman and too congested. Max Lerner suggests that most Americans embrace technology warmly, although some always remain suspicious. However, he sees the embrace of technology as causing the frugal values of the past to be replaced by greater consumption and higher standards of living. These documents should help us to reconsider the place of technology in *Death of a Salesman* and to determine how technology seems to be working for or against the Loman family.

FROM HENRY ADAMS, "THE DYNAMO AND THE VIRGIN," IN
THE EDUCATION OF HENRY ADAMS
(1907; Boston: Houghton Mifflin, 1918, 380–81)

He led his pupil directly to the forces. His chief interest was in new motors to make his airship feasible, and he taught Adams the astonishing complexities of the new Daimler motor, and of the automobile, which, since 1893, had become a nightmare at a hundred kilometres an hour, almost as destructive as the electric tram which was only ten years older; and threatening to become as terrible as the locomotive steam-engine itself, which was almost exactly Adams's own age.

Then he showed his scholar the great hall of dynamos, and explained how little he knew about electricity or force of any kind, even of his own special sun, which spouted heat in inconceivable volume, but which, as far as he knew, might spout less or more, at any time, for all the certainty he felt in it. To him, the dynamo itself was but an ingenious channel for conveying somewhere the heat latent in a few tons of poor coal hidden in a dirty engine-house carefully kept out of sight; but to Adams the dynamo became a symbol of infinity. As he grew accustomed to the great gallery of machines, he began to feel the forty-foot dynamos as a moral force, much as the early Christians felt the Cross. The planet itself seemed less impressive, in its old-fashioned, deliberate, annual or daily revolution, than this huge wheel, revolving within arm's-length at some vertiginous speed, and barely murmuring—scarcely humming an audible warning to stand a hair's-breadth further for respect of power—while it would not wake the baby lying close against its frame. Before the end, one began to pray to it; inherited instinct taught the natural expression of man before silent and infinite force. Among the thousand symbols of ultimate energy, the dynamo was not so human as some, but it was the most expressive.

FROM FREDERICK L. ALLEN, "FASTER, FASTER," IN *THE BIG CHANGE*
(New York: Harper, 1952, 188, 190–91)

Meanwhile the war-induced prosperity was speeding technological change on a quite different level. The jingle of cash in the pocket was preparing innumerable ordinary Americans to buy and use more machines just as soon as these became available. And after V-J Day the rush was on.

Everybody, to begin with, seemed to want new automobiles, which had been unavailable for purchase during the war. There was hot competition for the joy of getting a new car fresh from the assembly line; people talked about the number of months or years that they had "had their name in" with dealers; there was a lively racket in ostensibly used cars; and it was years before the automobile manufacturers could catch up with the demand. After they had done so, in the single year 1950 they sold more than eight million vehicles—which was more cars than had existed in the entire United States at the end of World War I.

But that wasn't the half of it. During these postwar years the farmer bought a new tractor, a corn picker, an electric milking machine; in fact he and his neighbors, between them, assembled a formidable array of farm machinery for their joint use. The farmer's wife got the shining white electric refrigerator she had always longed for and never during the Great Depression had been able to afford, and an up-to-date washing machine, and a deep-freeze unit. The suburban family installed a dishwashing machine and invested in a power lawnmower. The city family became customers of a laundromat and acquired a television set for the living room. The husband's office was air-conditioned. And so on endlessly.

• • •

At the mid-century a thoughtful observer of the startling progress of American technology is likely to feel a bewilderment akin to that which Adams felt in 1904. For the application of power to the circumstances of American life has not only increased at a dizzy pace since Adams's time, but has seemed to be accelerating sharply, with the promise of further leaps ahead. In the latter nineteen-thirties many economists had come to the conclusion that the United States had arrived at a "mature economy"; instead, we have been witnessing a technological revolution comparable to that which followed the introduction of steam, and far more rapid. During the fifteen years from 1935 to 1950 American technology took a stride forward at least as impressive as that which Henry Ford's assembly line dramatized in earlier years; and from all appearances this was not the culmination, but merely a preliminary phase, of a process of change which in time would profoundly alter the working and living conditions of the people.

FROM JOSEPH A. SCHUMPETER, "CRUMBLING WALLS," IN
CAPITALISM, SOCIALISM, AND DEMOCRACY
(New York: Harper, 1947, 131–33)

We have seen that the function of entrepreneurs is to reform or revolutionize the pattern of production by exploiting an invention or, more

generally, an untried technological possibility for producing a new com-
modity or producing an old one in a new way, by opening up a new
source of supply of materials or a new outlet for products, by reorgan-
izing an industry and so on.

• • •

To undertake such new things is difficult and constitutes a distinct
economic function, first, because they lie outside of the routine tasks
which everybody understands and, secondly, because the environment
resists in many ways that vary, according to social conditions, from simple
refusal either to finance or to buy a new thing, to physical attack on the
man who tries to produce it. To act with confidence beyond the range
of familiar beacons and to overcome that resistance requires aptitudes
that are present in only a small fraction of the population and that define
the entrepreneurial type as well as the entrepreneurial function. This
function does not essentially consist in either inventing anything or otherwise creating the conditions which the enterprise exploits. It consists
in getting things done.

• • •

Technological progress is increasingly becoming the business of teams
of trained specialists who turn out what is required and make it work in
predictable ways. The romance of earlier commercial adventure is rapidly
wearing away, because so many more things can be strictly calculated
that had of old to be visualized in a flash of genius.

On the other hand, personality and will power must count for less in
environments which have become accustomed to economic change—
best instanced by an incessant stream of new consumers' and producers'
goods—and which, instead of resisting, accept it as a matter of course.
The resistance which comes from interests threatened by an innovation
in the productive process is not likely to die out as long as the capitalist
order persists. It is, for instance, the great obstacle on the road toward
mass production of cheap housing which presupposes radical mechanization and wholesale elimination of inefficient methods of work on the
plot. But every other kind of resistance—the resistance, in particular, of
consumers and producers to a new kind of thing because it is new—has
well-nigh vanished already.

Thus, economic progress tends to become depersonalized and autom-
atized. Bureau and committee work tends to replace individual action.

• • •

Rationalized and specialized office work will eventually blot out personality, the calculable result, the "vision." The leading man no longer

has the opportunity to fling himself into the fray. He is becoming just another office worker—and one who is not always difficult to replace.

FROM MELVIN RADER, "TECHNOLOGY AND COMMUNITY: THE MANDATES OF SURVIVAL"
(Scientific Monthly 66 [1948]: 504–5)

Even the mere frequency of inventions has a disturbing effect upon the folkways of the old neighborhood life. Modern inventions are not only numerous but are increasing at a fast, cumulative pace. Most of these inventions are unpredictable, and a great many of their effects are unforeseeable. Consequently, men cannot prepare for the unknown future, and they find that the old ideas and prophecies do not apply. They feel bewildered, as though they had awakened after a severe earthquake to find the old landmarks scarcely recognizable.

The cumulative effect of these factors—mobility, communication, economic insecurity, modern technological warfare, and frequency of invention—is a disorientation more radical than the world has known for many centuries. When the mind is subjected to rapid shifts in time, space, rank, and expectation, impressions are multiplied beyond the individual's power of synthesis. Faced by this disjunctive multiplicity of experience, many minds have floundered in their effort to achieve life organization. The technological revolution has transported them to

> . . . . the waste beyond God's peace
> To maddening freedom and bewildering light.

The quiet, intimate, stable pattern of the small community or family group has, in consequence, been severely shaken.

No doubt the restless and sophisticated man of today is posterior in point of evolution to the stable "Philistine" type of the old-fashioned neighborhood and primary group; he is possibly higher in scale of "intelligence" and certainly wider in range of experience. Others besides Marx have spoken of the "idiocy" and dullness of rural and village life. Most city dwellers, indeed, would be reluctant to leave their cramped quarters for the more spacious and beautiful environment of the small town or countryside. To some extent, their reluctance is the result of a kind of blindness, like that of the city dweller who takes a portable radio when he goes into the country for an "outing" lest he feel bored in contact with earth and sky without the commercial advertising and continual mechanical din of the radio programs. On the other hand, many people have good reason for their reluctance to leave the great city. It affords more opportunity for varied experience, critical choice, purposive association, and many-faceted cultural experience. The small, relatively static community, in contrast, has less stimulus and challenge, less dramatic appeal, more stodgy conservatism, more intolerance toward variations in personality.

Life in the metropolitan environment, however, is now becoming so congested and hectic, so routinized in its mechanical regiments, so casual in its human contacts, that relatively few of the inhabitants can find any deep happiness or intimate companionship. The happy life, like music, has its melody and its harmonic background, its essential motifs and subsidiary phrases, evolving in an orderly and continuous pattern. Such organic development of personality occurs only when there is a considerable degree of organicity in the stuff of experience, whereas the environment of the machine-age man is disorganic in its confusion, profuse novelty, fragmentation of experience, and mechanized routines. The high rates of crime, juvenile delinquency, insanity, and suicide in the great urban areas are one indication of the human toll that is being exacted.

• • •

It is doubtful if the ideal of the brotherhood of man, which even now is honored more in the breach than in the observance, can be long sustained in this metropolitan environment. Modern technology and its giant spawn, industrialism, have so atomized human relations, so specialized human activities, so externalized human contacts, so entangled human nature in a net of technical functions, that the loving, intimate, comprehending relations of man to man have given way increasingly to the hostile, abstract, uncomprehending relations of "pressure groups" and mass organizations one to another. A face-to-face community, in contrast, is required for the appreciation of personality in its fullness and integrity.

As an illustration of the callousness of people in a great city, I might cite an Associated Press dispatch from Chicago dated August 13, 1947. It tells how a man was waylaid and robbed and then left late at night in an area of cheap bars and flophouses, to stumble along barefoot, shirtless, gagged, and with hands bound. He wandered into one saloon and then another to secure aid. In each case, the bartender took one look and ordered him out. He then approached a couple walking along the street and, with the gag in his mouth, tried by a pleading expression on his face to enlist help; but the two passers-by walked briskly away. Finally, he managed to work loose his hands, removed his gag, and went into another saloon to tell his story. The bartender, who consented to listen, tossed him a nickel to call the police. This misadventure, although extreme, illustrates the indifference—the lack of sympathy and understanding—that only a great city can breed.

FROM MAX LERNER, "THE CULTURE OF SCIENCE AND THE
MACHINE," IN *AMERICA AS A CIVILIZATION*
(New York: Simon and Schuster, 1957, 222–23, 226–27, 232–33)

I have tried to describe science in the phrase that Max Weber used of it: *Wissenschaft als Beruf*—science as discipline or calling. To a great degree this describes the place of science in a civilization like the American. There are some who in their overzealousness for science succeed only in distorting it. One group makes a cult of scientific neutrality. It makes of science not a method for handling experience and organizing observations but an end in itself—a dedicated, superhuman, almost inhuman way of life: in Nietzsche's words, "the last, most subtle asceticism." It regards scientific culture as the only important culture today, forgetting in its overrationalism that much of what men do and think is unreasoned, arising from the promptings of the unconscious self. It shades off into another group, which expects science to remake society with a conscious rationality of purpose.

• • •

Most Americans, however, with an organic optimism largely bred out of their experience of technological gains, are not troubled by these anxieties. They see science, and especially technology, as a means in the quest for an attainable good, and they feel certain that the good need never be explicitly defined but is implicit in the scientific quest. They regard the television eye and the electronic brain as proof that science has never lost the secret of mastery. They live within the realm of science and technology much as the American farmer once lived with the soil, as something close to their mood and experience. It is a medium in which they move much as they move in the air that they breathe.

Yet the gap between the scientist and the ordinary man, as they confront each other, is still an open one. The scientist is skeptical of every certainty except that of the method which makes him skeptical; he doubts everything except what enables his doubts to be productive of a new formulations. He tries to rid himself of any scared-cow beliefs in social institutions except for the open society without which he cannot breathe as a scientist. The common man, on the other hand, does seek certainties and is fearful that the scientist may destroy them. He wants a universe which is closed and comfortable, compact and finished. The universe of the scientist is still an expanding one, discontinuous and open. To keep it thus the scientist requires the willingness of an open society to let him follow his nose and give him the right to be wrong, both as scientist and as citizen. . . .

Given these changes, and the changing patterns of work in America . . . there is a problem which has baffled students of American society, especially those who come to it from the experience of European history. Here (they argue) is a working population cut off from the soil, severed from its tools and from the idea of work as craft and calling: why does it not become the victim of revolutionary movements and demagogues? Granted that the unique conditions of American history have played hob with the idea of a self-conscious revolutionary proletariat, why has not America retraversed the experience of the Roman Empire, whose landless, rootless, tool-less population was used by adventurist leaders? Or the similar experience of Hitler's Germany?

Behind these questions there is the running theme of alienation and its political effects, which has been emphasized in the literature of Socialism and psychiatry from Marx to Erich Fromm. Most Americans, especially the industrial and white-collar classes, have been alienated from some crucial life experiences—from the soil, from independent enterprise, from the ownership of tools, from the sense of craft and the dignity of work, from the feeling of relation to the total product. One might expect this to turn the American into the "formless" man whom Nietzsche dreaded and whose emergence in the modern machine world Ortega y Gasset has described, and thus into easy material for either revolutionary or reactionary adventurers.

The catch is in the failure to see that men uprooted from one kind of social and institutional soil can become rooted in another. The loss of some of the old life values may affect the long-range survival of the culture, but what counts for the cohesion of a culture in the generations immediately ahead is whether people have (or think they have) what their culture has taught them to value. While the American has been alienated by the machine from his old role as independent farmer-artisan-entrepreneur, his culture still has a strong hold on him. The loss of a sense of independence in the productive processes has been replaced by a feeling of well-being in consumption and living standards. The pull of property, no longer in tools or productive land but in consumers' goods; the sense of power and pleasure in the means of sight and sound and movement placed at his disposal by the communications revolution; the glorying in what makes the world of drama and entertainment accessible; the whole range of popular culture; the feeling of access to new gradients of income and experience: these form the new soil in which the American has found new roots.

The values of income, consumption, status, and popular culture are a different set of values from those of soil and craft and small-scale productive property, and in that sense the whole ground tone of American civilization has changed under the Big Technology. But the point is that in their own way they are values, not emptiness or formlessness. Even more strikingly, it is the Big Technology that has raised living standards, created leisure, carried through the communications revolution, and set the conditions for the new popular culture. That is to say, it is the machine itself that has cut American industrial, white-collar, and professional workers away from the machine and has transferred their interest and life energies from the making of goods to the making of money with which to buy and enjoy the goods.

STUDY QUESTIONS

1. Adams describes the dynamo as having a moral force similar to that of the cross in Christianity. What exactly are the implications of this? How would you describe Adams' reaction to the dynamo? Is it one of approval or disapproval?

2. How fast has technology grown in America in the twentieth century, and in what ways does Allen see this as problematic?

3. What machines do the Lomans feel that they must have? How necessary are these machines in actuality?

4. How does Schumpeter see mechanization as affecting America's business society, and how does he see the romance of commercial adventure being lost?

5. According to Schumpeter, who or what is the "entrepreneurial type?" What importance have personality and will power in a technologically advanced society? How does this clash with what Willy tells his sons? Who do you think is right, Schumpeter or Willy?

6. Do the Lomans have any resistance to new products and ideas? Does Willy have "vision?" What would Schumpeter feel is the use of such vision?

7. What does Rader see as the effect of the growth of technology on society, and how is this depicted in *Death of a Salesman*?

8. Why does Rader feel that the older sense of community has been destroyed by modern technology? Is this evidenced in *Death of a Salesman*?

9. Rader talks of people's lives being "organic" or "disorganic." What does he mean by this, and which term best describes the Lomans?

10. Could Rader's story of the man who was waylaid, robbed, and treated with indifference by the people he asked for help take place in the society we see depicted in *Death of a Salesman*? Do any similar events occur in the play?

11. Do any of the characters in *Death of a Salesman* see science as an "end in itself?" If so, how does this affect their humanity?

12. Does Lerner see technology as helping or hindering social development toward a better life? Does he see Americans as embracing or rejecting technology?

13. Does Willy Loman have the personality of what Lerner describes as a "scientist" or a "common man?"

14. Why does Lerner wonder whether Americans may wish to rebel, and what does he think has stopped them from doing so?

THE HAVES VS. THE HAVE-NOTS

American materialism has become somewhat notorious, both in terms of the American desire for the best of everything from services to goods, and the overwhelming abundance of goods and services available to satisfy those desires. This section explores how, in the search for the "good life," Americans, like the Lomans, have surrounded themselves with a plethora of things above and beyond the mere necessities of life. However, these goods are only available at a price, and not everyone in American society can afford all that the advertisers convince them that they must have to be considered happy. All dream of the high life, but few can afford it, and so four out of five Americans become trapped in a rat-race, a life Lerner describes as one of "worry, work and scrimping." Competitiveness lies at the heart of the American business culture. The drive to keep up with your neighbor becomes a spur to consumption and ensures that no one is ever satisfied, as all are ever hungry for more.

The drive for success creates a very competitive society in which people's standing in the community becomes measured by how much more they have than others. To "keep up with the Joneses" people sacrifice themselves on the treadmill of acquisition, striving to get a better job, higher income, a more opulent residence, and entrance into the best clubs. This often leads to rather joyless lives as people expend all of their time and effort in pursuit of the great god of wealth and prestige. Consider, for example, how far Willy is motivated by his desire to beat his neighbor Charley. Alexis de Tocqueville notes that Americans, because they are always striving for more, are never satisfied. In this light, to what extent can we see Willy and his family as typical Americans?

Thorstein Veblen's *The Theory of the Leisure Class* was a pioneering study on the way Americans perceive wealth. In his chapter on conspicuous consumption, he explains how consuming various goods becomes a mark of status and takes over every American household. Money for necessities gets spent on luxury goods to make the family seem more prosperous to outsiders. What items, for example, do the Lomans own that they really cannot afford? Are such items really necessary to their existence? Ironically, people have to work harder just to appear to be able to afford leisure, but how much leisure does a man like Willy ever actually enjoy? The essential meaning of Veblen's term "conspicuous consumption" and how this can be applied to people like the Lomans are very important. This should also lead us to consider in what other ways people can show themselves to be wealthy.

While most people seek to increase status through possessions, Vance Packard explains how advertisers play to this by emphasizing a product's generous size and expense, and by using testimonials of the rich and famous. We see evidence of the effectiveness of these techniques in Willy's desires for a Chevrolet and a General Electric refrigerator. They are techniques that could also be used to the Lomans' advantage. Hap and Biff clearly understand the way such techniques operate, as their plans to start a sporting goods business show, but it is unlikely that they will be able to raise the capital to begin such an enterprise. Packard concludes that giving in to the advertiser's art and trying to keep up with everyone else will inevitably cause great stress, which we see manifest in Willy's guilt at not being able to provide his family with more. The advertising copy for the American Face Brick Association, which blatantly appeals to people's desire to appear superior, is a good example of the techniques used to convince people like the Lomans to buy products, whatever the cost.

FROM ALEXIS DE TOCQUEVILLE, "WHY THE AMERICANS ARE SO RESTLESS IN THE MIDST OF PROSPERITY," IN *DEMOCRACY IN AMERICA*
(Trans. Henry Reeve. New York: Adlard and Saunders, 1838, Vol. 2, Book 2, Chapter 13, 144–46)

In certain remote corners of the Old World you may still sometimes stumble upon a small district that seems to have been forgotten amid the general tumult, and to have remained stationary while everything around it was in motion. The inhabitants, for the most part, are extremely ignorant and poor; they take no part in the business of the country and are frequently oppressed by the government, yet their countenances are generally placid and their spirits light.

In America I saw the freest and most enlightened men placed in the happiest circumstances that the world affords; it seemed to me as if a cloud habitually hung upon their brow, and I thought them serious and almost sad, even in their pleasures.

The chief reason for this contrast is that the former do not think of the ills they endure, while the latter are forever brooding over advantages they do not possess. It is strange to see with what feverish ardor the Americans pursue their own welfare, and to watch the vague dread that constantly torments them lest they should not have chosen the shortest path which may lead to it.

A native of the United States clings to this world's goods as if he were certain never to die; and he is so hasty in grasping at all within his reach that one would suppose he was constantly afraid of not living long enough to enjoy them. He clutches everything, he holds nothing fast, but soon loosens his grasp to pursue fresh gratifications.

In the United States a man builds a house in which to spend his old age, and he sells it before the roof is on; he plants a garden and lets it just as the trees are coming into bearing; he brings a field into tillage and leaves other men to gather the crops; he embraces a profession and gives it up; he settles in a place, which he soon afterwards leaves to carry his changeable longings elsewhere. If his private affairs leave him any leisure, he instantly plunges into the vortex of politics; and if at the end of a year of unremitting labor he finds he has a few days' vacation, his eager curiosity whirls him over the vast extent of the United States, and he will travel fifteen hundred miles in a few days to shake off his happiness. Death at length overtakes him, but it is before he is weary of his bootless chase of that complete felicity which forever escapes him.

• • •

Their taste for physical gratifications must be regarded as the original source of that secret disquietude which the actions of the Americans betray and of that inconstancy of which they daily afford fresh examples. He who has set his heart exclusively upon the pursuit of worldly welfare is always in a hurry, for he has but a limited time at his disposal to reach, to grasp, and to enjoy it. The recollection of the shortness of life is a constant spur to him. Besides the good things that he possesses, he every instant fancies a thousand others that death will prevent him from trying if he does not try them soon. This thought fills him with anxiety, fear, and regret and keeps his mind in ceaseless trepidation, which leads him perpetually to change his plans and his abode.

If in addition to the taste for physical well-being a social condition be added in which neither laws nor customs retain any person in his place, there is a great additional stimulant to this restlessness of temper. Men will then be seen continually to change their track for fear of missing the shortest cut to happiness.

It may readily be conceived that if men passionately bent upon physical gratifications desire eagerly, they are also easily discouraged; as their ultimate object is to enjoy, the means to reach that object must be prompt and easy or the trouble of acquiring the gratification would be greater than the gratification itself. Their prevailing frame of mind, then, is at once ardent and relaxed, violent and enervated. Death is often less dreaded by them than perseverance in continuous efforts to one end.

FROM THORSTEIN VEBLEN, "CONSPICUOUS CONSUMPTION,"
IN *THE THEORY OF THE LEISURE CLASS*
(New York: Macmillan, 1899, 73–74, 84–85)

The quasi-peaceable gentleman of leisure, then, not only consumes of the staff of life beyond the minimum required for subsistence and physical efficiency, but his consumption also undergoes a specialisation as regards the quality of the goods consumed. He consumes freely and of the best, in food, drink, narcotics, shelter, services, ornaments, apparel, weapons and accoutrements, amusements, amulets, and idols or divinities. In the process of gradual amelioration which takes place in the articles of his consumption, the motive principle and the proximate aim of innovation is no doubt the higher efficiency of the improved and more elaborate products for personal comfort and well-being. But that does not remain the sole purpose of their consumption. The canon of reputability is at hand and seizes upon such innovations as are, according to its standard, fit to survive. Since the consumption of these more excellent goods is an evidence of wealth, it becomes honorific; and conversely, the failure to consume in due quantity and quality becomes a mark of inferiority and demerit.

• • •

The basis on which good repute in any highly organised industrial community ultimately rests is pecuniary strength; and the means of showing pecuniary strength, and so of gaining or retaining a good name, are leisure and a conspicuous consumption of goods. Accordingly, both of these methods are in vogue as far down the scale as it remains possible; and in the lower strata in which the two methods are employed, both offices are in great part delegated to the wife and children of the household. Lower still, where any degree of leisure, even ostensible, has become impracticable for the wife, the conspicuous consumption of goods remains and is carried on by the wife and children. The man of the household also can do something in this direction, and, indeed, he commonly does; but with a still lower descent into the levels of indigence—along the margin of the slums—the man, and presently also the children, virtually cease to consume valuable goods for appearances, and the woman remains virtually the sole exponent of the household's pecuniary decency. No class of society, not even the most abjectly poor, foregoes all customary conspicuous consumption. The last items of this category of consumption are not given up except under stress of the direst necessity. Very much of squalor and discomfort will be endured before the last trinket or the last pretence of pecuniary decency is put away. There is no class and no country that has yielded so abjectly before the pressure of physical want as to deny themselves all gratification of this higher or spiritual need.

FROM VANCE PACKARD, "SELLING SYMBOLS TO UPWARD
STRIVERS," IN *THE HIDDEN PERSUADERS*
(New York: McKay, 1957, 106–10, 112, 114–15)

While American society presents an over-all picture of stratification, most of the individuals at the various layers—excepting only the benighted nonstrivers near the bottom—aspire to enhance their status. This trait, which if not peculiarly American is at least particularly American, offered an opportunity that the depth merchandisers were quick to exploit. It needed to be done with some deftness as no one cares to admit he is a social striver.

Lloyd Warner spelled out the inviting situation to ad men in these words: "Within the status systems something else operates that is at the very center of American life and is the most motivating force in the lives of many of us—namely what we call social mobility, the aspiration drive, the achievement drive, the movement of an individual and his family from one level to another, the translation of economic goods into socially approved symbols, so that people achieve higher status."

As the merchandisers became symbol-conscious, the markets for many different products began taking on new and exciting dimensions. Mr. Martineau for example pointed out that among automobiles the Buick and Oldsmobile were particularly valued by highly mobile people as symbols that they were going somewhere. Such owners "are striving," he explained, "but don't yet want to say they are in the Cadillac class."

A home-furnishings designer, in 1956, explained the facts of life about what people are really reaching for in decorating their home. This designer, George Nelson, asserted that the typical wife was more concerned about creating an impression than with solving a problem. She wants to show that her husband is rising fast in the dry-goods business and is really a great big success.

• • •

The depth probers studying the most effective ways to sell status symbols to American strivers concluded that most of us are vulnerable to one of three merchandising strategies.

One is to offer bigness. Millions of Americans were believed to equate, subconsciously, biggest with best, best at least at making a big impression. A kitchen-range maker found himself in trouble because he accepted as fact the explanation many people gave for preferring a large kitchen range rather than a smaller one of equal efficiency. The customers had explained, almost unanimously, that they had bought the bigger stove in order to have more work space. With this in mind the company put engineers to work, and they brought out a moderate-sized stove with all working elements engineered more compactly to permit an unusually large work space. The stove was a dud. Salesmen couldn't move it off the floor. The firm called in a Connecticut market-research firm with staff psychologists who examined the problem and concluded: "People are willing to pay a great deal more for a little space they don't really use because what they are interested in is not so much the space itself as the expensive appearance of a large range." . . .

A second way merchandisers found they could sell us their products as status symbols was through the price tag. By seemingly inverse logic, many discovered they could increase their sales by raising their price tag, in the topsy-turvy merchandising battle of the mid-fifties. . . .

The third strategy that merchandisers found was effective in selling products as status symbols was to persuade personages of indisputably high status to invite the rest of us to join them in enjoying the product. The testimonial can be a mighty effective selling device, *Printer's Ink* pointed out, cynics to the contrary. This is particularly true where the celebrity has some plausible ground for being interested in the product. Testimonials by celebrities were not a new discovery but in the early fifties they were placed on a systematic basis.

• • •

All the social striving encouraged by these various strategies of symbol-selling has a cost, too, emotionally. Economist Robert Lekachman indicated this when he stated: "We can only guess at the tensions and anxieties generated by this relentless pursuit of the emblems of success in our society, and shudder at what it might give rise to during an economic setback."

ADVERTISING COPY FOR THE AMERICAN FACE BRICK ASSOCIATION
(*Literary Digest*, 30 October 1920)

The use of Face Brick in the homes of the average family has greatly increased in the last few years. More and more, people are thinking of home-building in terms of permanent investment.

First cost is not the important financial factor in building. Upkeep, depreciation, fire-safety and insurance rates determine the ultimate economy of your expenditure. And beauty, too, has a tangible value in case you ever wish to sell or rent—not to mention the satisfaction it gives you to live in an artistic home.

The difference between frame and brick upkeep and depreciation amounts in five years to more than twice the initial excess cost of brick.

Even if you are not ready to build now, now is the time to think matters over and formulate your plans. "The Story of Brick" and "The Home of Beauty" will help you to a decision.

• • •

A•F•B•A
USE FACE BRICK
—it Pays

"THE STORY OF BRICK"
An artistic booklet with attractive illustrations and useful information for all who intend to build. The Romance of Brick, Extravagance of Cheapness, Comparative Costs, How to Finance the Building of a Home, are a few of the subjects treated. Your copy is awaiting your request. Send today.

"THE HOME OF BEAUTY"
A book of fifty designs of attractive small Face Brick houses, selected from four hundred drawings entered in a national architectural competition. The houses represent a wide variety of architectural styles, with skillful handling of interior arrangements. Sent on receipt of fifty cents in stamps.

STUDY QUESTIONS

1. How does Tocqueville describe Americans as opposed to other nationalities, and how does he explain the differences? What does Tocqueville see as the biggest advantages and disadvantages of being American?

2. What does Tocqueville see as the biggest American fear? Can this be applied to Willy Loman?

3. What does Willy "consume" that is not really necessary for his subsistence? What does he want that he does not have? Why does Veblen suggest Willy might want such things?

4. Why is Willy so annoyed when his wife tries to mend her stockings? What would Veblen say was the reason?

5. What does Veblen suggest provides a good reputation in an industrial society such as the United States? Is this something that Willy has? What does leisure have to do with a person's reputation? Does Willy have any leisure time?

6. How do people show that they have "pecuniary strength"? How does Willy try to do this? Does such an urge have any harmful side effects?

7. What does Vance Packard see as particularly American traits? To what extent are the members of the Loman family the type of upward strivers described by Packard?

8. How does Packard see a car as a symbol of status? What kind of car does Willy drive, and how does this affect his status?

9. What would Packard notice Linda doing to try to create a good impression with her home? What problems does she tend to ignore?

10. What does Packard suggest are the three most effective merchandising strategies? Do the Lomans show an awareness of any of them? What does economist Robert Lekachman see as the final cost of such sales techniques? Have the Lomans paid the price?

11. What are the implications behind the subject areas in the "artistic" booklet "The Story of Brick" offered by the American Face Brick Association?

12. Why would someone want to put face-brick on their home?

13. What is the difference between a regular home and the "artistic home" promised by the Brick Association? Are they telling the truth? Is first cost really not the important financial factor in building? Why would they tell their customers this?

14. What, apart from bricks, is the Brick Association selling to their customers?

TOPICS FOR WRITTEN OR ORAL EXPLORATION

1. Would Willy Loman support the "gold-digger" or the "honest laborer" in Thoreau's "Life Without Principle," and why? Do any of the characters in *Death of a Salesman* prefer what Thoreau calls "real profit" over money?

2. Write an imaginary letter from Willy or Ben Loman to Thoreau in response to his essay "Life Without Principle."

3. What do you think Tocqueville believes Americans must do to live honorably? Consider whether or not Miller would agree with Tocqueville's definition of American honor. Could Willy Loman or any other character in *Death of a Salesman* be called an honorable man?

4. Write an essay on what you think Tocqueville would have said about America in the 1940s and/or today. Would he see it as having changed a lot, or as being essentially the same?

5. Summarize what Lerner means by the "commercial spirit." To what extent does Miller show it as having penetrated into every area of American culture in *Death of a Salesman*?

6. Who seems to have the most power in *Death of a Salesman*, the individual or big businesses? Write an essay that explains how the various characters in the play might view this issue, and try to account for any differences of opinion.

7. Write a description Willy might have included in his autobiography about the same exhibition that Adams attended; consider how Willy might view the way in which technological advances would change his life.

8. Write an essay on how World War II affected the American economy and how this is depicted by the desires and designs of the Loman family.

9. Write an essay in which you consider whether or not any of the characters in *Death of a Salesman* fit Schumpeter's description of the "entrepreneurial type." Include any characters in the play who want

to be the entrepreneurial type but fail, and a discussion of whether or not Miller offers reasons why they fail.

10. Imagine that Howard Wagner has decided to advertise for a new salesman. Write the advertisement he might put together to attract what he would see as the right kind of salesman.

11. List the essential differences between the old and new life values Lerner discusses, and suggest which of these values Willy Loman displays.

12. In "Why the Americans Are So Restless in the Midst of Prosperity," Tocqueville attempts to describe a whole nation. Is this description supported by the characters and events of *Death of a Salesman*? What kind of letter would Charley write to Tocqueville (if he were still alive) in response to his essay?

13. Who is Willy Loman trying to impress, and why? How does he go about trying to impress others, and what is it that he sees as "impressive?" Write a letter from Willy to his brother Ben that provides answers to these questions.

14. Write what you think Vance Packard might say about Willy's selling techniques, or about Biff and Hap's business ideas.

15. How would Vance Packard advertise the Loman brothers' business if they actually got it going?

16. Write a journal entry by Linda Loman in which she explains what she wants for her home and family.

17. Write an essay on the degree to which economic interests and forces of the time are to blame for the difficulties faced by the Loman family.

18. Create an advertisement for a common household product using the same selling strategies employed by the American Face Brick Association.

SUGGESTED READINGS

Business vs. Morality

Drucker, Peter F. *The New Society*. New York: Harper, 1950.

Gras, N.S.B. "Capitalism—Concepts and History." *Bulletin of the Business Historical Society* 16, no. 2 (April 1942): 21–34.

Trachtenberg, Alan. *The Incorporation of America: Culture and Society in the Gilded Age*. New York: Hill and Wang, 1982.

Turner, George Kibble. "The Way of Capital with the New World." *Saturday Evening Post* 193 (8 January 1921): 16, 92, 95, 97.

Humanity vs. Technology

Giedion, Sigfried. *Mechanization Takes Command*. New York: Oxford University Press, 1948.

Mumford, Lewis. "Let Men Take Command." *Saturday Review of Literature* 31 (2 October 1948): 7–9, 33–35.

Potter, David. *People of Plenty*. Chicago: University of Chicago Press, 1954.

The Haves vs. the Have-Nots

Allen, Frederick L. "The All-American Standard." In *The Big Change*. New York: Harper, 1952. 209–33.

Davis, J. S. "Standards and Content of Living." *American Economic Review* 35 (March 1945): 1–15.

Lerner, Max. "The Wilderness of Commodities." In *America as a Civilization*. New York: Simon and Schuster, 1957. 249–58.

Montagu, Ashley. "The Pursuit of Happiness." In *The American Way of Life*. New York: Putnam's, 1967. 27–33.

4

American Business Culture

There are three generations of salesmen in *Death of a Salesman*, that of Willy's father and his hero Dave Singleman, that of Willy and Charley, and that of Willy's sons and his boss, Howard Wagner. In the play, Miller creates a history of the career of the traveling salesman in America in the stories of these characters, and through them he suggests some of the larger reasons for Willy's business failure and his personal disintegration.

The profession of traveling salesman began in the United States with the Yankee peddler in the early nineteenth century. Peddlers would buy up cheap, portable manufactured gadgets in the early industrial centers of the Northeast, pack them in a wagon or peddler's pack, and set off for the rural South or the frontier villages of the West, where they would travel from small town to small town, selling their wares at a high profit. They generally traveled in a wide circuit, following the mild weather south in the winter and north in the summer, and returning once or twice a year to the city for new merchandise. These men were entrepreneurs, operating completely on their own, free to buy and sell whatever they wanted and to travel wherever they liked. Willy Loman's father, born in the mid-nineteenth century, was a peddler. Ben tells Willy that their father was a "very wild-hearted man" who would "toss the whole family in the wagon" and drive right across the country, through Ohio, Indiana, Michigan, Illinois, and all the Western states. Miller emphasizes the elder Loman's independence by indicating that he even manufactured the products he sold, the flutes he made along the way. According to Ben, he was also a great inventor who made more in a week with one gadget than a man like Willy could make in a lifetime. It is the elder Loman that Miller evokes with the play's flute music, "small and fine, telling of grass and trees and the horizon." It speaks of a lost age when the traveling salesman was free and independent, living by his wits and his own hard work.

It is significant that Willy's father traveled west, away from the urban centers of the country, and eventually left his family to go to America's last frontier, Alaska. During Willy's childhood in the 1890s, the Yankee peddler was already an outmoded figure, living on the fringes of society. He had been replaced by a figure who served the interests of the larger manufacturers more efficiently, the drummer. Beginning in the late nineteenth century, drummers, usually young men with pleasant personalities, were sent by large manufacturing firms or wholesalers to greet small retail merchants who came from outlying areas to the industrial centers to buy their stock. The drummers would go to hotels, railroad stations, and boat landings, greet the merchants, help them to make their way around the city, and offer them free entertainment in hopes of securing their orders for merchandise. As competition between wholesalers intensified, the drummers were sent on the road with sample cases and catalogs, going out to the merchants rather than waiting for them to come to the city. These were the original traveling salesmen, and they spent six to nine months a year on the road, living in hotels and sleeping cars.

Dave Singleman is Miller's example of the drummer, Willy's hero. When Willy was young, in the first decade of the twentieth century, he met Dave Singleman, a salesman who had drummed merchandise in thirty-one states. Singleman was eighty-four years old at the time Willy met him, and still making his living as a salesman. According to Willy, he could go into twenty or thirty different cities, pick up a phone, and call the buyers, who would give him orders. Willy decided then that he wanted to be a traveling salesman because he wanted to become like Singleman and be "remembered and loved and helped by so many different people."

Willy's own career as a salesman began in the early part of the twentieth century, when, as Willy tells his sons, "personality" was the salesman's greatest asset. His job was to make friends with buyers and merchants so that they would buy what he was selling. The product itself was not all that important. With the growth of mass production, however, the pressure increased on the salesman to "move merchandise," to sell as much as possible in order to keep up the volume of production. As Willy came into his maturity, married, and raised his sons during the 1920s, there was a good deal of pressure on him to sell merchandise, but it was relatively easy to do so, since the American economy was enjoying one of its greatest periods of prosperity. Willy was able to support his family and to buy a house, the cars that were necessary for his work, and the new "big ticket" appliances that were being invented for the home, such as a refrigerator.

There was a debate among salesmen at this time over the best approach to selling merchandise. While there were many like Willy, who put all their faith in personality, friendship, and personal loyalty, there was a new way of thinking about salesmanship. The earlier assumption had been that good salesmen are born, not made. During the teens and twenties, salesmanship was beginning to be treated as a profession to be learned. The new interest in psychology led experts to think about the psychology of the buyer and how best to manipulate it, as well as the psychological traits that made for the best salesmen. With mass production and increased competition, buyers and merchants began to think more about profit margins and customer satisfaction than about their own personal relationship with the salesman. There was more interest in the quality of the product and the salesman's knowledge about it. Companies began to train employees in the methods of salesmanship and to educate them about the products they were selling.

With the stock market crash in 1929 and the Great Depression that followed it, competition among salesmen became more and more cutthroat. One-third of Americans were unemployed at the height of the Depression, and the demand for consumer goods dropped precipitately. Willy Loman's job got harder and harder. As Willy tells Ben in one of the daydream sequences that take place in 1931, "business is bad, it's murderous." Using all of the tricks that Willy has learned in a lifetime of selling, including seducing the buyer's secretary and bribing her with stockings, Willy is barely able to eke out a living for his family.

The definitive end of the Depression did not come until World War II, when American manufacturers were geared up to manufacture war materiel. With most of the younger men in the military, cutting down the competition, middle-aged salesmen like Willy made an adequate living during World War II despite the fact that the manufacture of consumer goods was severely restricted. In the postwar period, when the "real" time of the play takes place, there was a pent-up demand for things like new cars, tires, brand-name liquor, and nylon stockings, which had not been available during the war. The enormous American war industry was being retooled to produce consumer goods, and the advertising business was expanding rapidly as Americans were "educated" to desire things like vacuum cleaners, televisions, and air conditioners, which had not been manufactured in large quantities before the war. Young men were returning from the military eager to resume the lives that had been interrupted by the war. The newly invigorated American business sector seized on this youthful and energetic workforce, displacing the women and older men who had been employed during the war. Men like Willy Loman, sixty-three years old in 1948, were being displaced by the younger generation everywhere.

Hap Loman and Howard Wagner are typical members of this younger generation. Hap is not a salesman, but one of two assistants to the assistant buyer of a large department store. His job is more secure than Willy's, and it carries a regular salary rather than the precarious commission that Willy lives on. Unlike his father, though, Hap does not use his salary to support a family. Instead, he lives a carefree bachelor life, more interested, as Linda tells him, in his apartment and his car and his women than in helping his family.

After the war, the profession of selling changed along with everything else. As Willy says, "Today, it's all cut and dried, and there's no chance for bringing friendship to bear—or personality." Willy misses the respect, comradeship, and gratitude that had been a vital part of the business relationships of his youth. Howard Wagner, who has taken over the business that employs Willy after the death of his father, Frank, is pragmatic and impersonal in his treatment of the aging salesman. When Willy admits that he can't handle the road anymore, Howard refuses to consider finding him something to do in New York, as his father would have done, explaining, "It's a business, kid, and everybody's gotta pull his own weight." When Willy loses control, showing his desperation, Howard fires him, telling him that he is not in a fit state to represent the firm.

During the forties and fifties, the professional salesman became increasingly driven by things like market studies and demographics. Willy's plea for loyalty and humane treatment—"you can't eat the orange and throw the peel away—a man is not a piece of fruit!"—is irrelevant to Howard's way of thinking. The new way of thinking was that a salesman's job was not to sell a product—any product—to a buyer because he liked and trusted the salesman, but to learn as much as possible about a particular product, identify its market, and bring the product to the buyer, any buyer. The two human beings, salesman and buyer, were becoming the least important elements of the transaction. Willy's complaint that salesmanship was becoming "cut and dried" is meaningless to a man like Howard, who is interested only in the bottom line of profit and loss. That is exactly the way he wants it to be.

WHEN WILLY WAS YOUNG

When Willy Loman began his career as a salesman in the early part of the twentieth century, businessmen talked more about the character traits that would make one successful than about techniques of salesmanship. Market studies and demographics would have been foreign concepts to these men. The selections in this section provide a sense of what the life of a traveling salesman was like in the teens and twenties, and how the salesman thought about himself and his profession. They suggest how Willy might view his own vocation as a salesman, and illustrate in more depth the models that may have affected his thinking.

In O. R. Geyer's article, a real-life Dave Singleman, James Fenlon, the oldest living traveling salesman in 1916, attributes his success to the fact that he has never used tobacco and has always behaved as a gentleman should. In "What Makes a Good Salesman?" Harry G. Petermann defines his perfect salesman and outlines the type of man he prefers to hire. The excerpts from J. Annan's diary give clear examples of how salesmen of this period saw themselves and others, and gives us insights into how a salesman might feel after a fairly unproductive trip. The "Self-Analysis Chart," from a textbook on salesmanship by John G. Jones, shows that salesmen at this time thought of success as something that was achieved because of one's character and abilities. And character was something to work on. Businessmen were constantly invited to examine themselves to determine where there was room for improvement. Willy could probably have accepted failure more easily on these terms, but with what he saw as his own ability and character, he felt that success must be certain.

During the twenties, the focus began to shift from character to technique. Salesmen were beginning to ask whether they should use the same sales pitch on everyone, as illustrated in "Facts that Beat Eloquence in Salesmanship." Salespeople were beginning to think it would be a good idea to find out about a piece of machinery before they tried to sell it to someone. They were beginning to think they should try to identify a need for the item in a potential customer before they tried to sell him a product. George W. Hopkins shows that these were matters of debate in the twenties, when Willy Loman was in his prime. Willy's belief that being knowledgeable about the product and the customer's needs did not matter because "personality wins the day" was old-fashioned even in the twenties.

FROM O. R. GEYER, "THE OLDEST TRAVELING SALESMAN"
(*American Magazine* 81 [March 1916]: 53)

The dean of traveling men in America is James Fenlon of Des Moines, Iowa. He has held down his job for seventy years and today the eighty-nine-year veteran continues to "look after his trade" with all of the energy and all of the success that has characterized his work in his younger days.

Mr. Fenlon gained his title several years ago in a contest conducted by an Eastern publication desirous of locating the country's oldest traveling man. For a time it seemed as though some of the seventy-year veterans would carry off the honor, but the aged Iowan finally was convinced that he ought to throw his hat into the ring.

The contest stopped then and there, and the editor wrote a letter calling Mr. Fenlon the dean of all traveling men, promising to write again should anyone dispute the title. Having waited five years for such a letter, Mr. Fenlon feels that there can be no questioning of his right to the honor to-day, so he does not hesitate to claim it.

For the last thirty-two years Mr. Fenlon's specialty has been windmills and pumps. During these years the winds of southern Iowa have battled Don-Quixote-like against a host of fifty-seven thousand windmills the veteran has sold. This number may be increased to sixty thousand within a short time, as Mr. Fenlon spends three or four days out of each week traveling through the southern part of the state in the interest of the firm he represents—and farmers in the West have plenty of money for farm improvements this year.

When he started on the road seventy-two years ago, there was no such individual as a "traveling salesman." "People just rode on horseback and sold goods," he says. He was seventeen years old when he called on his first customer, and he has been calling on them ever since. His success he attributes to the fact that he never used tobacco in any form and that he always acted as a gentleman should. "A salesman cannot afford to take on a handicap by entering a man's office with a pipe or cigar stuck into his mouth," declares Mr. Fenlon.

His trade is the envy of every traveling man who carries a similar line, and the mass of correspondence he takes care of would tax the resources of the ordinary business man. Half an hour after receiving a call he will be on his way to the station to travel half way across the state to get an order.

Recently, when he was taken severely ill, the president of his firm wrote that he wanted to keep the dean of the force on the pay roll as long as he lived, even if he never made another trip. "Your name is worth the salary to us," wrote the president. But Mr. Fenlon refused to stay retired.

In addition to working at his calling, Mr. Fenlon found time to serve in three wars—Mexican, Civil, and the patriotic war in Canada which preceded the union of Upper and Lower Canada.

FROM MERLE CROWELL, "WHAT MAKES A GOOD SALESMAN?"
(*American Magazine* 81 [April 1916]: 43–45, 102)

This is a story of the hundredth man—why he is chosen from the ninety and nine.

It is a study of the salesman and the customer—two terms that include all of us—as made by Harry G. Petermann, who hires men, "builds" men, and places men for the United Cigar Stores Company, with its chain of a thousand stores.

Suppose you were to walk into Petermann's office someday to ask him for a job as clerk. This is done by twelve thousand men every year. Right away you would step into the sweep of a pair of strong-lensed blue eyes. For a moment those ocular searchlights would hold you; perhaps by the time Petermann had asked you to sit down you would have come to notice the clean-cut features behind them.

Before you could clear your throat to launch your first carefully pre-pared phrase Petermann might have nominated you for a position behind the counter (provided that you panned out as well as you appeared on the surface), or he might have decided definitely that you wouldn't do. In the second sad eventuality, he would merely be waiting for a short cut to tell you so without hurting your feelings. Your failure might be due to any one of half a dozen reasons, and you might not be in the least to blame for the one really responsible.

• • •

What to Look For First in Picking a Salesman

Suppose that nature had been unduly generous in your physical make-up. Suppose, for instance, that you weighed more than two hundred pounds.

In the background of those blue eyes there is always a picture of a thousand cigar stores, some of which pay as high as thirty-five thousand dollars a year for rent. High rents demand economy of space; every square inch is precious.

"Won't do! Won't have working room behind the counter! Would be in his own way!" runs Petermann's thought as he sizes you up.

Suppose, to the contrary, that nature had used a short yardstick; suppose you were less than five feet three inches tall.

"Won't do!" thinks Petermann. "Customers would bulldoze him! Hold-up men would spot him as an easy victim! General impression wouldn't be up to par!"

The hold-up factor would play no minor part in the analysis, for in recent years thieves have developed a chronic habit of raiding cigar stores in New York and other cities.

Your suit might be a bit shabby, yet as long as it was neat, and your linen was clean, the fact would not count against you. But if you happened to be flashily dressed and shimmering with cheap jewelry, your doom would be sealed right away. Men who seek paste-diamond brilliance are likely to be untrustworthy and dishonest, Petermann believes.

As you sank into a chair your face would be swept by his eyes, but the chances are that the inspection would not settle your case beyond appeal. For Petermann believes that physiognomy and phrenology are still inexact sciences.

"Some employment directors will not take on a man who has the 'square' or 'flat' type of head." Petermann told me the other day. "I discount such ideas. If a man with a head as square as a cigar box can sell me his services I'll hire him.

"The face is always a contributing factor, and sometimes it's a deciding one. When a fellow comes in who has coarse black hair, a bulging forehead which looks like a misplaced fist, and the belligerent chin of a boxer, I check him up as quarrelsome, hard to adjust, prone to argument, and not pliable enough to cater to the demands of customers. 'Service first,' our slogan, would rule that fellow out right off the reel.

"If an applicant has small eyes set close together they flash me a warning that he has a low type of intelligence. Of course, skin diseases bar a man, if only for the mental effect on the customer. When a chap fails to look me straight in the eye I am prejudiced against him at the start; but if he has clear-cut features, a pleasant expression, and a forthright, cordial manner, I am prejudiced in favor of him."

• • •

How a Good Salesman Looks, Acts and Talks

In measuring up the men who stream in before him Petermann has always in mind an ideal salesman—one who feels he could step behind the counter and give one hundred per cent service. Sometimes, in an idle moment, Petermann makes tentative pencil sketches of this Hercules of the Havanas: he is twenty-six years old, five feet nine inches tall, and weighs one hundred and forty-five pounds. He lives in a central location, or near subway or elevated railway lines, and he pays not more than seventeen dollars a month rent. He has alert, well-spaced eyes, a bright, cheery expression, clear complexion and neat personal appearance. His head is longer than the average, rather than wider.

He talks plainly and to the point, and he meets one's eyes squarely when doing it. His voice is neither high-pitched nor harsh; he neither stutters nor mumbles; he uses good English and he carries himself with confidence.

In addition to these physical characteristics he has all those other assets of a salesman which Petermann has reduced to a science.

If Petermann should ask this paragon, "Why do you want to work for us?" the paragon would reply: "I have talked with some of your clerks and I believe that in time I can work myself up into a good position—a better one than the one I am holding down now."

Petermann has as definite ideas about the proper material for a sales-man as he has about the proper filler for a "perfecto."

"Other things being equal," he told me, "the fellow who has sold shoes or hats has the call. He has been schooled in pleasing people; he has patience raised to the *n*th power. You know how hard it is to satisfy the average buyer with a shoe or a hat. Well, some persons are just as finicky about their cigars.

"A barber is good material, too: he is polite, he has been used to meet-ing people and to pleasing them with his services. He has had, also, to work part of the time evenings and Sundays. Men who have worked in grocery stores, candy stores, or who have done any other kind of retail clerking are likely to be pretty fair material to pick from.

FROM J. ANNAN, "FROM THE DIARY OF A TRAVELING
SALESMAN"
(*Outlook* 122 [20 August 1919]: 606, 610–11)

Sunday Night.
I am on the sleeper bound for Erie, having just left my wife at the Albany station. Singular that, no matter how often I start off for a trip on the road, there is a mist in her eyes which she tries to hide by smiling bravely. One would think that it were for six months or a year and to some distant land I was going instead of on a three weeks' trip to a near-by State. Nevertheless it does seem good to hear a better good-by than a masculine

"So long! Hope your trip is successful." I envy the fellow who returns at night to his own fireside. Strange beds and hotel food wear on one after a while. Sometimes it seems as if all the chefs had learned the art of cooking in a school where they drowned the food in one kettle of a highly seasoned liquid which removed all individual flavor. A trout might be a bluefish (perhaps it is).

Although my berth has been made up, I am sitting in the smoking compartment, listening to the heavy rain and waiting for the rest to get settled for the night. Years of travel have made me selfish enough to prefer waking others up when I retire to being wakened myself. Besides, berths were never made for one of my length. Absolute sleep, the kind that "knits up the raveled sleave of care," is impossible for me.

• • •

Tuesday Night.

Lowering clouds and rain beating against the windows by my breakfast table this morning. Not a pleasant prospect for a day's work, but with a mental "Cheer up! The worst is yet to come," I attacked a hearty breakfast to put me in a good physical shape. A full stomach can forgive any weather and almost any insult. I put on raincoat and rubbers, and with umbrella raised I started out to see the first of ten customers. Around the corner my umbrella was turned inside out, a wreck, and I faced the gusts of rain chastened in appearance but decidedly unchastened in spirit. I reached my first place, and with my best smile entered. Gloom sat enthroned here. The proprietor looked as if his family and friends had died, his money was lost, and a mortal sickness was upon him. I told a funny story. He eyed me with disfavor. I told another. He looked at the puddle of water which my raincoat was making on the floor. I tried a sad anecdote, which cheered him up a little, and at the end of an hour I sold him about a quarter of what I should.

The next call was no better. Everything was wrong. The times were bad, the present Administration rotten, the last one rottener, and the next one will probably be worse. I cheered him up with an expenditure of a lot of vitality and sold him a small bill of goods. The next man was busy, and I made an appointment to take him to lunch. Then I saw two others who did not buy anything, and came back for my luncheon appointment. Wet as I was, I enjoyed the meal. Over coffee my customer agreed to buy a larger line than I had expected, and, furthermore, he was good for it.

The afternoon was a different story. Not one of the remaining customers bought anything, and wet clothes and soggy shoes did not add to my cheerfulness. What little I may have had disappeared before my last call, I fear. This kind of weather makes me feel as if I was living in the trenches with water up to my knees, and without the consolation of shooting some enemy. I feel very much riddled myself, and, if it were not for the fact that I have given hostages to fortune, I would cease this peripatetic life, even if it does make one a sort of philosopher.

• • •

Friday.

Happy faces are the rule in trains. I presume the feeling of "homeward bound" shines out, as it should. What a queer world this would be, indeed, if there were none to greet us! There looms the Capitol amid the city's lights. Now for a leisurely taking down of bag and coat. Not too fast, for that would show excitement unbecoming in one so staid. Every one is laughing and talking and crowding to the door as we slowly pull across the river. Down the platform and under tracks to the station. There *she* is with eyes softly aglow, a tender smile of welcome, and a shy—a very shy—kiss, with mantling cheek.

"Home, Thomas, and don't stop at every corner for passengers."

FROM JOHN G. JONES, *SALESMANSHIP AND SALES MANAGEMENT*
(New York: Alexander Hamilton Institute, 1919, 171–72)

SELF-ANALYSIS CHART

Analyze yourself by making your own standing with regard to each of the qualities listed below. For convenience use the following scale:

1. Nearly perfect.
2. Good.
3. Above the average.
4. Average.
5. Below the average.
6. Deficient.
7. Almost wholly lacking.

Obviously the qualities listed are not all equally important. Their relative importance depends, in part, on the work you are doing or for which you are being considered.

Your analysis, when completed, should show a few "1's," a large number of "2's" and "3's," a smaller number of "4's," very few "5's," and no "6's" or "7's." Remember that one or two striking defects, no matter how excellent a man's other qualities may be, are often enough to disqualify him for a high grade of duties. You should endeavor as quickly as possible to remove the "5's," "6's" and "7's" from your analysis.

I. Physical Qualities.

  (a) Chiefly inherent—subject, however, to some cultivation.

    1. Proper size and structure of body
    2. Correct conformation of face and head
    3. Physical vitality
    4. Correct age (depending on position)

  (b) Chiefly acquired and subject to cultivation.

    5. General good health
    6. Erect carriage
    7. Impressive and pleasing facial expression
    8. Pleasing voice and enunciation
    9. Personal neatness
    10. Appropriate dress and pleasing appearance
    11. Bodily control (e.g., ability to sit quietly and absence of nervousness)
    12. Quickness of bodily movements

II. Mental Qualities.

  (a) Chiefly inherent.

    13. Quickness of thought
    14. Imagination
    15. Good memory
    16. Reasoning ability

  (b) Chiefly acquired.

    17. Good elementary education
    18. Higher general education
    19. Special education in business
    20. Special education in salesmanship
    21. Habits of thought and study
    22. Office experience
    23. Selling experience
    24. Executive experience
    25. Correct conception of the proposition
    26. Detailed knowledge of the proposition
    27. Accuracy of observation
    28. Concentration
    29. Sound judgment
    30. Resourcefulness
    31. Ability to talk well

32. Ability to write well
33. Organizing ability
34. Attention to details
35. Habits of punctuality
36. Ability to develop
37. Breadth of view
38. Fair-mindedness

III. Temperamental Qualities.

   (a) Chiefly inherent.

39. Will power
40. Energy
41. Liking for your work

   (b) Chiefly acquired.

42. Courtesy
43. Tact
44. Truthfulness
45. Integrity
46. Loyalty
47. Enthusiasm
48. Industry
49. Self-control
50. Self-confidence
51. Stability
52. Courage
53. Aggressiveness
54. Ambition
55. Sincerity
56. Cheerfulness
57. Good business habits
58. Good personal habits
59. Poise
60. Helpfulness
61. Initiative
62. Discretion
63. Willingness to accept suggestions
64. Power to dominate
65. Persuasiveness
66. Fixity of purpose
67. Sympathy

FROM "FACTS THAT BEAT ELOQUENCE IN SALESMANSHIP"
(*Literary Digest* 67 [30 October 1920]: 62, 64)

A successful Chicago salesman carefully reads the papers each day to inform himself on current events for the benefit of his farmer customers. He has found that the man on the farm, lacking opportunities for daily contact with his fellow men, likes to discuss world happenings with somebody, and immediately becomes friendly toward a salesman who can favor him in this respect. After the general discussion is over, the customer is ready to talk business, and if he is in the market for the salesman's goods, the latter generally goes away with his order. This is a good illustration of a salesman's knowing his "prospects," which is one of the chief principles of salesmanship. There is one other, equally important. It is that the salesman should know his goods. A third might be added to the effect that he should avoid getting into a rut and ought to bear in mind constantly that every selling transaction presents certain features a little different from those of all the sales that have gone before, and hence each requires individual handling. A party with chronic liver complaint can't be sold by the same methods employed in dealing with a man in perfect health and exuberant spirits, and the sales psychology applying to a farmer differs from that of a poet. Further illustrations of the advantages of a salesman's knowing his goods and his public are furnished in a recent article in *System* (Chicago) by J. C. Thorpe, who writes on selling the customer who "has to be shown." Mr. Thorpe is the president of a company most of whose business is with farmers, and hence the article treats particularly of dealings with that class, but farmers are not the only customers who have "to be shown," and what Mr. Thorpe says is equally applicable to the selling of any other class of buyers. In training his salesmen, it appears that Mr. Thorpe emphasizes particularly the importance of their knowing the "prospects." He puts much of his argument in the nutshell of this concrete example:

Not long ago one of our salesmen learned that a farmer prospect was financially interested in some producing oil-wells in Oklahoma, and that the study of the petroleum industry occupied most of his spare time. The salesman's very slight knowledge of the oil business was increased by reading a pamphlet on practical oil geology. When he made his first call on the prospect, he found it easy to divert the conversation to oil. An hour's visit ensued, during which time the farmer talked most, encouraged by intelligent questions from the salesman. As the hour drew to a close, the prospect rose, slapped the salesman on the shoulder, and said: "Well, boy, we've had a good visit, all right. We haven't talked much about automobiles, and

I guess that's what you really came for. But I do like that sedan of yours. Bring her around May 1, and I'll give you a check." "A freak reaction!" do you exclaim? Not at all. Making that sale in that way was just as natural a result as could be. The prospect had somewhat of an interest in the car to begin with, but the courteous and complimentary attitude of the salesman, in the subject near his heart, made it easy for him to reach a decision.

The importance of a salesman's knowing his goods is illustrated by several instances from Mr. Thorpe's experience. Most customers ask numerous questions about the goods they buy, and unless the salesman is able to give satisfactory answers he stands in danger of losing the sale. The writer relates the following:

A few months ago a farmer of my acquaintance walked into the salesroom of an automobile dealer who had just taken on a line of power farm machinery. He was met by a young man who had achieved success in selling motor-cars, and who, because of this achievement, had been assigned by his employers to have charge of tractor sales. He had had no special training in farm machinery, was densely ignorant of farm operations, and hence without a workable knowledge of the application of mechanical power on the farm. He did know, however, the specifications of the machine down to the last nut and bolt.

The farmer was interested in mechanical specifications, but he was more interested in knowing the constants of performance— whether the belt horse-power was sufficient to pull a 26-by-46 separator under most trying conditions brought about by heavy, damp straw, or whether the tractor would pull three plow bottoms seven inches deep through the rubbery gumbo that spotted his fields. These and other similar suggested questions the young salesman could not answer intelligently; he at last appealed to his employer for aid, but without success.

Seeing no possibility of securing the desired information, the farmer left the salesroom with this parting injunction: "Young man, I like your appearance. I believe you'd tell me the truth if you knew it. Just let me give you this advice from a man who is old enough to be your father: Don't try to sell another tractor until you know a lot more about what your machine will do and why it is preferable or necessary for a farmer to use mechanical power."

This farmer, in describing this experience, told me that he went to that salesroom ready to buy that particular machine but his confidence was so upset by the inability of the salesman to tell him what he most desired to know that he looked elsewhere and purchased another machine. This farmer could not make allowances for ignorance and was susceptible only to argument that showed an accurate knowledge of the machine and what it would do. The incident points to principles previously suggested, but in a specific way to the importance of really "knowing the performance of the goods you have for sale."

FROM GEORGE W. HOPKINS, "THE REAL 'STAR SALESMAN' IN MODERN BUSINESS"
(*American Magazine* 93 [April 1922]: 70)

We had a period when we thought that a first-class salesman was a man who could burst in anywhere, fill up the place with a freshet of language, and get out again with an order. Young salesmen studied the methods of these men, and tried to do likewise. A good many thought that salesmanship was mostly a matter of front and talk; that a salesman simply had to have a good act, like a vaudeville performer, and that he could put the act on anywhere.

But a salesman is not a one-man circus. Salesmanship is simply the ability to read human nature, and to get there first. Modern business is built on the platform of service to the other fellow. But before you can serve the other fellow, you must *know* him.

If all people were both wise and wide-awake there would be no use for salesmen. A wise and wide-awake man would know what he wanted, and if a manufacturer advertised properly he would know which manufacturer had the best offering. Then he would simply go and buy, and save the cost of being sold to. But people do *not* know what they want, until someone has shown or explained a new article to them.

Salesmanship is not trying to persuade people to buy something they do not want. That kind of salesmanship is, indeed, practiced, but not for very long; and no one makes any money out of it. Real salesmanship is demonstrating an article, or whatever it may be, in terms of the person who, it is hoped, will buy it. It is the development of a need, that already exists, into a present want. It is an operation performed first on the intellect and only secondly on the pocketbook of the prospect.

Any man can be a salesman, if he sufficiently wants to be, provided he has just two qualities:

1. A liking for people—to be with them, to mix around, to prefer to be with someone rather than to be alone.

2. An ability to express himself.

Without them, he cannot sell.

Liking to be with people may be overdone. A man may have such a rich gift of gab as to forget that the words he utters ought to convey some meaning. On the other hand, a thin-lipped man will not commonly like people; he will prefer to be alone. Such a man can rarely develop into a salesman. I would never bother even trying to train him. Neither would it be worth while to go forward with anyone whose manner of speech or choice of words was such that I could only with difficulty, or after a long time, discover what he was talking about. An effusive man, one who almost fawns, is one who does not understand people and probably does not like them, and has adopted his manner to conceal a lack of knowledge.

STUDY QUESTIONS

1. To what does O. R. Geyer attribute James Fenlon's success? Does his business practice resemble the life that Willy ascribes to Dave Singleman?

2. Compare the treatment that Fenlon receives from his employer in 1916 with the attitude of Howard Wagner in the play. How does Miller indicate that the relationship of employer and employee has changed between the time of Willy's youth and 1948?

3. According to Merle Crowell in "What Makes a Good Salesman?" how important were a person's physical characteristics to their business success early in the twentieth century? How does Willy Loman's thinking reflect these ideas, both positively and negatively? It is now illegal to discriminate in hiring employees on the basis of physical characteristics such as weight or disabilities. Is physical appearance still an important part of business success?

4. What are the characteristics of Harry Petermann's ideal salesman? How are they related to the job of selling? Judging by this standard, what would you say are Willy Loman's chances for business success? How would Biff, Hap, and Howard Wagner compare to the ideal salesman?

5. What are the drawbacks of the salesman's life on the road as J. Annan describes them? How does the life he lives relate to the cheerful demeanor that his job requires him to exhibit to customers?

6. How does J. Annan's depiction of his wife relate to Willy Loman's view of Linda? Does Annan's portrait of his wife seem realistic? What characteristics in a wife seem to be most valued by the traveling salesman?

7. Does John G. Jones' chart suggest that salesmen are born or made? Is it possible, as he says, to change the personal characteristics listed in Section III?

8. Which of the characteristics that Jones lists are related to business success today? Have the qualities that we associate with successful businessmen changed since 1919? How are virtue and good character related to success in business?

9. "Facts that Beat Eloquence" and "The Real 'Star Salesman'" suggest methods of salesmanship that were new to the 1920s. How do they suggest that the salesman needs to change his tactics? What do they suggest are the most important factors in making a sale? Does Willy Loman seem to have learned these lessons?

THE DEPRESSION

The next two documents give polar opposite views of the salesman's predicament during the Great Depression, from the right and the left politically and economically. "Wanted: Salesmen" blames the salesman for his own lack of success, warning that "with the boom years over, customers can't be expected to come along and take goods as fast as they are made." Salesmen have had it easy during the twenties, it warns, and they had better learn to get out and hustle if they want to succeed. Has Willy been unable to adapt to this change in the system? "Born to Be a Salesman" is a story from a magazine for young people. It is about a young salesman who is "radicalized" into thinking that the best hope for sales to pick up is to help all Americans "make a decent kind of American living." The question here is, has Willy recognized that the times have changed and that he needs to reassess his position in the light of these changes? Arthur Miller has suggested in his autobiography, *Timebends*, that one of the most devastating things about the Depression was that at the time people thought their business failures were their own fault, compounding their sense of defeat and worthlessness. Like other businessmen during the Depression, Willy feels the need to cover up his failure, claiming to Charley and Linda that he is the exception in this "murderous" economy, that he can still sell because he has "important contacts." Unable to admit his own failure, Willy could not begin to see the failed economy as a universal problem that needed a response that went beyond individual success or failure.

"WANTED: SALESMEN"
(*Literary Digest* 113 [21 May 1932]: 41–42)

Of course, there has always been a demand for first-class salesmen.

But the present business situation has created a special demand. We have solved our problems of production. Now, "like a well-geared machine, production can be trusted largely to run itself." But we must have real salesman [*sic*] to sell the goods.

At least so runs the talk in the Department of Commerce at Washington, according to J. C. Royle, writer of newspaper letters on business topics. Obviously, he points out, there is no point in producers being ready to turn out huge volumes of goods if there are no customers for the goods. With the boom years over, customers can't be expected to come along and take goods as fast as they are made. And "as a result of the change, a call has gone out for salesmen"—

It is not true that salesmen are born not made, but for years producers ceased to make them. The sales of the born salesmen have not suffered terribly during the depression, but the amount of goods handled by the poor salesmen or those who needed training has been pitiable.

As a result sales executives are going into the byways and the hedges for salesmen prospects, feeling they can teach a fair prospect any particular line if he has an innate inclination toward the sales field.

Also, a good many high-priced sales managers are scurrying around looking for other jobs. Some are going out on the road themselves to see at first hand how conditions were changed since they were accustomed to write up their day's orders and swindle sheets in the lobby of the Eagle Hotel.

The salesman who allows a customer to sell him a hard-times story instead of selling the customer goods is not likely to have a salary or a drawing account long.

In 1929, the last year for which figures are available, the retail salesmen were paid over $5,134,000,000. They did not sell sufficient goods to justify themselves. They are urged to do so now under spur of necessity. They are not being asked the impossible either.

JOSEPH STAROBIN, "BORN TO BE A SALESMAN"
(*Champion of Youth* 1, no. 4 [September 1936]: 10, 15)

His mother always said that Jimmy Randall was born to be a salesman.

The neighbors swore, as they sat in the orchard after the harvest drinking the Randall cider, and the brown bread that Grandma Randall baked better than any of them, that there weren't a thing in the whole blessed catalogue that Jimmy couldn't sell.

"At a good commission, too," added Uncle Oliver after a long draught on his pipe, "a darn fine sum of money can be made in selling. The future of this country and every living soul in it depends on selling. Selling is the thing,["] he avowed, pointing his hot pipe like a little Colt, "there wern't nothing like it."

None of this was ever lost on Jimmy Randall.

Week after week, while the roads were good, he bicycled up and down all of Northwest Agawash county, selling brushes, honing straps, suspenders, dresser sets, subscriptions to the Platte gazette, and whole sets of Scott, Dickens, and Twain.

And when the company brought through the electric extension, Jimmy was the first to bring around vacuum cleaners, toasters, grinding machines and triple action clothes irons.

Jimmy had a complete file of the neighbors for miles around. He knew just what they had bought of him last Spring, just what they still owned on the installment, and precisely what was the chance of working up a sale on something or other this year. He had a complete record of which companies and which articles gave the best commissions, discounts, advances, bonuses, prizes, emblems, buttons, and trophies.

Jimmy Randall had selling down to a system.

Roughly speaking there were two types of sales propositions. The first kind is where you got some sort of little gadget, useless or useful, for disposing of so many hundred other little gadgets. For instance, a real Daniel Boone hunting knife, autographed by the president of the Daniel Boone memorial foundation, and retailing normally for $7.75 was given free, if you sold one hundred bottles of Dew Drop Hair Restorer and Refurbisher at the low price of 25c. per bottle.

By a series of such enterprises, Jimmy had secured two World Wide stamp albums, four jackknives, two baseball bats, a pair of genuine silver cuff buttons as well as a host of other items too numerous to include here, and too bulky for Jimmy's chest in the attic.

By essentially the same type of transaction, but in this case involving a subscription to the Annual Almanac for 25 years plus a copy of Movie Stars 1910–1930, Jimmy had secured part of a bicycle. I say part, because there was $15 in cash to be paid in addition in three months time.

The cash came from ordinary sales operations, the second of the two categories. You got a discount and a commission for selling so much of something at such and such a price.

Selling is the thing, Uncle Oliver had said, that this country needs. Jimmy was out to help his country as well as himself.

For four years after he graduated high school, Jimmy had odd jobs, selling. First it was in the Platte hardware store. Then it was books, up and down the countryside in an old Model T, until folks complained that there was a definite limit to the education that folks could absorb.

Then for a while Jimmy was selling chicken feed with Vitamin C in it, but Agawash did not go for this vitamin angle at all. It caused somewhat of a scandal when a caustic note appeared in the Gazette about "a certain well known young salesman in these parts was selling chicken feed with medicine in it; it was claimed that the chickens laid eggs, which if you ate, would cure you of aching bones, cataracts, and tonsil trouble."

After which, Jimmy went back to magazines, with Old Tar disinfectors, as a sideline.

These were hard times in the county. The farmer was not selling his crop at livable prices. The land was lying barren, and the cattle getting thin and sometimes dying, and the Ford lay in the barn with the tires off because gasoline prices were up too high. The government was talking crop reduction. The farmers said they couldn't see how the country was going to have recovery by not planting anything at all. When the salesmen came to the front door, they were told that the farmer couldn't buy anything until he began to sell at decent prices, and the salesmen left scratching their heads.

It was about this time that Jimmy saw a notice about a salesman's convention in Indianapolis. He lost no time in getting a letter of recommendation from the mayor of Platte as the best salesman in the county. He wrote letters to all the big companies announcing that he was representing the market of Platte and the surrounding territory of Agawash.

"I figure," he remarked to Uncle Oliver, at the railway station, "that this convention will get me a start with some big company. Then watch me start selling," he shouted. ["]I'm gonna sell this county, state and nation right into recovery."

For he who helps himself, thought Jimmy, helps his country.

He spent four nights in a stuffy furnished room preparing his speech for the convention. When it opened he was thrilled to meet the managers of all the big companies and hobnob over the rail with salesmen from all over the state, chewing the rag.

There was no doubt; everyone remarked that here was a young man, a hard-hitting, double-barreled young man, who was going to go far, very fast.

The further, the faster; the sooner, the better, replied Jimmy Randall.

The first sentence in Jimmy's ten-minute address hit the keynote of the entire convention.

"There is nothing wrong," he shouted, "absolutely nothing wrong with our great nation."

The thousand salesmen rose to their feet as one man, their mighty cheers echoing from every beam and rafter.

"What we must do," he continued at a shout, "is to go out to the people of the United States and sell them the goods that they need, which now lie in the warehouses, clutter the railroad sidings, and block the wharves.

"My friends," he lowered his voice, "we have dedicated our lives, and the lives of our families who are dear to us, to the noble cause of our profession. Yet we have been accused of bringing on this depression by too much selling. I say that we must fling this challenge back to our accusers by vowing that ours is the great job of selling this great country back on its feet."

Once again the entire audience rose to a crescendo of applause. He continued:

"Why, do you fellows realize that the great majority of the American people do not consume enough foodstuffs, automobiles, bathtubs, pianos, etcetera, to maintain an American standard of living?

"Men, there is a world of things that the American people need. They need more milk, they need more shoes, they need hats, coats, clothing to shield their bodies from the wind and the rain . . . they need books and musical instruments, yes, radios, phonographs; they need new houses to live in; they need stoves, heaters, boilers, coolers, porches, rockers, curtains. My friends, there is a world of things that men and women need in this day and age in order to be happy and prosperous. There are millions who do not own autos, sleighs, cycles for the kiddies, little bungalows in the country. . . . I say that these are the things we have got to go out and sell them. . . .

"Yes, sir, we have got to maintain the American standard of living . . . and all of it seems to come from the fact that the people are not earning enough for the staples of life, not to mention the luxuries. Millions employed at low wages and millions unemployed at relief levels . . . why how can we carry on if the American people cannot buy what we are ready to sell? . . . I come to the conclusion that people can't buy our zippers, xylophones, airplanes and ashtrays . . . unless they begin to make a decent kind of American living . . . the kind of living that fits in with our great industrial and commercial progress. . . . We ought to help them do it. . . ."

Jimmy Randall paused for breath . . . and suddenly he felt a subtle enmity rising from the gathering. He expected applause: men jumping on their chairs, waving their handkerchiefs, stamping their feet.

But there was no applause.

From the far end of the chamber a low whistle carefully made its way through the aisles. Then, a rumble of booing, slowly like thunder on an early evening, late in summer. Then, a rising chorus of tumult, a roar that shook the rafters.

"Throw the goddam Bolshevik out of the window. . . ."

"Who let that fellow in with all that boloney? . . ."

And then someone arose in his chair and shouted, "Men, are we going to let this hunkie insult the American flag and the American people? . . ."

Jimmy whirled about, his head spinning, spinning like the turbans of the whirling dervishes of the Sahara, the carefully rolled turbans of the whirling dervishes.

Then there were cops, and men yelling, and fists flying, and the rumble of thunder, like the rumble of milk wagons in the morning, and somewhere newsboys shouting extra, extra, salesman Bolshevik, and newspapers selling, selling, selling.

STUDY QUESTIONS

1. Where does the author of "Wanted: Salesmen" place the responsibility for the poor sales record of the Great Depression? What is the proposed solution?

2. What does the play suggest about Willy's failure to do as well as he would like during the Depression?

3. What does Willy's conversation with Linda about his sales trip reveal about his own view of his failure to succeed, and hers?

4. What are Willy's and Linda's standards for success during the Depression? How do they jibe with general economic conditions in the country?

5. What solution to the sluggish economy does Jimmy Randall propose in "Born to Be a Salesman?" Why is he booed out of the sales meeting?

6. What is a Bolshevik? Is this an accurate description of Jimmy?

7. How does the view of the American economy presented in "Born to Be a Salesman" compare with that in *Death of a Salesman*? Which presents its views more clearly? Which one is more artistic?

THE STRANGE NEW WORLD

The Depression changed the way people looked at the traveling salesman. No longer the freewheeling, carefree life it had been earlier in the century, or the lucrative and enjoyable life it had been in the flush times of the twenties, the salesman's life was hard and precarious during the thirties. The instability of the salesman's income because of his dependence on commissions and the insecurity of his job in hard times made sales an increasingly unpopular occupation as the G.I. Bill made it possible for more Americans to go to college or business school and make other career choices. In the late forties, a movement began to professionalize the salesman, promoting sales as a career for college graduates. An important part of this movement was to emphasize the salesman's expertise and downplay his personality. Students were taught in business courses that the salesman's job was to learn everything he could about his product and about the market, to gather all the data he could and analyze it using the most sophisticated statistical methods—in other words, to make the job "cut and dried," as Willy would say. A number of books were written about salesmanship in the late forties and early fifties. They attempted to codify the knowledge that was the fruit of a lifetime of experience for a Willy Loman or a Dave Singleman. Unfortunately for veteran salesmen, the knowledge was expressed in a new language they didn't always understand, and it was based on different values, Howard Wagner's values, where the bottom line was everything. The documents that follow express the postwar view of salesmanship that Willy Loman is never able to comprehend. A study of what George Edward Breen et al. and Harry Simmons suggest may help us to understand just why Willy can no longer do a good job as a salesman.

FROM GEORGE EDWARD BREEN ET AL., "SELLING AS A
CAREER," IN *EFFECTIVE SELLING*
(New York: Harper, 1950, 1–16)

Considering the importance of the function of selling in our economic system and the large number of people now employed in selling, one would suppose that it is selected as the vocational goal by many young persons. Actually, however, a relatively small number of people seem to plan in advance of the completion of their education to become salesmen. In fact, there is evidence of an actual rejection of that possibility. In the 1947 Parlin Memorial Lecture, Mr. R. S. Wilson, Vice-President of the Goodyear Tire and Rubber Company, tells of a survey of approximately five hundred freshmen at Ohio State University.[1] Despite the fact that these men were in the College of Commerce of that institution only 7 percent stated that they would want their sons to be salesmen, while 89 percent would like to have them be physicians or lawyers. They had to select the occupation from a list of seven, including the two professions mentioned, three types of salesmen, bookkeeper, and auto factory worker. Had the choice been made between different business occupations such as accounting, advertising, banking, personnel work, or production management, salesmanship would, doubtless, have rated better. Nevertheless, there is a widespread resistance to selling as a career among young people, and many of those who do become salesmen or saleswomen do so by accident.

One reason why high-school and college graduates, in particular, do not plan to enter a selling career is that few, if any, schools have a prescribed curriculum leading to that goal. Different types of selling require varying combinations of talents and training. All selling requires personality traits which cannot be taught as such but can be acquired only by the individual's reaction to his environment and his willingness to apply himself to the task of developing his personality. In another chapter methods of acquiring greater sales ability will be discussed in detail.

The very need for self-application is a deterrent to interest in selling as a career. The large scale of many of our enterprises today tends to lessen the need for self-initiative on the part of people who work in them. Policies are determined, plans made, and problems solved by top management. Employees in lower echelons tend to follow instructions and carry out these predetermined policies. Even in our leisure time we are spectators of, rather than participants in, entertainment or sport.

The salesman is an employee, to be sure. He, too, is the recipient of instructions and policies which he must carry out. But his superiors cannot go into every prospect's office or home with him, or tell him what to do or say in each particular case. To only a limited extent can they plan his work for him. Even as an employee, the salesman more nearly pursues the principles of freedom of enterprise than any other type of employee.

---

1. R. S. Wilson, *Salesmanship Is a Profession*, Charles Coolidge Parlin Memorial Lecture, 1947, published by Philadelphia Chapter, American Marketing Association, p. 7.

Furthermore, the depression frightened many people into seeking the security that comes from a steady job with steady wages. Others seek security through union activity and seniority. The salesman's security comes from his confidence in his own ability and an active, creative attitude toward life.

Many people who have self-initiative and the desire to be creative, however, prefer one of the professions such as medicine, law, education, or the ministry. The prestige of these callings is high enough to compensate for the struggle that must be made to become successful in the field and the financial uncertainties that attend it. Salesmanship, on the other hand, is likely to be held in rather low esteem by the public. The survey mentioned above included questions to people in four typical American communities in various parts of the country. They were asked to rate the seven occupations as to the standing of each in the community. The three types of selling received 3 percent of the votes.

Expressions like "just another salesman," "high pressure," "the selling game," and "putting over a deal" indicate the general attitude, even among salesmen themselves. The salesman is often considered to be an undesirable character who feeds in a parasitical way off the fat of the land by foisting products of dubious value on an unsuspecting public at exorbitant prices. This attitude grows out of the normal consumer "sales resistance." But it is real, and since the average person is certain to be a consumer before he can ever be a salesman he naturally thinks of the vocation from the consumer point of view. To himself, he says: "I don't want to be a pest like that insurance salesman who hounds my dad," or "That encyclopedia salesman 'prevented' our having a vacation last summer, because it took all the family savings to buy his books." So young Mr. (or Miss) America looks for a nice job safely out of sight of the general public where he can work without risk of being thought an objectionable personage.

• • •

The Advantages of Selling as a Career

To sum up the advantages of selling as a career:

1. Selling is a tremendously important activity to both society and individuals.

2. There is a selling opportunity for everyone who can talk well, regardless of the formal education he has completed. Better selling jobs go to better educated people.

3. There is always some selling job open for the ambitious person.

4. Advancement possibilities are great and lead up three avenues: sales management within one's own or a similar organization; top management, which is more frequently turning to sales-minded men; and advertising, research, and government, which can utilize men with sales ability. Furthermore, one's progress is determined more by his own efforts than in many other lines of work.

5. Earnings average higher in selling than in other types of work in the same product field. The salesman is more likely than are salaried employees to determine the level of his own earnings by his own efforts, especially in times of depression.

6. There are non-monetary rewards not often given to non-selling employees.

7. Selling jobs often offer a chance to travel and see new places and faces.

8. The salesman is to a large extent his own boss, even though he may work for someone else.

9. The salesman deals with people and thus is constantly confronted with new and different problems in human relations.

The Disadvantages of Selling as a Career

1. It is sometimes difficult to get a start in the type of selling job or with the type of organization one would like.

2. It is easy to become a mediocre salesman, because the demands on self-initiative are so great.

3. Earnings are often low or non-existent for the first few months. At any time the exact amount of earnings may be difficult to predict.

4. Traveling salesmen spend many lonesome hours away from home, staying in hotels, eating in restaurants or on the road. One cannot always keep in close touch with one's friends or family and is tempted to seek refuge in dissipation.

FROM HARRY SIMMONS, *HOW TO SELL LIKE A STAR SALESMAN*
(New York: Henry Holt, 1953, 94–98)

Twenty-eight pint-size capsules that hold a gallon of helpful sales advice

CAPSULE 1: The only way to handle a customer complaint is to take the "plain" out of complain and put it into *ex-*

plain. Then make the adjustment snappy—and you'll make your customer happy.

CAPSULE 2: Although an army travels on its stomach, a business travels on its man power. And man power means you! Every business has its problems: Are you part of the problem or part of the answer? Are you a help or a hindrance to your business? According to your reply, your bank account either skyrockets or nosedives.

CAPSULE 3: Don't fool yourself by believing that dealers pay no attention to advertising. It is all a question of how it is presented. You can sell any good product with advertising—and your dealer knows it. He may be just "playing possum" to see how much advertising you can show him or to see where *he* enters the picture. Don't be bashful about telling him—and tell him plenty!

CAPSULE 4: Strike while the customer is hot and follow through with your urge for action. In other words, close on a high note of satisfaction, while your customer is full of enthusiasm.

CAPSULE 5: Reach for the order instead of applause. Many a man mistakes sociability for sales ability. He spends his time being a good-time Charley instead of a brass-tacks salesman. And then he complains about business being slow!

CAPSULE 6: Tall tales make funny stories, but sound selling talks its way to the cash register! It's just a question of whether you want your sales manager to laugh with you or at you.

CAPSULE 7: Agreement rather than argument means orders rather than alibis. The squared ring is the place to settle arguments. The customer pays dividends only on agreements—and your company pays off only on results. Which means more to you?

CAPSULE 8: Selective selling is common sense, good judgment, and wise economics all rolled into one. You cannot always sell profitably to every Tom, Dick, and Harry. Less volume at a profit beats the tar out of big volume at a loss. Of course, the ideal selling situation is big volume at a modest profit—that's how your really big profits roll up fast!

CAPSULE 9: We are not so much interested in the geography of a territory as we are in the possible customers and potential volume. Have you analyzed *your* territory lately?

CAPSULE 10: It is not the quantity, but the *quality* of calls that counts. In other words, not just calls and more calls, but more intelligent calls. If you can combine the two—perfect!

CAPSULE 11: Make big ones out of little ones! When it comes to making more sales, there is no more profitable method than to develop the customers you already have. Too many will-o'-the-wisp salesmen are like barbers. They think a "once-over lightly" is all that's necessary. They don't realize it takes tough gold digging to bring the real volume to the top.

CAPSULE 12: Divide your list of customers into three classes: casual, medium, good. Bear in mind that if you can devise ways and means to step up each customer just one classification, you will step up your total sales to a sensational figure. It's worth trying, isn't it?

CAPSULE 13: Competition is not only the life of trade; it is a godsend to selling! It is something for which to be grateful, when it teaches us so much about selling and gives us so much additional voltage through its constant prodding.

CAPSULE 14: Worrying about your competitor usually gets you nowhere in a hurry. To get *somewhere* twice as fast, forget your competitor and start thinking instead about your sales potential and building it up.

CAPSULE 15: New age groups. Every twenty-four hours a vast number of men, women, and children enter new age groups. They build up new habits, develop new needs and new wants, acquire new desires and new demands for the products you have to sell. Do you realize that every day a new market for your product has come of age?

CAPSULE 16: New wage groups. Additional wage groups and increasing wage levels bring the masses closer to the buying line, with a constantly rising curve of buying power. Many more dollars are going into pay envelopes and finding their way into stores, amusements, equipment, necessities, and luxuries. Are you getting your share?

CAPSULE 17: New markets everywhere. Your customers may open new branches, resulting in orders for new stocks and new supplies. Changes in buying habits due to increased quality and luxury buying are responsible for the quickening of sales activities. Population shifts and changes affect markets, old and new. Do you keep your eyes and ears open when you travel your territory?

CAPSULE 18: The poorest sales argument in the world is price; the best sales argument is quality. In between are many other constructive sales points that pave the way for profitable and self-respecting salesmanship. Is your list of constructive sales points ready for spontaneous use?

CAPSULE 19: Price-cutting is only an optical illusion. It builds nothing, tears down everything, deludes everyone; and in the long run it is expensive even to the buyer. As a rule, it results only in a vicious circle of reciprocal price-cutting in which everybody loses, nobody wins!

CAPSULE 20: Don't count your "price" chickens before they are hatched! You're liable to lose your shirt on the way down, unless you are able to let the price-cutter take the loss himself.

CAPSULE 21: Value is represented by a very simple formula— price divided by the amount of satisfactory service. That's always the true value and the real cost!

CAPSULE 22: John Ruskin once said: "There is hardly anything in the world that some man cannot make a little worse and sell a little cheaper; and the people who consider price alone are this man's lawful prey."

CAPSULE 23: If a salesman would only realize how little extra effort it takes to sell on a quality basis at a profit rather than on a price basis at a loss, he would become a candidate for the Medal of Honor. Not to mention the little detail that he would build more, deserve more, and earn more!

CAPSULE 24:   Helpmanship rather than salesmanship is the modern note in selling. Helping your customer to buy properly, to use correctly, and to sell efficiently will fill both your pockets with more profits and will build more real friendships for you on your customer list.

CAPSULE 25:   Product information. How much do you really know about your line? How often do you have to bluff your way through or play dumb when your dealer asks a question? Is that the way to build confidence? Is that the way to build sales? Is that the way to make money?

CAPSULE 26:   Handle your territory like an executive—contacting, prospecting, building friendships, developing interest, arousing enthusiasm and desire, routing yourself for greater efficiency, selling quality rather than price, and cutting down your sales cost by building up your sales volume. In other words, do a *complete* selling job and you will have a better chance of developing into a complete sales executive.

CAPSULE 27:   Prove to your dealers the dollars-and-cents of doing a better sales-management job all the way through. Tell them some of the specific things they can do, and show them how you can help. That won't hurt you a bit!

CAPSULE 28:   It is a well-known fact that the prospect's buying temperature never gets any higher than the salesman's selling temperature. Does that suggest the temperature on your sales thermometer?

STUDY QUESTIONS

1. According to George Edward Breen et al., what was the general view of the selling profession at the time when *Death of a Salesman* was produced? Does this differ from today's view?

2. According to Breen et al., what were the results of the survey of freshmen at Ohio State University about the desirability of selling as a career? Would you predict similar results now? Why or why not?

3. How would Biff Loman's view of selling as a profession compare with the view that Breen et al. ascribe to the next generation of high school graduates? How would you account for this difference?

4. How does Miller's representation of the salesman's life compare to Breen et al.'s description of it?

5. Are there other disadvantages to selling as a career than those Breen et al. mention? Are there other advantages?

6. What advice does Harry Simmons have for a salesman like Willy? Which "capsules" apply particularly to his problems?

7. Based on Harry Simmons' advice, how would you rate Hap and Biff's ideas for selling Loman Brothers sporting goods? Do they seem to understand the current marketplace?

8. How would you rate Harry Simmons' strategy for selling in today's marketplace?

TOPICS FOR WRITTEN OR ORAL EXPLORATION

1. Apply the test suggested by John G. Jones to one of the characters in *Death of a Salesman*, using his "Self-Analysis Chart" and his rating scale. Then write (1) an evaluation of the character's potential for business success based on these qualities, and (2) an evaluation of Jones' criteria. Do you agree with Jones about the things that are necessary for success in business? What sort of person does the chart describe? What is missing from his chart? What is no longer a factor in the business world?

2. Take the test of Jones' "Self-Analysis Chart" yourself, trying to be as objective as you can in assessing your own characteristics. Then write a comparative analysis of your potential for success as a salesman now and in 1920.

3. Make a list of the characteristics required to make a good salesman from Willy Loman's point of view, based on the statements that he makes in the course of the play. Then write an essay comparing and

contrasting Willy's view of the profession to that of Merle Crowell, John G. Jones, George W. Hopkins, Harry Simmons, or George Edward Breen. Does Willy's view of what is necessary for success coincide with the ideas of any of the "authorities" at the beginning or the end of his career?

4. "Wanted: Salesmen" and "Born to Be a Salesman" represent polar opposite ways of thinking about the solution to the economic crisis of the Great Depression in America. One locates business failure in the individual salesman, putting the responsibility on him to improve sales. The other locates it in the economic system, putting the responsibility on the country as a whole to improve conditions enough to create a demand for goods that will improve sales. Which of these points of view do you see reflected in *Death of a Salesman*? Does the play suggest that Willy is personally responsible for his failure, or that he is the victim of economic conditions and social forces that he cannot control? Write an essay in which you analyze the reasons for Willy's failure.

5. Harry Simmons' "capsules" suggest the changing view of the successful salesman during the postwar period. Salesmen were beginning to pay attention to marketing techniques that depended on the study of demographics (capsules 15, 16, and 17), the selling of service as well as products (capsule 24), and the salesman's knowledge about the product (capsule 25), as well as more traditional things like enthusiasm and energy. Write an essay in which you evaluate the potential for success of Willy Loman, Charley, Hap Loman, and/or Howard Wagner in this new business environment. What qualities are required for a salesman to succeed in this world? Do any of these characters possess them?

6. J. Annan's diary describes the loneliness of life on the road as well as its minor irritations and triumphs. Construct a diary like his for one of Willy Loman's sales trips to Boston in 1931, making use of the various things he tells the boys, Linda, and The Woman. Does Willy's experience differ appreciably from Annan's?

7. Willy's relationship with The Woman is one aspect of the salesman's life that is not touched on by the authorities on salesmanship and the salesman's life. Based on their statements in the play, try writing a private diary entry for Willy and for The Woman, in which each tells about the relationship from his or her point of view. From the little you learn about her, what do you think The Woman's motives for entering into the affair would be? What does each of them get from it?

8. Discuss as a group or think for yourself about the differences be-

tween the salesman's life on the road in 1920, in 1948, and now. Then write a traveling salesman's diary for the present, focusing on the kinds of things J. Annan writes about, but reflecting the conditions of the contemporary salesman's experience.

9. Working alone or in a group, make up your own advice "capsules" for selling a product you are familiar with in today's market. Which of the things Harry Simmons was concerned with in 1953 are still important? How have the methods for defining and reaching a particular market changed?

10. Try taking on the role of Biff Loman as he is preparing to pitch his idea about selling sporting goods to Bill Oliver. Write a memo in which you explain your idea to Oliver and try to sell him on investing in the business. How would Biff try to sell himself and his idea? How effective do you think he would be?

11. Taking on the role of Howard Wagner, write a diary entry in which you justify firing Willy Loman to yourself after his suicide, or a letter in which you justify the firing to a family member. How would Howard think about this issue? What kinds of justifications or explanations would he make for his behavior?

12. Taking on the role of Uncle Charley, write a letter to Biff Loman after the Requiem scene in which you give him advice for his future based on your own ideas about business success and failure. Explain how you look at Willy's inability to succeed in the way he hoped to, and what you think Biff should do to be happy in his own life.

SUGGESTED READINGS

Atherton, Lewis E. "Predecessors of the Commercial Drummer in the Old South." *Bulletin of the Business Historical Society* 21 (April 1947): 17–24.

Frederick, J. George. *1000 Sales Points: The "Vitamin Concentrates" of Modern Salesmanship*. New York: Business Course, 1941.

Friedman, Lee M. "The Drummer in Early American Merchandise Distribution." *Bulletin of the Business Historical Society* 21 (April 1947): 39–44.

Gross, Barry. "Peddler and Pioneer in *Death of a Salesman.*" *Modern Drama* 7 (February 1965): 405–10.

Hattwick, Melvin S. *The New Psychology of Selling*. New York: McGraw-Hill, 1960.

Ivey, Paul, and Walter Horvath. *Successful Salesmanship*. 3rd ed. New York: Prentice-Hall, 1953.

Kitson, Harry Dexter. *The Mind of the Buyer: A Psychology of Selling*. New York: Macmillan, 1929.

Leigh, Ruth Fagundus. *The Human Side of Retail Selling*. New York: D. Appleton, 1921.

"Sales Person Rising in the Business Scale." *Literary Digest* 66 (7 August 1920): 90, 92.

Scull, Penrose. *From Peddlers to Merchant Princes: A History of Selling in America*. Chicago: Follett, 1967.

Sprague, J. R. "Commercial Entertainment." *Saturday Evening Post* 192 (20 March 1920): 15, 72, 75, 77.

———. "The Importance of Being a Salesman." *Saturday Evening Post* 193 (29 January 1921): 14, 45–46, 48, 51.

Wheeler, Elmer. *Sizzlemanship: New Tested Selling Sentences*. New York: Prentice-Hall, 1940.

5

Family and Gender
Expectations

Sociological studies of American families speak of a common expectation among parents that their children will "do better" than
they have. Indeed, parents are dedicated to the idea that parents
whose children do not live wealthier and more accomplished lives
have somehow failed. The Lomans certainly appear to believe this,
and they live in an era when it is still possible for children to
surpass the achievements of their parents, as proven by Charley
and Bernard. Such an idea puts increasing pressure on each generation as the ceiling of opportunity draws closer, and it is understandable that Hap and Biff feel daunted by Willy's need for them
to be more successful than he is. American parents also have a
tendency to make things too easy for their children, providing for
their every need. Ironically, children thus treated often end up
lacking motivation, and failing because they are not used to having
to fend for themselves. This is what lies behind Willy allowing Biff
to run wild as a child and not disciplining him. Biff accordingly
lacks both direction and stamina as he grows older. On reading
Death of a Salesman we should consider whether or not Willy and
Linda Loman have offered Biff and Hap the kind of support children need from their parents. Have their expectations been responsible for souring the children's lives? We should also consider

what other family groups in the play can be compared to the Lomans. Do they offer any better parenting strategies?

Before judging the parenting skills of the Lomans, we should recognize that in the late 1940s, male and female roles remained fairly restricted and narrowly prescribed by a society that still largely felt that the male should be the guiding head of the household, providing the cash and moral rectitude, with the female being the subservient housekeeper and nursemaid, quietly supporting all of her husband's decisions. The selections in this chapter offer examples of such thinking by both men and women. Though women had won the vote, their expectations about their place in society had not substantially changed, and men continued to be forced into roles laid out for them since the nineteenth century. While it remained fine for a daughter just to get married, sons were expected to achieve greatness. Thus, every member of the Loman family is under pressure to behave in a socially predetermined way regardless of what they personally want to do. Willy acts as the family provider, while Linda takes a subservient back seat, and Hap and Biff struggle to make it big.

During World War II, many women called to assist in the war effort performed jobs outside the home which gave them new authority and ambition. To the dismay of many, some were reluctant to pass this authority back to the men on their return from the army. The "working girl" was becoming a social reality that some welcomed, but by which many more felt threatened. There are a number of examples of working women in the play, such as The Woman, Jenny, and Miss Forsythe, and it is interesting to note the way in which they are presented. To diminish the threat these women posed to males, they were often discredited and belittled wherever and however possible, largely to affirm old-fashioned opinions of what was right and proper for men and women to do.

THE FAMILY

The first three documents in this chapter explore how social critics see the typical American family. Alexis de Tocqueville describes American families as being less formal and their children as having greater freedom than their European counterparts; this he sees as a great advantage, as it allows for a greater possibility of love between family members. We need to look for evidence of love between the Loman family members. Andrew Truxal and Francis Merrill point out how a variety of social changes in America have affected families, making it necessary for them to be highly adaptable to survive intact during hard times. Applying their theories to the Lomans gives us an idea of the numerous pressures under which this family lives. Finally, Max Lerner explores the ways in which American families place great pressure on children to surpass their parents, and considers what damage that might cause. On what does Lerner suggest the average American child's attention is focused? Do his observations apply to Biff, Hap, and Bernard? It is important to determine to what degree Willy and Charley may be responsible for their sons' attitudes.

FROM ALEXIS DE TOCQUEVILLE, "INFLUENCE OF DEMOCRACY
ON THE FAMILY," IN *DEMOCRACY IN AMERICA*
(Trans. Henry Reeve. New York: Adlard and Saunders, 1838, Vol. 2,
Book 3, Chapter 8, 202–5)

In America the family, in the Roman and aristocratic signification of the word, does not exist. All that remains of it are a few vestiges in the first years of childhood, when the father exercises, without opposition, that absolute domestic authority which the feebleness of his children renders necessary and which their interest, as well as his own incontestable superiority, warrants. But as soon as the young American approaches manhood, the ties of filial obedience are relaxed day by day; master of his thoughts, he is soon master of his conduct. In America there is, strictly speaking, no adolescence: at the close of boyhood the man appears and begins to trace out his own path.

It would be an error to suppose that this is preceded by a domestic struggle in which the son has obtained by a sort of moral violence the liberty that his father refused him. The same habits, the same principles, which impel the one to assert his independence predispose the other to consider the use of that independence as an incontestable right. The former does not exhibit any of those rancorous or irregular passions which disturb men long after they have shaken off an established authority; the latter feels none of that bitter and angry regret which is apt to survive a bygone power. The father foresees the limits of his authority long beforehand, and when the time arrives, he surrenders it without a struggle; the son looks forward to the exact period at which he will be his own master, and he enters upon his freedom without precipitation and without effort, as a possession which is his own and which no one seeks to wrest from *him*.

When men live more for the remembrance of what has been than for the care of what is, and when they are more given to attend to what their ancestors thought than to think themselves, the father is the natural and necessary tie between the past and the present, the link by which the ends of these two chains are connected. In aristocracies, then, the father is not only the civil head of the family, but the organ of its traditions, the expounder of its customs, the arbiter of its manners. He is listened to with deference, he is addressed with respect, and the love that is felt for him is always tempered with fear.

When the condition of society becomes democratic and men adopt as their general principle that it is good and lawful to judge of all things for oneself, using former points of belief not as a rule of faith, but simply as a means of information, the power which the opinions of a father exercise over those of his sons diminishes as well as his legal power.

• • •

In a democratic family the father exercises no other power than that which is granted to the affection and the experience of age; his orders would perhaps be disobeyed, but his advice is for the most part authoritative. Though he is not hedged in with ceremonial respect, his sons at least accost him with confidence; they have no settled form of addressing him, but they speak to him constantly and are ready to consult him every day. The master and the constituted ruler have vanished; the father remains.

Nothing more is needed in order to judge of the difference between the two states of society in this respect than to peruse the family correspondence of aristocratic ages. The style is always correct, ceremonious, stiff, and so cold that the natural warmth of the heart can hardly be felt in the language. In democratic countries, on the contrary, the language addressed by a son to his father is always marked by mingled freedom, familiarity, and affection, which at once show that new relations have sprung up in the bosom of the family.

FROM ANDREW G. TRUXAL AND FRANCIS E. MERRILL, "SOCIAL
CONFLICTS IN THE FAMILY," IN *THE FAMILY IN AMERICAN
CULTURE*
(New York: Prentice-Hall, 1947, 604–5, 621–22)

The Nature of Social Conflicts. The forms of all institutions are determined by their milieu. The family is no exception. As Arthur W. Calhoun points out, ". . . the family is in no sense an independent institution capable of being fashioned, sustained, or modified at will to suit the fancy. It is part and parcel of an organic civilization and must undergo such evolution as will keep it in correspondence with co-existing social institutions . . ." If this close relationship characterizes the adjustment between members of the family, it also exists in their maladjustments and conflicts. In the preceding chapter, we considered the factors growing out of the personalities in the family which tend to bring about conflict. Many other factors impinge upon the little group from outside and have no conceivable connection with the personalities except as outside tensions are translated to the family through its participants. It is clearly an arbitrary matter whether a given tension is said to originate in the individual or the outside society, since the ultimate expression takes place in the orbit of the family. We shall be concerned here with some of the elements from the outside world which modify the attitudes of the members of the intimate family.

Among these social elements are the social influences brought to bear upon husband and wife which have left their mark upon the adult personality; the conflicts engendered or intensified by the occupation of husband or wife; the possible threat to the husband's ego when the wife is working and the imminent threat thereto when he himself is *not*; and other external factors that make harmonious adjustment in marriage more difficult. These factors are all related to the position in the social structure occupied by the family. This does not mean "social position" as usually interpreted, involving the presence or absence of social status. We refer to the role of the family in the congeries of institutions comprising its immediate and more remote social world. The ecological position of the family in the large city; its place in the various ethnic communities making up the large metropolitan center; the religious affiliations of the family members and their attitudes toward them; the economic status of the family and the occupational status of the breadwinner; these and many other elements are reflected in each individual family and influence it as a functioning unit. These influences may make either for harmonious family adjustment or for conflict.

• • •

In his study of the family in the depression, Angell suggested that the two most important criteria of stability are integration and adaptability. When found together in a particular family, these conditions seem to assure its future integrity in the face of the most severe crisis. Family integration is defined in terms of the "many bonds of coherence and unity running through family life, of which common interests, affection, and a sense of economic interdependence are perhaps the most prominent." Adaptability is a function not so much of the ability of the individuals to make rapid adjustments but of the adaptability of the family as a unit in surmounting obstacles. Families lacking adaptability are often characterized by a materialistic philosophy that makes it difficult to adjust to changed material standards of living; by a rigidity in the family mores which will not allow the wife to work because her traditional role is confined to the home; and finally by an irresponsibility on the part of one or all of the members that makes self-discipline difficult or impossible. Families that measure negatively in the key criteria of integration and adaptability were adversely affected by the depression. Families drawn together by common interests and able to adjust to the changing times came through with greater success.

One of the situations most productive of conflicts involves family roles. The husband in our society has traditionally been the breadwinner, a position that seems both obvious and inevitable until we consider the many cultures in which he assumes no such role. The individualism of a pioneer society intensified this cluster of attitudes whereby the burden of family support rested squarely upon the husband. Failure to measure up to this role causes an acute sense of frustration and inferiority.

FROM MAX LERNER, "GROWING UP IN AMERICA," IN *AMERICA AS A CIVILIZATION*
(New York: Simon and Schuster, 1957, 571–72)

On the formal level the qualities [the child] is taught, both in the family and the peer groups, are those that will fit him best into the competitive race: to be resourceful, industrious, persuasive, friendly, popular, an easy mixer, strong of purpose, inventive, self-reliant. The emphasis in a mobile society built on immigration is on outdoing your parents—getting a better education, marrying into a better social stratum, making more money, living in a better neighborhood and with higher living standards. The traits stressed are those of packaging your abilities in the best salesman's fashion, and of a constant quality of *push*. These traits, inculcated and renewed in each generation, take on a cumulative strength in the culture. They leave little room for the withdrawn and reflective personality, who may be detached from the competitive struggle. In fact, when American parents or teachers find these traits in a boy, they may regard them as signs that he is "badly adjusted" and in need of therapy.

Some American scientists, like W. H. Sheldon, see the physical constitution as shaping temperament and even character, and a number of biologists stress the "built-in" mechanisms which set the frame for all growth. Yet there is little of determinist thinking in the attitude of most Americans toward the growing-up years. The pluralism of stocks, the high living standards, and the strides in medicine, all tend to disarrange any preconceived frames of physical growth for Americans and put the stress on will. Similarly, the stress in popular thinking about personality and career is not on the limits but on the potentials of development. "Be a king in your dreams," said Andrew Carnegie to the young American. "Say to yourself, 'My place is on the top.' "

Thus the young American grows up to see life as a cornucopia spilling its plenty into the lap of those who are there to take it. Within the limits of his family's income, and sometimes beyond it, there are few things denied to the growing son and daughter. Their attention is focused on what they can *get*, first out of their parents, then out of life. The growing girl learns to get clothes and gifts from her father and later from her husband. The boy fixes his attention on a succession of artifacts, from a toy gun and an electric train to a car, preferably a convertible. Their levels of aspiration stretch to infinity. Often the parents are blamed for this pliancy and indulgence, yet it is also true that the culture, with its sense of plenty, contains the same principle of infinite possibility. It tells the boy that if only he wants something hard enough, even the Presidency of the nation, he can achieve it. This spurs his striving but it also sets unrealizable goals, since his capacities may not equal the tasks he sets himself, or his class and status handicaps may be too crippling. Thus he misses the sense of security which one gets from the compassable. No limits are set to his goals, and often he reaches for incompatible sets of goals. Rarely does he learn the tolerance of deprivation or the recognition of limits which are a matter of course in less dynamic cultures and which exact a lesser psychic toll than the sense of infinite possibility.

STUDY QUESTIONS

1. Tocqueville describes the members of American families as displaying great independence. Is this true of the Lomans?

2. What does Tocqueville see as the difference between a father in an aristocracy and one in a democracy? Which seems to be more reflective of your own experience? Which type seems most like Willy Loman? How much power does Willy have over his family? How ready are his sons to consult with him and take his advice?

3. What are the dangers of setting unrealizable goals for people? Must limits always be negative, or can they sometimes be positive? What kind of limits do the Lomans face?

4. What do Truxal and Merrill suggest are the social factors that cause conflict in families?

5. What does Angell see as the best means for a family to remain stable, and how do these means operate? Are they operating in the Loman family?

6. Do the Lomans have any common interests? Could they be called a harmonious family?

7. What does Lerner see as the lessons that Americans tend to teach their children, and in what ways are these qualities necessary for a successful life in a competitive society? What kind of pressures does an insistence on being "a king in your dreams" put on the average child?

8. What are the similarities and dissimilarities between the families described by Tocqueville, Truxal and Merrill, and Lerner? Which description seems to be the closest to your own family? Which is the closest to the Lomans?

ROLES OF FATHERS VS. MOTHERS

What exactly are the roles that fathers and mothers should play? Is there an ideal mode of behavior, or does it vary from family to family? Can the problems of the Loman children be blamed on a poor upbringing? Do children need different things from their mother and father, or are parents' tasks essentially the same? What is it that Biff and Hap need from their parents? These are all questions that need consideration. Whether or not one subscribes to more old-fashioned views of parenting or to the latest trend, there is no real consensus about the best way to raise a child, but there have been many people who think they know what it takes. The following selections offer a variety of views from popular magazines on the proper roles of parents. We should consider how far Willy and Linda might have been influenced by such theories.

The author of "The Greatest American Invention" gives a picture of an ideal, romantic father figure who acts as his children's friend, model, and provider. In contrast to this is a portrayal of the nurturing mother who always knows her place. Although we should be able to see the obvious limitations in such roles, they are ones that Willy and Linda seem to be trying to fulfill. Marion Chase Baker briefly outlines what she sees as the duties of all women in society, which seem to consist of the need to teach young girls to look pretty and keep out of trouble. How far might such views have influenced Linda? Amey Eaton Watson suggests that while a mother raises the children, they also need a father's input. We need to consider how the various parents in *Death of a Salesman* have divided their duties toward their offspring; have any achieved an effective balance between mother and father, and are some of them lax in any areas of parenting? Clifford Olcott warns against fathers becoming too dependent on their wives, as the family identity could suffer, but he also suspects that many fathers have not been pulling their weight in rearing their children.

FROM "THE GREATEST AMERICAN INVENTION"
(*Outlook*, 23 July 1919: 463–64)

We of the United States are sometimes humblest about our noblest achievements and braggarts about less worthy ones. Parents and teachers, pastors and publicists, are to-day solicitous about American education, all alike eager to subdue and strait-jacket it to that pitiful dead level called standardization—this American education which by some high and happy hazard has produced a power of initiative and of energy beyond that of any other nation in the world. Better not shackle our schools or our homes, but let them go on with their liberty for incessant experiment, for back of both has been one pervasive but modest influence, one potent but unnoted person. Our armies of the field and our armies of the factory were due both to the American school and to the American home, and yet we have never been proud of the child-training of either. We boast of our electricity, our industry, our inventions, but the greatest thing America has ever produced is the great American "daddy."

"Daddy" is the most influential person we have ever given birth to, and he is also the humblest. He is still pretty young; as a National type he does not belong to the time of our grandfathers—he has only just begun to be a grandfather himself. He is found in every class in this country, but he is not found at all in any other country or in any other period. Yet perhaps from time to time there were in the past potential daddies.

• • •

It has remained, however, for the American daddy to solve the problem of parenthood better than history has ever before solved it, and much better than the mother has yet solved it, although that is hardly her fault, poor thing! There is a subtle division of parental labor and parental privilege implicit in the fact that an American household calls its male head "daddy," while it calls its female head "mother." In the nature of things, mother is a generic term, belonging to every time and country, as static in its implication as it is stanch. Mother is mother all the world over, but daddy, in the American tongue, is a word instantly whimsical with individuality. Daddy, however, is a sad rogue really, walking off with all the poetry of parenthood and leaving the prose to mother. The dentist and the doctor, the teacher and the oculist, are mother's affair; tonsils and adenoids are under maternal management; candy and toys and holidays are the paternal prerogatives. It is not fair, of course, but it will grow fairer as the woman recognizes her equal rights with the man in utter, irresponsible enjoyment of children.

It may be inherent in the laws of nature that mothers cannot enjoy children so much as fathers may. Perhaps a mother cannot sufficiently separate herself from what was once flesh of her flesh and bone of her bone to be able to regard her offspring as separate entities. Yet the consummation of happy irresponsibility is to be recommended as a goal for mothers no less than for fathers. Mothers are prone to an anxious and insistent dominance that involuntarily shapes a child's character into a maternal likeness, eventually entailing upon the mother herself the deadliest ennui rather than the delight due to intercourse with a fresh and independent personality. In spite, however, of the still imperfect evolution of the maternal attitude, the development of parental responsibility is to-day peculiarly promising. What daddy has already accomplished mother will later attain, because the constant attitude of woman toward man's privileges is first to covet, then to appropriate.

One special advantage the present-day father possesses which enables him both to be his son's boon companion and to let his son be his, and that is that to-day old age has become obsolete. Young people now have greater liberty to become enjoyable entities because old people are too busy with their own affairs to bother their children so incessantly as in the days when at fifty the old were laid upon the shelf, where they had nothing whatever to do but cavil at the antics of the oncoming generation. Now that a man goes on experimenting with business or statesmanship until he dies, he has less impulse to live in his son's life, being too much absorbed in his own. In fact, no one who has lived his own life adequately has any desire to live again in another's life. Only those who are feeble and frustrate desire by means of another's existence to right their own mistakes. Any live man or woman prefers to watch while younger folk essay the great adventure each after his own vision. The wise American daddy knows well that discreetly letting his children have their own way is the only means of making them unfailingly entertaining as friends.

Within the last forty years the world has made an incalculable advance in the sheer abandoned joy of intercourse between parents and children, first securely established and made uniform by the one and only American daddy. Little as we have noted the fact, daddy is so far our greatest contribution to the march of civilization.

FROM MARION CHASE BAKER, "MOTHERCRAFT"
(*Survey*, 24 September 1921: 709)

The meaning of "mothercraft" as the term is used in this article is restricted to a definite, carefully planned course of study, usually given in about twelve lessons to classes of young girls. The earlier of these lessons are concerned with carriage, posture, correct habits of eating and sleeping and other principles of good health. The classes then take up the right care of the baby in the home. Using a large doll as model the teacher, who is ordinarily the school nurse or some other qualified person, explains the application of the laws of health to the diet, bathing and sleeping, emphasizing the relationship of the clean happy home to child life. When the course is finished the girls write essays summarizing what they have learned.

FROM AMEY EATON WATSON, "STANDARDS IN PARENTHOOD"
(*Survey*, 26 July 1919: 622)

At this time when so much emphasis is being placed upon standards in child protection and development, a growing appreciation is being shown for the work of parents, upon which in the main depends the production of socially desirable children. Parenthood is in fact beginning to be thought of as it has seldom been before. In the article on Mothers and—Mothers [the SURVEY, for May 3] J. Prentice Murphy says:

> Maternity represents the most continuously exacting individual responsibility known to society. As our community standards have been raised, they have always been preceded by the raising of the standards of maternity care, for every other standard in the community is affected by the care and training which the mother gives her child. The married woman, living under the most normal conditions—and these involve the protection of a husband, a good home, proper physical care, sufficient food, adequate social life, education, opportunities for self-expression and for recreation—still has a most exacting responsibility in the rearing and training of her children. No protection she can possibly receive detracts one iota from the respect and admiration due to her for the great personal service she renders to her family and to the state when she gives intelligent care to her children.

It should be borne in mind here that in the article quoted Mr. Murphy was concerned in discussing motherhood. The present writer believes that Mr. Murphy would agree with her in emphasizing the fact that for the highest type of parenthood we need the contribution of two happily mated individuals—in other words, that efficient fatherhood as well as efficient motherhood is a vital contribution to the family and to the state, a contribution which we need to stress and evaluate far more than is generally done today.

• • •

The following standards were offered tentatively as a basis for a discussion of constructive parenthood . . . :

1. Every child to be born should be consciously desired and purposively conceived in love by *both* parents. In other words, parenthood should be voluntary, deliberate and based on mutual love.

2. Every child born should have a sound heredity and be free from congenital disease and defect.

3. Before any child is conceived, its potential parents should be certain that they will have the economic necessities of life, i.e., at least enough to build up health and maintain physical efficiency in their child.

4. Adequate parenthood must depend on the intelligence of both parents and the willingness of both to exercise responsibility without cessation during the period of dependence of their offspring on the following points:
   a. Physical development, including a rational diet, attention to the laws of hygiene, care in sickness and in health.
   b. Mental development, including home training, training for industrial efficiency, and training for cultural enjoyment.
   c. Moral and spiritual development, including daily training in right habit formation and character, training for citizenship and social service, education for an understanding of sex and parenthood, education in the religious and spiritual life.

5. Adequate parenthood must include on the part of both parents an understanding of the value of membership in a social group and of the great desirability of the conscious acceptance by both parents of the decisions and customs of their social group as expressed by law.

FROM CLIFFORD OLCOTT, "FOR FATHERS ONLY"
(*Parent's Magazine*, October 1945: 140–42)

From the time a man hands out his first cigar with "Boy" or "Girl" on it, he is tremendously interested to know just how to make himself rate as his child's ideal of a father. If you're aspiring to that most soul-satisfying goal here are a few tips.

• • •

One of the first points to master in order to win children is the art of being gentle. Your influence over your child will be a thousand times stronger if you make kindness in your speech and in your manner an everyday virtue. You won't have polite and charmingly behaved children if you shout commands for everything you want. . . .

. . . If you want to teach gentleness, then first of all, practice it. Obedience is often a virtue, but there's no credit to you in having obedient children if they are forced into it with fear and resentment. That type of obedience is never sincere and can not be lasting. Unless you first of all make your children want to obey you with the fullness of their hearts, you have profited absolutely nothing. Defiance follows close upon the heels of forced obedience. Take for example a father calling his young son in to supper. A father who yells angrily, "Get in here and wash those hands—and I won't tell you again!" has no consideration for the boy's self-respect with the rest of the gang. The child will feel indignant and is apt to talk back. Thus will start an evening of tempers or sullen resentment and no peace whatever. But take the father who handles the situation gently and with the ease of a diplomat. He treats his son with the respect he would offer a business associate. Perhaps he goes out to second base where his boy stands, taps him on the shoulder and whispers. "Son, what do you say we surprise Mother tonight and be in for dinner before she calls us?" This father, by his attitude of good comradeship alone, will have his son throwing down his mitt and saying, "So long, fellows, see you after we eat!" He and his dad will go off to enjoy their meal together.

To be a success with the children, be a personality on your own. Don't relinquish your own identity by turning over to your wife all the decisions and matters concerning the children. Don't become the type of father who perpetually says: "Go ask your mother!" This seems, to some fathers, to be a good universal answer for any request from a nickel for an ice cream cone to the meaning of a strange new word. Certainly you are just as capable of deciding as your wife is, whether it's too close to lunch time for the ice cream cone. As to the new word, how about you and the young questioner exploring the dictionary or encyclopedia together? If you pay attention to the requests of your children, that in itself will help to make you a popular person. If you can get them to tell you what they are really thinking and feeling you are gaining their confidence and that is beyond price. You can hold that confidence by making the things that are important to them important to you, too. . . .

My next suggestion as to a way to put you over with the kids is: Say "Yes" as many times as possible. Even if you've just settled yourself in a comfortable chair when your son says, "Can you fix my bike pedal?" show interest and if you can't fix it then promise to do so later—and keep your promise. Too many noes, from you in response to what seem like inconsequential matters may cause your children to lack the courage to come to you with the big problems that will crop up in their lives later on. So by all means pay attention now to small requests for help.

• • •

Plan and look ahead with your children. Show them that their futures are important to you and that you will do everything you can to help them. If your Johnny wants to become a doctor, plan with him each step of the way he will have to follow to get there. If you can't see him through, financially, then work it out with him, somehow, that the two of you saving together might meet the expense. Otherwise, plan with him how he can accomplish the goal on his own; but let him know that you are with him all the while, in your interest if not in the actual help you can give him. . . . There's no greater satisfaction to be had in this life than for a father to know he has contributed to the success his children have achieved.

STUDY QUESTIONS

1. Why does "The Greatest American Invention" claim that the "daddy" is the "greatest thing America has ever produced" and the "greatest contribution to the march of civilization"? Do you agree?

2. What kind of father is depicted in "The Greatest American Invention"? How typical is he? Are any of the fathers in *Death of a Salesman* like this?

3. In "The Greatest American Invention," what is the writer's attitude toward mothers, and how is this conveyed? Is the author male or female?

4. What does the writer suggest is the difference between the terms "daddy" and "mother"? What difference applies to the terms "father" and "mommy"? Is Willy Loman a "daddy" or a "father"? Is Linda Loman a "mommy" or a "mother"?

5. How does the writer divide the tasks of parenting between the mother and the father? What does the writer see as the inherent dangers within motherhood?

6. What does Baker see as the essential lessons of "mothercraft"? What kind of mothers will be produced by the young girls who follow her guidance?

7. Does Baker feel that girls need to learn anything in school other than how to be good mothers? Would Baker see Linda Loman as a good mother?

8. How does J. Prentice Murphy describe the role of a mother? What is it that Watson wishes to add to Murphy's advice, and why?

9. How does Watson divide the tasks of parenting between the mother and the father?

10. What do you feel is the order of importance for the standards Watson suggests? Do you agree with all of her standards? Do the Lomans live up to these standards? If not, in what areas do they seem to be most lax?

11. Would either Marion Chase Baker, J. Prentice Murphy, or Amey Eaton Watson approve of Linda Loman as a mother? Do you?

12. What is the core of Olcott's advice to fathers? Is it realistic? What does his advice seem to imply about the behavior of many American fathers? Does Willy Loman follow his advice? Does Willy "plan" with his children in the way that Olcott suggests?

13. Olcott warns of the dangers of saying no to children too many times

and believes that a father should say yes as often as possible, but is this always a good thing? Has Loman said too many noes or too many yeses to Biff and Hap?

14. Would the author of "The Greatest American Invention" or Clifford Olcott approve of Willy Loman as a father? Do you?

PROVIDERS VS. COWBOYS OR PLAYBOYS

Twentieth-century American society appears to promote a variety of roles toward which males might wish to aspire. While on the one hand society applauds the man who marries, has children, and provides them with a good home and everything they might desire, on the other hand, society also displays a tremendous respect toward figures who represent none of these reliable qualities. Willy is struggling for respect as a provider, but he is ever attracted to what seem to be the more glamorous lives of pioneers and cowboys who live close to nature, or playboys who live only for themselves. What is more, his two sons seem to be even more drawn to these romantic modes of life and are determined not to be tied down to the role of provider that Willy has been forced to accept.

American pioneers and cowboys have reached the stature of mythic heroes in the eyes of many, and this seems to include Biff and his father. The cowboy, especially, has been popularly associated with a sense of romance and freedom. There is also a sneaking envy of the playboy figure, a man whose attractions allow him to live a high life full of the proverbial wine, women, and song, a life very close to the one Hap currently lives. Clearly cowboys and playboys offer a major contrast to the good provider, the family man who works hard on the road like Willy, or keeps busy in an office five days a week. In light of the documents that follow, taken from social studies, an advertisement, a collection of songs, and a popular magazine, try to ascertain which of these types it is that society really condones and promotes. This should help us to better understand the roles the characters in *Death of a Salesman* reject or try to fulfill.

In "The American Father" Ashley Montagu discusses ways in which a father is expected to provide for his children. He claims that many fathers tend to spend too much time in pursuits beyond home and become estranged from their families, which is, in many ways, what has happened to Willy. Montagu insists that fathers should be authority figures for their children, not pals. Children copy their fathers, and so the best fathers provide strong values for them to emulate. This is something about which Willy has been particularly lax. The advertising copy for Cutler desks tries to create a sense of the potential romance of business, to make the man's provider role seem more attractive and less restricting. But are men like Willy, stuck in thankless jobs they have begun to hate, really that easily fooled?

Americans have ever held a romantic view of the great wild West, seeing it as a land of beauty and freedom—a desert landscape first settled by adventurous pioneers, then later spotted with cattle and cowboys. The cowboy, who epitomizes the Western viewpoint, stands for daring individuality, masculinity, and a simple code of honor. He is consistently depicted as suntanned and carefree, constantly confronting the exciting dangers of the wide-open spaces he inhabits, mastering wild cattle, wild horses, and wild terrain. The scorching sun, heavy winds and rain, loneliness and isolation, continual thirst and exhaustion of this harsh and violent world seemed to create characters who were self-reliant, crude, and powerful. It is little wonder that Willy and Biff are drawn to such figures.

While Frederick Jackson Turner outlines the attractions of the pioneering character, the various songs from John Lomax's collection cover both positive and negative images of the life of a cowboy. Barrett Wendell's introduction to this collection tells about the romantic charm of the cowboy, but Wendell also admits that the cowboy's era is really over by the twentieth century, and the dream of being a cowboy is one of nostalgia. What appears to have happened to the cowboy over the years, and what might be the appeal of becoming a cowboy in the 1940s to someone like Biff?

In "Sex and the Double Standard" (1947) Waverly Root responds to a letter sent by a woman who complains of what she sees as a double standard in the way people treat men and women in sexual matters. Root suggests that she wrote only because she herself wants more freedom to have sex without censure. He then imposes his view that women are generally too emotional to commit adultery properly anyway. Root feels it is better for the husbands to play around, because they are naturally polygamous. This is a typical view from the 1940s. Might such a stance go some way toward justifying Willy's adultery? In "Sex and Sex Education," written twenty years later, Ashley Montagu suggests that American men take sex too casually and women get hurt. In America, he tells us, men are encouraged to act like playboys. We should ask why

Hap has chosen the irresponsible life he leads and whether Willy and Linda have failed as parents by not inculcating better values.

FROM ASHLEY MONTAGU, "THE AMERICAN FATHER," IN *THE AMERICAN WAY OF LIFE*
(New York: Putnam's, 1967, 233–35, 238–40, 242)

It is not surprising to learn from these researches that inadequate fathers are remote from their children in what has become an increasingly acceptable social way. Superficially the family appears adequately socially and emotionally organized, the husband seeming to exercise the usual controls. That is to say, he *seems* to be the head of the family, to play the dominant role, to be aware of his obligations, and so on. In fact, the husband's role as father is ill defined and weak. The breadwinner in such families does not participate in the making of family decisions or in discipline of the children. The mother in these families has taken over these obligations. Remaining on the outskirts of the family, such men were found to be neither happy nor unhappy with this arrangement. Social participation in the lives of their children was either negative or minimal. There was no involvement, such fathers pursuing a recreational and social life separate from or at most tangential to that of their children. Investigation of such men indicated that they had themselves not experienced satisfactory relationships with their fathers. . . .

The unfulfilled and unfulfilling father in such families, achieving none of the gratifications which come from involvement as a parent with his children, is naturally dissatisfied with the diminished position in which he finds himself in the home. Under such conditions he tends to seek release from this attenuated status and to find expression for himself in the diversion of his available free energy into channels in which he can feel more adequate. The result of this usually is a worsening of his inadequacies as a father by overinvestment in gratifications obtained from activities away from the home.

• • •

So little do many men understand their role as a father and so little do they take that role seriously that many a father has experienced some difficulty in thinking of himself as such, except in the narrow technical sense. Instead, with the best of intentions, such fathers often think of their children as pals, buddies, friends. Good intentions are no substitute for the work that almost anything worth doing requires. It cannot be too often repeated that the father who treats his children as if they were his pals and encourages them to call him by his first name serves his children ill. Children are not the equals of adults, still less of their parents, and should not be treated as such. Children are growing and developing human beings, who need all the guidance they can receive from people whom they can trust, respect, and follow. Children don't want to be treated as equals, still less as pals. What they want is a firm hand at the helm, which will serve to pilot them into the safe harbor of their own growth and developmental abilities, upon which they may safely make their landfall. If they don't receive the help of father, they will have a hard time dropping anchor anywhere.

Children learn through the imitation and repetition of acts modeled on and conditioned by their parents. These are the images upon which the clay that is the child is molded. . . .

The role of the father should be to behave toward the members of his family in such a manner that he confers survival benefits upon them in a creatively enlarging manner—in brief, to be loving toward them; to love with the firmness and the fairness which enables one to say "No" when that should be said and equally to say "Yes" when that is indicated; to build up a sense of justice, responsibility, courage, resoluteness, integrity, resourcefulness, honesty, sincerity, kindness, thoughtfulness, gentleness, and compassion—all traits that are within the power of a loving father to communicate and to make part of his children.

The romance of business is not dead. Ideals have not grown old, only stronger. We still build as it has been our ideal to build, for three generations, desks fit for a man to put his fist on when he means the thing he says and means it hard.

There is a Cutler dealer near you who sells the desks that express success. Write for his name and for descriptive literature.

FROM FREDERICK JACKSON TURNER, "PIONEERS' IDEALS AND THE STATE UNIVERSITY"
(*Indiana University Bulletin*, 15 June 1910: 6–29)

The first ideal of the pioneer was that of conquest. It was his task to fight with nature for the chance to exist. Not as in older countries did this contest take place in a mythical past, told in folk lore and epic. It has been continuous to our own day. Facing each generation of pioneers was the unmastered continent. Vast forests blocked the way; mountainous ramparts interposed; desolate, grass-clad prairies, barren oceans of rolling plains, arid deserts, and a fierce race of savages, all had to be met and defeated. The rifle and the ax are the symbols of the backwoods pioneer. They meant a training in aggressive courage, in domination, in directness of action, in destructiveness.

To the pioneer the forest was no friendly resource for posterity, no object of careful economy. He must wage a hand-to-hand war upon it, cutting and burning a little space to let in the light upon a dozen acres of hard-won soil, and year after year expanding the clearing into new woodlands against the stubborn resistance of primeval trunks and matted roots. He made war against the rank fertility of the soil. While new worlds of virgin land lay ever just beyond, it was idle to expect the pioneer to stay his hand and turn to scientific farming. Indeed, as Secretary Wilson has said, the pioneer would, in that case, have raised wheat that no one wanted to eat, corn to store on the farm, and cotton not worth the picking.

Thus, fired with the ideal of subduing the wilderness, the destroying pioneer fought his way across the continent, masterful and wasteful, preparing the way by seeking the immediate thing, rejoicing in rude strength and wilful achievement.

But even this backwoodsman was more than a mere destroyer. He had visions. He was finder as well as fighter—the trailmaker for civilization, the inventor of new ways.

• • •

The pioneer was taught in the school of experience that the crops of one area would not do for a new frontier; that the scythe of the clearing must be replaced by the reaper of the prairies. He was forced to make old tools serve new uses; to shape former habits, institutions and ideas to changed conditions; and to find new means when the old proved inapplicable. He was building a new society as well as breaking new soil; he had the ideal of nonconformity and of change. He rebelled against the conventional.

Besides the ideals of conquest and of discovery, the pioneer had the ideal of personal development, free from social and governmental constraint. He came from a civilization based on individual competition, and he brought that concept with him to the wilderness where a wealth of resources, and innumerable opportunities gave it a new scope. The prizes were for the keenest and the strongest; for them were the best bottom lands, the finest timber tracts, the best salt-springs, the richest ore beds; and not only these natural gifts, but also the opportunities afforded in the midst of a forming society. Here were mill sites, town sites, transportation lines, banking centers, openings in the law, in politics—all the varied chances for advancement afforded in a rapidly developing society where everything was open to him who knew how to seize the opportunity.

FROM JOHN A. LOMAX, ED., *COWBOY SONGS AND OTHER FRONTIER BALLADS*
(New York: Macmillan, 1922, 20–21, 96–97, 117–18)

THE COWBOY'S LIFE

The bawl of a steer,
To a cowboy's ear,
Is music of sweetest strain;
And the yelping notes
Of the gray cayotes
To him are a glad refrain.

And his jolly songs
Speed him along,
As he thinks of the little gal
With golden hair
Who is waiting there
At the bars of the home corral.

For a kingly crown
In the noisy town
His saddle he wouldn't change;

No life so free
As the life we see
Way out on the Yaso range.

His eyes are bright
And his heart as light
As the smoke of his cigarette;
There's never a care
For his soul to bear,
No trouble to make him fret.

The winds may blow
And the thunder growl
Or the breezes may safely moan;—
A cowboy's life
Is a royal life,
His saddle his kingly throne.

Saddle up, boys,
For the work is play
When love's in the cowboy's eyes,—
When his heart is light
As the clouds of white
That swim in the summer skies.

THE COWBOY

All day long on the prairies I ride,
Not even a dog to trot by my side;
My fire I kindle with chips gathered round,
My coffee I boil without being ground.

I wash in a pool and wipe on a sack;
I carry my wardrobe all on my back;
For want of an oven I cook bread in a pot,
And sleep on the ground for want of a cot.

My ceiling is the sky, my floor is the grass,
My music is the lowing of the herds as they pass;
My books are the brooks, my sermons the stones,
My parson is a wolf on his pulpit of bones.

And then if my cooking is not very complete
You can't blame me for wanting to eat.
But show me a man that sleeps more profound
Than the big puncher-boy who stretches himself on the ground.

And then between me and love lies a gulf very wide.
Some lucky fellow may call her his bride.
My friends gently hint I am coming to grief,
But men must make money and women have beef.

If I had hair on my chin, I might pass for the goat
That bore all the sins in the ages remote;
But why it is I can never understand,
For each of the patriarchs owned a big brand.

Abraham emigrated in search of a range,
And when water was scarce he wanted a change;
Old Isaac owned cattle in charge of Esau,
And Jacob punched cows for his father-in-law.

He started in business way down at bed rock,
And made quite a streak at handling stock;
Then David went from night-herding to using a sling;
And, winning the battle, he became a great king.
Then the shepherds, while herding the sheep on a hill,
Got a message from heaven of peace and goodwill.

THE OLD SCOUT'S LAMENT

Come all of you, my brother scouts,
And join me in my song;
Come, let us sing together
Though the shadows fall so long.

Of all the old frontiersmen
That used to scour the plain,
There are but very few of them
That with us yet remain.

Day after day they're dropping off,
They're going one by one;
Our clan is fast decreasing,
Our race is almost run.

Oh, the days of elk and buffalo!
It fills my heart with pain
To know these days are past and gone
To never come again.

We fought the red-skin rascals
Over valley, hill, and plain;
We fought him in the mountain top,
And fought him down again.

These fighting days are over;
The Indian yell resounds
No more along the border;
Peace sends far sweeter sounds.

But we found great joy, old comrades,
To hear, and make it die;
We won bright homes for gentle ones,
And now, our West, good-bye.

FROM BARRETT WENDELL, "COLLECTOR'S NOTE," IN *COWBOY
SONGS AND OTHER FRONTIER BALLADS*
(New York: Macmillan, 1922, n.p.)

Most cowboys . . . were bold young spirits who emigrated to the West for
the same reason that their ancestors had come across the seas. They loved
roving; they loved freedom; they were pioneers by instinct; an impulse
set their faces from the East, put the tang for roaming in their veins, and
sent them ever, ever westward.

That the cowboy was brave has come to be axiomatic. If his life of
isolation made him taciturn, it at the same time created a spirit of hos-
pitality, primitive and hearty as that found in the mead-halls of Beowulf.
He faced the wind and the rain, the snow of winter, the fearful dust-
storms of alkali desert wastes, with the same uncomplaining quiet. Not
all his work was on the ranch and the trail. To the cowboy, more than
to the goldseekers, more than to Uncle Sam's soldiers, is due the conquest of the West. Along his winding cattle trails the Forty-Niners found
their way to California. The cowboy has fought back the Indians ever
since ranching became a business and as long as Indians remained to be
fought. He played his part in winning the great slice of territory that the
United States took away from Mexico. He has always been on the skirmish
line of civilization. Restless, fearless, chivalric, elemental, he lived hard,
shot quick and true, and died with his face to his foe. . . .

The big ranches of the West are now being cut up into small farms.
The nester has come, and come to stay. Gone is the buffalo, the Indian
warwhoop, the free grass of the open plain;—even the stinging lizard,
the horned frog, the centipede, the prairie dog, the rattlesnake, are fast
disappearing. . . .

The changing and romantic West of the early days lives mainly in story
and in song.

FROM WAVERLY ROOT, "SEX AND THE DOUBLE STANDARD"
(*American Mercury* 65 [October 1947]: 403–8)

"You leave untreated," my female correspondent writes, "a point to which I have been accustomed to cling in defending not only American over French morals, but 'Anglo-Saxon' morals in general over 'Latin' morals in general . . . namely, the issue of masculine fidelity in marriage."

"In Latin culture," she continues, ["]almost the entire burden of upholding sexual virtue falls upon the shoulders of women in the wife-mother class, permitting to masculine instincts absolutely free rein both before and after marriage. . . . Wives have no choice but to shrug their shoulders. . . ."

The most interesting point of this letter, to my mind, is that it objects to the double standard not so much because it caters to the male, but because it "cruelly" restrains the female. In other words, why should the boys have all the fun? Now, this is an understandable attitude and one with which, like most males, I am ready to sympathize. (After all, how can the boys have fun if there are no girls to have fun with?) But my correspondent, in the tradition of that Puritanical morality which we still honor with lip service in the United States, would redress the unfairness of the situation by imposing on men the restraint she finds cruel because it is now applied to women.

Twenty years ago, with the brashness of youth, I, too, had no doubt that the double standard was all wrong, but my solution was to allow the girls the freedom I enjoyed. I was then a *naif* dissenter from the majority opinion and certainly at odds with my New England upbringing. Today, when I find myself coming around to the opinion that the double standard is a natural development from the fact of masculine and feminine differentiation, I seem still to be a dissenter, for the truth is that the American *jeune fille* participates fully, as my correspondent puts it, in erotic play.

To be sure, the girls, unwilling to forego an advantage, have not thrown away all of the double standard; they have dispensed only with that part of it which limited their own sexual freedom. Women still have the advantage in sidestepping unwanted advances. When a man makes a pass at a girl who doesn't welcome it, society stands behind her like a wall in her resistance. With a word, she can render his conduct contemptible, and he can only crawl away in complete apologetic abjection. He has demonstrated himself to be a cad, a churl and a bounder.

But let us suppose that the lady approaches the man. For him, she is prepared to make the supreme sacrifice. She offers him her virtue, her all. Let us assume he does not covet her all, but can any gentleman spurn such an offer? Not with impunity. Escape is difficult, and even if achieved, the ungrateful and usually graceless flight of the recreant proves him a cad, a churl and a bounder.

• • •

. . . [I]t can be said that our mores permit men and women to follow different paths of sexual conduct because men and women react differently to sexual situations. This is not precisely a new discovery. Byron informed us long ago that while love is of man's life a thing apart, 'tis woman's whole existence. At the same time, one can make out a good case for the argument that male love is more dependable and more profound than female love. Where the essential difference comes in, I should say, is in the different emphasis placed on the physical act of love by men and by women. . . .

To woman, if one may speak in generalizations, the physical act is of enormous importance. To man, it is a detail. Thus a man may be, in the physical sense of the word, unfaithful to a woman without ever having wavered, in his mind, from his devotion to her. But a woman who has been physically unfaithful to a man is obsessed with a sense of guilt; this establishes a psychological barrier between herself and her mate, a barrier which does not appear in the mind of the physically unfaithful male, whose conscience usually does not trouble him excessively though he may be apprehensive of being found out. . . . For the purpose of the reproduction of the species, it is advantageous for women to be constant and for men to be inconstant. . . . A man with a beautiful wife becomes unable, in a year or so, to see her beauty, for the familiarity of her appearance dulls for him the sensations it evokes in others. In the same way, though it is grievous to admit it in the presence of ladies, a sexual diet limited to one woman eventually palls on the most moral of men. From observation of the marriages of my friends, I would estimate that most husbands begin to tire of their wives in about ten years.

What happens then? The man of the single standard maintains a fidelity which, whether he admits it to himself or not, is irksome to him. He envies bachelors. His wife gradually assumes the aspect of an obstacle between himself and a fuller life. This is particularly true if, as a young man, he forebore to sow wild oats. He now sees the period approaching when his sexual opportunities will end and he begins to regret that he has accepted so few of them. He has reached the dangerous forties and his marriage is in peril.

. . . Logically, a woman should be more flattered than angered that her husband is attractive to other women, successful with them and still prefers her. What value should be put on the approval of a man who has known the merits of no other women? What does he know of England who only England knows? The approval of a connoisseur should be more highly prized than that of an ignoramus.

FROM ASHLEY MONTAGU, "SEX AND SEX EDUCATION," IN *THE AMERICAN WAY OF LIFE*
(New York: Putnam's, 1967, 78–79)

The real difficulty, as I see it, is not that too much but that too little is made of sex. Christian, Puritan, Fundamentalist, and other influences have served to obscure and pervert the understanding and meaning of sex, not alone in America, but wherever these influences have made themselves felt. The result is, particularly in America, that sex is equated with sexual intercourse and all the titillations that lead to that climactic experience. Instead of the uniquely beautiful enchantment that sex should be, it has been degraded to the crass status of a male relief mechanism for the pressures of the sex drive. This is principally a male psychosis, and this male attitude toward sex is extremely hard on the female and is not a little responsible for the frequent unhappiness of the American wife.

No one having taught him anything of the meaning of sex, except what he has picked up adventitiously, the American male at about sixteen discovers yet another dimension of the process of growing up into which he must enter and which he must conquer. And since sexual conquests are considered to be the mark of a genuine he-man and are made in the context of a pseudoromantic glow, aided and abetted by TV, the movies, the press, and the like, in which love constitutes the theme and sex its realization, sex and love come to be identified as one.

STUDY QUESTIONS

1. What does Montagu see as the increasing trouble people have with the role of the husband/father, and what is the root cause?

2. Montagu describes a tendency in offspring to emulate their parents. In what ways are Biff and Hap imitating their father? How has Willy's attitude toward them, and his treatment of them, affected their lives? In what ways do you see yourself as imitating your mother or father?

3. Why does Montagu see it as wrong and dangerous for a father to try to be a "pal" to his children? How does Willy treat his children? Is he a good provider?

4. What does Montagu believe that the ideal role of a father should be? How do Charley, Willy, and Willy's father measure up?

5. To what senses is the advertisement for Cutler desks appealing? What do the manufacturers offer the people who buy their desks beyond a piece of furniture? Why might a businessman be attracted to such advertising?

6. What kind of man sits behind a Cutler desk? Would Willy be that type? What picture might the company place with this text?

7. How does Turner characterize the American pioneer? What kind of person would make a good pioneer? Why might the role of pioneer appeal to a man like Willy Loman?

8. What type of men become cowboys, and why? How does Wendell characterize the typical cowboy, and how is the cowboy portrayed in the various songs? What is the implied alternative to a cowboy's way of life?

9. What do these songs suggest are the chief responsibilities, pleasures, rewards, and drawbacks of being a cowboy? Are they being realistic or presenting an ideal? Do they omit any aspects of a cowboy's life?

10. Why does the song "The Cowboy" depict Biblical figures as cowboy types?

11. What is implied in the songs about a cowboy's relationship to the land? What is it that the old scout is lamenting in the final song?

12. What is it that concerns Root's female correspondent, and how does Root respond to her concern? Is he fair?

13. What does Root seem to think of men and women who sleep around? What would he think of Willy's extramarital affair?

14. What does Root's argument suggest about attitudes toward men, women, and marriage in the 1940s?

15. What does Root see as the sexual differences between men and women? What is he trying to justify by this? Can we accept his logic?

16. What does Montagu mean by saying that the real difficulty is that "too little is made of sex"?

17. Why does Montagu think American men have extramarital affairs, and what is the result of this for their wives? How does Willy's affair affect his relationship with Linda?

18. What does Montagu say has influenced the male attitude toward sex, and how does this suggest that Americans tend to view men who sleep with a lot of women?

HOMEMAKERS VS. CALL GIRLS

While twentieth-century America seems to influence its men to adopt contradictory roles that require them to stay with their women or use them and leave them, the options open for women are no less contradictory. What may be surprising is the far narrower range of role possibilities allowed to women than to men, especially in the earlier part of the century, and the lack of any median between the extremes by which these few roles were judged. While a man could be applauded for both responsibility and irresponsibility, women were given little leeway. Women of Linda Loman's generation were taught that if they were to go against the dictates of proper behavior, even in so minor a way as to attempt to be independent or to get a job, then they could be instantly reduced to whoredom by the social watchdogs, as the following selections from popular magazines show. We should consider how far this is borne out by the female characters in the play.

Despite the sexual politics of the 1920s, when American women voted for the first time and demanded equal rights with men from the workplace to sexual practice, many women still preferred the older models of womanhood, as they made them feel safer in their well-defined roles as domesticated housewives whose duties were to raise children and look after their husbands. Such roles were consistently reinforced by popular culture, as shown in the advertisement for Congoleum rugs. The 1940s and 1950s were not a time when a lot of women took risks to expand their domesticated horizons; many, like Linda, seemed content to run the home.

Ethel Wadsworth Cartland expounds on the joys of being an old-fashioned mother and despises married women who wish to stay independent and unburdened, calling them parasites. Sheila Kaye-Smith's diatribe against the "new woman" who strives to be independent and compete in male spheres illustrates that it was definitely not just men who felt that women's roles in society should be restricted to the home. Kaye-Smith insists that it is unnatural for a woman to want to be independent and free, as women are meant to marry and raise children. Where does this place such characters as The Woman or Miss Forsythe? Does it partly explain the way men in the play tend to view and treat the "independent" women they meet? The advertisement for Congoleum rugs carries the strong suggestion, as did many advertisements in the first half of the twentieth century, that it is a woman's job to make both the home and herself attractive. How can women fight against such societal pressure? Is it suprising that the potential of an apparently strong woman like Linda can be so reduced in such a society?

FROM ETHEL WADSWORTH CARTLAND, "WANTED: MOTIVES
FOR MOTHERHOOD"
(*Outlook* 129 [12 October 1921]: 223–24)

When I had been only four months married, a college friend, herself now the mother of several children, who had been very kind to me, advised me not to have a family—at least not for some time. She was an influential woman in the town. I know she thought she was doing me a kindness in endeavoring to show me how to avoid having children, but she could not read my heart. Every time she introduced the subject my whole nature went into uncontrollable revolt. I gently changed the subject; but in a few days she again attempted to advise me about this. Again I refused to talk about it, and a third time she vainly broached the subject. But every time she spoke a voice within my heart cried loudly, despairingly, to me:

"If you do not have your children now, you will never dare to have them. You are twenty-six years old, and that is a very good age at which to begin having children. Later on you will be afraid. You will do as others do. You will have excuses—every one does. You will be sorry when it is too late for us. We call to you to give us birth!"

• • •

But, oh, these popular "best-seller" books and cheap popular magazines! Everywhere is the insipid girl's face on the cover, with the whole reading public apparently bowing down before the pretty, idle, inane, slouching, and dilettante girl, conspicuous for no achievement (not even for simple innocence) and renowned only for a physical beauty skin deep, and maybe not as deep as that. Bah! she is the girl who sees only the pocketbook and can be purchased like a top or a whistle by any little callow lad whose father's shoes are too big for him! Not a word—not a word anywhere of that daring woman who like the diver descends the awful depths of the unknown to seek the living "pearl that hath no price." Not a word of that mature, thoughtful woman with a mind as well as a face who labors conscientiously day and night, like the engineer who goes tapping, tapping, tapping with his hammer all over the great black engine, noting with scrupulous nicety its every part and condition before he trusts a hundred lives to its speed.

American parents! For how long will you continue to buy and read and have in your house for your boys and girls to read the vapid moonings of the young lovers—in what is designated their calf love—no more like real love than moonlight is like sunlight? At the age of adolescence, of all ages the most unbalanced and dangerous, you give them ever that which renders them still more so! When in her depressed and weary condition the expectant mother reads these books and magazines, she realizes perhaps for the first time what is the real psychological teaching of such trash. The pretty young girl travels ideally along on the insecure edge of a man's brute passion, so delightfully dangerous on paper, meets all these happy but wholly impossible adventures, and ends with the so-called *birth of love* in her own soul, but which, sad to tell, the discerning reader recognizes as nothing but the awakening of the sex impulse in the immature heroine. Some time, later on, not in the story, the poor, foolish heroine would in real life awaken to her bitter delusion, perhaps to seek the divorce court for incompatibility of temper.

In every way we are rushing the immature girl into the limelight to her own harm, asking too much of her in public and not enough of her in private life.

A former neighbor proudly remarked to me once that *her* daughter washed no dirty old dishes nor was tied down in any other way. She, the mother, did all the dishes and the family housework herself. She wanted her daughter to *enjoy herself* while she was young! Yes, the mother meant well, but what was the result? She unfitted a naturally able and willing girl for any serious responsibility in life, through which alone life's greatest and most lasting happiness can ever come.

Another friend aspires socially for her daughter, and rushes her day and night from one festivity to another. Any young man who has an automobile at his disposal may take the girl out at any time. What is the result? The undisciplined, ignorant girl, too much away from her mother at this critical age, is very indiscreet in her conduct (to put it mildly). Certainly she will make a shallow if not wicked woman.

These two types of girlhood are met everywhere, and become the childless wives we meet every day. They will accept no responsibility. They are parasites, as their mothers trained them to be.

FROM SHEILA KAYE-SMITH, "THE NEW WOMAN"
(*Living Age*, November 1921: 355–56)

Woman now has very nearly the same political and educational advantages as man, but you cannot be much impressed by the use she has made of them. Politics have surely never been more treacherous or commercial than they are in these Utopian days, when woman has the vote, and education seems to have persuaded some women to think that their highest aim in life is to produce a feeble imitation of their brothers. Marriage is going out of fashion as a vocation, and a great deal of nonsense is talked about men and women working together side by side and being independent of each other. I have even heard it said in praise of the modern woman that she does not look upon marriage as her aim in life, but looks forward to entering a profession and earning her living independently of male support.

To me this schoolgirlish contempt of natural emotions is just as bad as early Victorian prudery. If a woman does not look forward to marriage as the central hope of her life it means either that she intends to pursue her love affairs anti-socially, or, worse still, that she does not mean to have any at all. Of course, there is that most recent product of the age, that standby of modern journalism, the superfluous woman. But people forget that she is merely a passing phenomenon, and not a fact of Nature, and that there is no reason why ideals, morals, and economics should be altered to meet her case. It would be better if we set ourselves to get rid of her problem by improving the conditions of child-life, so that we do not every year preventably lose so many boy babies, and also by doing our best to make this country fit for other men besides heroes to live in. Nature intended the sexes to be equally balanced, so that neither man nor woman should have to live alone; but a selfish and muddled civilization has spoiled Nature's work, and every year thousands of the best of our men are driven overseas to create a superfluous man problem in Canada or Australia.

The result is that economic reasons urge women into professions for which they are physically and temperamentally unfitted, and conditions for the male worker are made still worse by the consequent lowering of standards both in work and wages. Surely the war ought to have taught us that most professions are unsuited to women, both for physical and for temperamental reasons. They stepped into the men's places and did their best, but they were not, generally speaking, successful. Those who worked under or with women in the war can testify to the nervous instability—showing itself in ill-temper, injustice, and petty tyranny—to which even the most charming and capable women succumbed after long hours of taxing and responsible work. A woman's nervous energy was meant to be consumed by other things. Of course, I am not saying that all professions are unsuited to women, but in these days of her recovered freedom she has shown a strange lack of discrimination. Woman is at her best in the more decorative ways of life—in the production and distribution of beautiful necessities, or in those professions most akin to motherhood, the care and education of children, or medical attendance of her own sex. Her brain power and nervous energy are essentially different from a man's, and she makes a mistake when she tries to use them in the same way. It is partly due to her confusion of equality with identity. To prove herself man's equal, as she always has been, she has paid him an unnecessary compliment of imitation, and she will never establish herself fully in popular opinion as his equal until she realizes that her equality lies in her difference. She is man's mate and completion, not his competitor, and her development lies along parallel, not similar, lines. If she merely tries to follow in his footsteps it will lead to much stumbling and weariness, and perhaps at last to the terrible tragedy of Eve's growing old.

ADVERTISEMENT FOR CONGOLEUM RUGS
(*Literary Digest*, 8 May 1920)

The design on the floor is Congoleum Gold-Seal Art-Rug No. 500. The 9x10½ retails at $14.25.

"*Isn't this Rug a Joy!*"

"*I used to think this kitchen a dull, cheerless place; but since I've had this lovely Congoleum Rug I actually am finding excuses for staying in the kitchen!*

"*Wouldn't Grandma have reveled in a rug like this! Gran'dad used to say you could eat off her kitchen floor!*"

But this modern housewife keeps her floor just as spotless and immaculate as her grandmother's without any back-breaking scrubbing or sweeping. She has something her grandmother never dreamed of—a sanitary, waterproof rug!

And as to expense—if this Congoleum Rug had cost as much as other rugs, it would have been a good investment for it certainly saves trouble in cleaning—but it *cost only $14.25!*

In a twinkling a damp mop wipes away every sign of the morning's baking and kitchen work and restores the charming fresh color.

The kitchen is only one of a dozen places where Congoleum has been found to give complete satisfaction.

3 x 4½ feet $2.40	7½ x 9 feet	$11.85
3 x 6 feet 3.20	9 x 9 feet	14.25
6 x 9 feet 9.75	9 x 10½ feet	16.60
	9 x 12 feet 19.00	

Prices in the Far West and South average 10% higher than those quoted; in Canada prices average 25% higher. All prices subject to change without notice.

Congoleum Company
INCORPORATED

PHILADELPHIA   SAN FRANCISCO   CHICAGO
MINNEAPOLIS   DALLAS   BOSTON   MONTREAL

CONGOLEUM
GOLD SEAL
RUGS

Look for the Gold Seal

You are always perfectly safe if the rug you buy has the Gold-Seal Guarantee pasted on the face. The salesman will tell you that the pledge "Satisfaction guaranteed or your money will be refunded," means exactly what it says.

STUDY QUESTIONS

1. What does the Congoleum rug advertisement imply about an average woman's desires, and what does it suggest that a "modern house-wife's" main concerns should be? Would Linda buy a Congoleum rug?

2. What stereotypes of women does this advertisement reinforce? How do today's advertisements sell products to women? Have their techniques changed?

3. Why do you think Cartland's friend advises her to wait to have a family? Why is Cartland so disgusted with her friend's advice?

4. How does Cartland view a woman's role in society, and what does she think of women who refuse to have children?

5. What does Cartland think of the ways in which women are presented in popular books and magazines of her time, and what does this imply about how she believes women should behave?

6. What does Cartland mean when she describes married women without children as parasites? What else does she imply about women who remain independent and unburdened by children?

7. Why does Kaye-Smith object to women working, and why does she feel that women are unsuited to work? How does she portray such women?

8. What does Kaye-Smith think of "The New Woman"?

9. Why does Kaye-Smith see talk of women working beside men and being independent as nonsense? What would she think of Miss Forsythe and Letta?

10. What does Kaye-Smith suggest about the sex lives of women who do not see marriage as the "central hope" of their lives?

TOPICS FOR WRITTEN OR ORAL EXPLORATION

1. Write a piece explaining what you think your family's expectations are for you, and explain how their expectations have influenced decisions you have had to make.

2. Write a letter Tocqueville may have written to a friend, making clearer what he implies in his essay are the main differences between American families and those he has witnessed elsewhere.

3. Are the Loman family relationships closer to Tocqueville's description of an aristocratic family or to that of his democratic model? Explain which model seems closer to describing the Lomans.

4. Write a description of what Tocqueville sees as the more usual roles of fathers and children in a family, and point out if any of these fit the Lomans.

5. Make a table of the social conflicts that Truxal and Merrill describe, and show where and how each one operates in the Loman family.

6. What do Truxal and Merrill see as the dangers inherent in insisting on the father as the traditional head of the family? Does Willy Loman reflect any of these dangers? Write a piece in which you imagine that you are Truxal and Merrill, analyzing Willy Loman's position in his family.

7. Compare and contrast the descriptions of parental roles in the section titled "Roles of Fathers vs. Mothers." Which come closest to the way Willy and Linda Loman behave?

8. How would you describe the roles that your mother and father play in your family?

9. Write a journal entry that Marion Chase Baker, J. Prentice Murphy, or Amey Eaton Watson might have written describing what they think of Linda Loman.

10. Write an article Marion Chase Baker might submit to a magazine describing what she thinks of today's mothers.

11. Clifford Olcott worries about who has control in the household. Write an essay that explores who has control in the Loman family—Willy or Linda.

12. How involved is Willy Loman in the lives of his children, and what are his "activities away from the home"? Write a letter from Willy to his brother Ben, asking for advice and confidentially discussing these issues.

13. Create an advertisement for an everyday product used by men in which you exploit the male desire to live more adventurously.

14. Explain why men like Willy and Biff Loman are attracted to the idea of becoming pioneers or cowboys, and decide whether either would be any good at such a life.

15. Write the lyrics of what you feel might be a typical "cowboy" song.

16. Explain how you feel people today view pioneers and cowboys. What images of pioneers or cowboys do we still employ in our language, advertising, culture, and everyday outlook?

17. The correspondence in "Sex and the Double Standard" was written in 1947. Do we see evidence of this double standard in the sexual habits of men and women in *Death of a Salesman*? Do any double standards still exist in society today? Write a dialogue between any two characters that illustrates such double standards.

18. Write a response Root's female correspondent might have given to his article.

19. Imagine that you are Linda Loman and that you have just read Root's article. How might you respond? Write a letter in which you explain your reaction to a family member.

20. Consider carefully how today's society commonly perceives women, and create an advertisement for an everyday product that targets women in particular.

21. Write a response to Ethel Wadsworth Cartland and Sheila Kaye-Smith.

22. Write the transcript for a talk show interview in which Sheila Kaye-Smith outlines what she sees as the duty of all women. Give the show's other guests—Linda Loman, Jenny, Miss Forsythe, and Letta—an opportunity to respond.

SUGGESTED READINGS

The Family

Truxal, Andrew G., and Francis E. Merrill. *The Family in American Culture*. New York: Prentice-Hall, 1947.

Roles of Fathers vs. Mothers

Cheley, F. H. "Why One Father Succeeded with His Sons." *Good Housekeeping* 72 (February 1921): 48.
Monroe, A. S. "Adventuring in Motherhood." *Good Housekeeping* 70 (May 1920): 28–29.
Turner, M. S. "Fathers." *Delineator* 94 (June 1919): 7.

Providers vs. Cowboys or Playboys

Deutsch, Albert, ed. *Sex Habits of American Men*. New York: Prentice-Hall, 1948.
Devereux, Mrs. A. "Pioneers." *Atlantic Monthly* 128 (1921): 336–40.
Everhart, H. R. "Master of the House." *American Home* (December 1946): 81–82.

Homemakers vs. Call Girls

Hutchins, Grace. *Women Who Work*. New York: International Publishers, 1934.
Lundberg, Ferdinand, and Marynia F. Farnham. *Modern Woman: The Lost Sex*. New York: Harper & Brothers, 1947.
Wilcox, L. C. "Woman's Place in the World." *Delineator* 94 (May 1919): 39.

6

Sports and American Life

At seventeen, Biff Loman defines himself as a football hero. His father describes his appearance on the football field as "like a young god. Hercules—something like that. And the sun, the sun all around him . . . A star like that, magnificent, can never really fade away!" At thirty-four, however, Biff is a self-described bum, no longer a hero, but a failure who has not been able to live up to the mythic success that was predicted for him by his father. Willy's is not the only point of view toward sports that Miller provides in the play, of course. While Biff is idolized by his family, particularly his father and younger brother, his Uncle Charley is more skeptical about football as the foundation for a successful life. When Willy tells Charley that the day Biff plays at Ebbets Field is the greatest day of his life, Charley responds, "Willy, when are you going to grow up?" Willy's angry retort is that Charley will be laughing out of the other side of his face when the game is over because "they'll be calling him another Red Grange. Twenty-five thousand a year." Biff fails math, loses his college scholarship, and winds up an aimless drifter, unable to find a job that pays more than the minimum wage. The play's irony is clear. But is it specific to Biff's life and experience, or is it a cultural irony, endemic to American values and mores? The following selections will help us to explore these possibilities.

In 1930, addressing the annual convention of the National Collegiate Athletic Association (NCAA), Frank Parker Day, the president of Union College, expressed a deep concern about the increasing professionalization of college athletics, particularly football. The recent Carnegie Report on college athletics had, in Day's view, clearly shown that "the great majority are not in any sense truly amateur, and that our athletics are riddled with pretense, hypocrisy, double-dealing, and deceit." College sports had been "capitalized" like so many other things in American culture. In this case, Day asserted, "we have capitalized the spirit of young men to make a vast show for the public. . . . Our college athletics are no longer college affairs, they are spectacles for the public." The transformation of amateur athletics into a business for profit was an issue when Biff Loman was playing football in the early 1930s, as it continues to be at the beginning of the twenty-first century. While Willy sees his son as a hero, loved and admired by everyone because of his athletic prowess, and unquestionably destined to succeed because of this, the play suggests another reality, in which, in sports as well as the rest of American life, "business is definitely business," and Biff the discarded athlete will wind up on the ashheap, just like his father the discarded salesman, as soon as he fails to make the grade. *Death of a Salesman* underlines with deep irony the faith in athletics as a means to a better life that Willy articulates: "Without a penny to his name, three great universities are begging for him, and from there the sky's the limit, because it's not what you do, Ben. It's who you know and the smile on your face!"

Willy Loman would have come to maturity at a time when sports and leisure were being established as a central part of the American way of life. In the general prosperity that followed World War I, Americans had more money to spend on spectator sports and sporting equipment, and as the forty-hour week became the norm for working Americans, they had more time and opportunity to pursue leisure activities. The amount of money that Americans spent on sporting equipment and other goods related to amusement nearly doubled during the decade of the 1920s. Americans spent $30 million to attend sporting events in 1921, and $66 million in 1929. The Jazz Age mentality of the twenties undermined what was left of American Puritanism in the national psyche, making the pursuit of pleasure a positive goal rather than a sin. Liberated from whalebone corsets and other confining clothing, women took up sports in increasing numbers, and the tennis racquet or the golf club was as much as sign of liberation in the hands of the "flapper" as the cigarette or highball glass. As Foster Rhea Dulles wrote in *A History of Recreation: America Learns to Play*, "millions of urban workers—men, women and children—were finally enjoying the organized sports that had been introduced by the fashionable world half a century and more earlier" (2nd ed. New York: Appleton-Century-Crofts, 1965: 364).

Above all, however, this was the era of two uniquely American spectator sports, baseball and football. During the twenties and thirties, American men and boys played and watched these sports with equal ardor. At the same time, spectator sports became enormous businesses for both sporting goods manufacturers and team owners. As Stephen Hardy explains in the article included here on Albert Goodwill Spalding, the economic alliance among sporting goods manufacturer, college athletic association, and star player began in the 1890s and has escalated to this day, when a single endorsement for a shoe can mean millions of dollars to a star professional player, or a considerable amount to an "amateur" university team. It is no surprise that Hap and Biff Loman conceive their "one-million-dollar idea" as a promotion scheme for sporting goods:

> You and I, Biff—we have a line, the Loman Line. We train a couple of weeks, and put on a couple of exhibitions, see? . . . We form two basketball teams, see? Two water-polo teams. We play each other. It's a million dollars' worth of publicity. Two brothers, see? The Loman Brothers. Displays in the Royal Palms—all the hotels. And banners over the ring and the basketball court: "Loman Brothers." Baby, we could sell sporting goods!

This idea is characteristic of the Lomans in its disregard for reality. Hap doesn't explain why the public would be interested in seeing two brothers who had never gotten beyond high school athletics compete against each other. But it is also typical of the culture and the times in many ways. The goods themselves are incidental. As Vance Packard suggests, it is the brand name and its association with a publicity campaign that matters (see Chapter 3). And the publicity campaign needs a celebrity's endorsement, whether it be by a team or an individual, rather than a demonstration of the quality of the goods. This principle was discovered very early on by Spalding and other manufacturers, and it drives sporting goods advertising to this day./If Biff Loman had gone on to be a football star at the University of Virginia, and then on to pro football, Bill Oliver might well be interested in backing him. As it is, Oliver's interest in backing Biff, presuming that Oliver has any kind of business sense, must surely be nil.

Another aspect of the sports mania that escalated in the United States during the first half of the twentieth century was the application of the model of competition deriving from sports to life in general, and particularly to business. It is useful to assess how far the Lomans may have been influenced by such models. Popular magazines from the twenties are full of advice articles like the one by Allan Harding included here. If life lessons were to be derived from team sports, their reasoning went, they ought to be applicable to the business world. Businessmen were advised to develop "team spirit" on the job, subordinating their own individual interests to the good of the team. Advice like Harding's seems to fly in the face of democracy: "So long as a man is your leader—whether he is your boss in business, or your captain, or your quarterback . . . give him your absolute loyalty, play his game to the limit, shut your mouth against making any criticism of him, and shut your ears against listening to any such criticism!" This kind of thinking seems more suggestive of the fascism that was dawning in Europe in the early twenties than of American democracy, but its authoritarian outlook was not the only "lesson" Americans were deriving from sports.

"If a business man did not play golf, had no polo handicap, loathed wearing himself out at squash, tennis and badminton and didn't like to sneak off to a baseball game," said a popular magazine in the forties, "he could still be a business man, maybe, in some European capital (if there is some European capital with any business left). But he couldn't be an American business man. American business men would refuse to do business" with him (from an unidentified clipping). The typical businessman at the time the play is set considered sports the essence of Americanism, and American character was thought to be expressed through sports. Besides teamwork and respect for authority, athletes were expected to learn hard work, dedication, concentration, and "sportsmanship"—playing by the rules, not taking an unfair advantage, neither gloating over winning nor sulking over losing. They were expected to show no emotion, whether in response to pain or injury, to loss, or to victory. Learned in childhood, these values were supposed to extend to one's business or profession in adulthood. Someone who had never been an athlete, it was thought, could never fully learn these values, and so could never be fully trusted or become a full player in the business world. Willy Loman takes this notion to the extreme, believing that success at athletics is all that is needed for success at business, but he was not alone in his thinking. It is Charley's skepticism that is out of sync in the 1930s, not Willy's enthusiasm.

AMATEUR SPORTS

This section examines various perspectives on high school and college sports at the time *Death of a Salesman* is set. The front cover of *St. Nicholas*, a popular children's magazine, illustrates the notion of the sportsperson as popular hero. A young boy who has evidently won the game for his team rides on the shoulders of two bigger and older boys while the crowd cheers them on. Such might have been the scene with Biff after he had helped win the game at Ebbets Field. Willy pictures Biff from this time as a "young god. Hercules." The novels by Burt Standish and F. Scott Fitzgerald—one an example of early young adult fiction, the other an important work of fiction by a significant American writer—both portray student athletes. While Standish in Frank Merriwell evokes the popular sporting hero of the day, with his physical prowess, courage, modesty, and sense of fair play, Fitzgerald's Amory Blaine is a sportsman of a different kind. Which character behaves more like Biff? Can we see the attitudes of either Frank or Amory depicted in any of the other characters in *Death of a Salesman*?

The final two documents are speeches by former athletic heroes Walter Camp and George Garrett. Camp, addressing the NCAA in 1921, offers his opinions of what team sports can do for a boy's character. Garrett reminisces about the differences between playing high school and college sports in his youth, at the time the play is set, which leads us to wonder how Biff would have fared had he made it to college.

FRONT COVER ILLUSTRATION FROM *ST. NICHOLAS FOR BOYS
AND GIRLS* MAGAZINE
(November 1920)

This cover of *St. Nicholas* Magazine is a good illustration of the admiration with which young athletic heroes were treated in the early twentieth century.

Burt L. Standish's Frank Merriwell was the hero of a series of books for boys that was immensely popular from the early years of the twentieth century through the 1920s. Merriwell was a baseball and football hero who embodied all of the qualities and values that proponents of school sports said would come from participating in them. He defined the sports hero for two generations of boys that included Arthur Miller, who was born in 1915, and presumably his characters Biff and Hap Loman. In the following excerpt, the conclusion of *Frank Merriwell's Schooldays*, Frank is being pursued by his athletic rival, Leslie Gage. Frank, who is rock-climbing, is hanging by a rope off the edge of a cliff. Earlier in the book, Leslie had drugged Frank to take him out of a baseball game where the two boys were pitching against each other.

FROM BURT L. STANDISH, *FRANK MERRIWELL'S SCHOOLDAYS*
(New York: Street and Smith, 1901, 249–51)

Far below the sea was rolling and roaring up against the base of the bluff, but he did not pause to look down there.

The eagle left her nest, and began to circle about, screaming her alarm.

Frank was about half way to the ledge, when he heard a shout from above. Looking upward, he was astonished to see the face of Leslie Gage, who was peering down at him.

There was a fierce look of triumph on that face—a look that turned cold the blood of the boy who was dangling by that slender line against the face of Black Bluff.

"I have you now, Merriwell!" cried Gage, hoarsely and triumphantly. "You'll never bother me after today!"

Then he held out his hand, and Frank saw it contained an open knife.

At this moment Frank Merriwell was numb with horror, for he fully understood his enemy's murderous purpose.

Gage meant to cut the rope!

"It's quite a little drop down there," mocked the young man above, "and I think it will fix you all right. I swore to get you out of my way by fair means or foul, and I am going to keep my word now."

Then he started to cut the rope. To do so, he leaned a little farther over the edge, lost his balance, uttered a shriek of horror, and fell.

Clinging to the rope, Frank saw the dark form of his enemy shoot past and go whirling downward.

It seemed that he had been saved by the hand of Providence.

Gage struck on the ledge, and lay there, motionless, one leg hanging over the edge, his white face upturned to the sky.

"It is retribution!" thought Frank Merriwell.

For some moments he was too unnerved to do anything but cling to the rope. Finally, he recovered and continued the descent until the ledge was reached.

Gage lay there, white and ghastly, apparently dead.

Shuddering with horror, Frank drew his foe back from the brink, and then, unmindful of the screaming eagles and the young eaglets, proceeded to tie one end of the rope securely about Gage's waist.

When this was done, Frank summoned all his strength and determination, and climbed to the top of the bluff, where he rested a few minutes, and then drew Gage up.

From that spot he succeeded in carrying his unconscious foe back to the camp, although he was forced to rest many times in doing so.

Astonishing, and almost impossible though it seemed to Frank, Gage was not dead, although the doctor said he might be injured internally, so that he would not recover from the fall.

But the fellow was not even injured that much, although he was confined to the hospital for two weeks. It was one of those peculiar instances where a terrible fall is sustained without resulting fatally, or even breaking a bone.

But Leslie was in no condition to play ball when the day came for the game with Eaton.

Frank Merriwell filled Leslie's place, and Bartley Hodge supported him behind the bat.

The game resulted in a score of nine to three, in favor of Fardale, and when the game was finished, everyone but the "sore-heads" acknowledged that Fardale's battery was the best the academy had ever put into the field.

Burrage had captained the team through this game, but he immediately resigned in favor of Merriwell, who was accepted by acclamation.

"What are ya goin' to do with Gage when he's well, me boy?" asked Barney.

"Vat vas dat?" put in Hans. "Vy, he should make him one lovely fight before soon and break his face in."

"No, no," said Frank, laughingly. "Gage has been punished enough. The score is settled. We will forget the foul business and all the other rotten things, and let him try to regain his prestige."

"Vich same he never vill already," said Hans, excitedly.

"Not while I'm alive!" cried Barney, putting up a brawny fist.

"Come," said Frank, "not one of us would hit a man when he's down. Gage is down in more senses than one, and I guess, Hans, you're right when you say his prestige is forever lost. But let's agree to treat the fellow decently, and not harbor enmity against him."

Hans shrugged his shoulders.

"Vell," he said, only half satisfied, "vot you say, Frankie, it vas as good as done."

"And you, Barney?"

"Me boy, I am wid ya every time!"

"Good!" cried Frank, delightedly; "we're at peace with all the world."

The three boys turned their faces once more toward the cadet camp at Fardale. Many struggles, temptations, defeats, and triumphs were still in store for them, some of which will be related in the next volume of this series, entitled FRANK MERRIWELL'S CHUMS. But for the present all went well, and so we bid them adieu.

In his novel *This Side of Paradise* (1920), F. Scott Fitzgerald is credited with defining the generation of the Jazz Age. His main character, Amory Blaine, is no Frank Merriwell. Arrogant, self-centered, and insecure, Amory wants to play football for all the wrong reasons, according to the code of sportsmanship. He wants to be noticed by his fellow students; he wants to be famous; he wants to be, in Willy Loman's words, "well liked." He sees sports as the quickest way to achieve this. Fitzgerald uses inflated literary language and grandiose references to myth to describe Amory's prep school victory to convey Amory's way of thinking about himself. But his description is not entirely ironic. At some level, Fitzgerald too takes football very seriously.

FROM F. SCOTT FITZGERALD, *THIS SIDE OF PARADISE*
(New York: Scribner, 1920, 34–35)

HEROIC IN GENERAL TONE

October of his second and last year at St. Regis' was a high point in Amory's memory. The game with Groton was played from three of a snappy, exhilarating afternoon far into the crisp autumnal twilight, and Amory at quarterback, exhorting in wild despair, making impossible tackles, calling signals in a voice that had diminished to a hoarse, furious whisper, yet found time to revel in the blood-stained bandage around his head, and the straining, glorious heroism of plunging, crashing bodies and aching limbs. For those minutes courage flowed like wine out of the November dusk, and he was the eternal hero, one with the sea-rover on the prow of a Norse galley, one with Roland and Horatius, Sir Nigel and Ted Coy, scraped and stripped into trim and then flung by his own will into the breach, beating back the tide, hearing from afar the thunder of cheers . . . finally bruised and weary, but still elusive, circling an end, twisting, changing pace, straight-arming . . . falling behind the Groton goal with two men on his legs, in the only touchdown of the game.

Walter Camp was one of the most important figures in the development of American football as we know it, as a game distinct from rugby. He played at Yale from 1876 until 1881 and coached from 1888 to 1892. Among the innovations with which he is credited are the eleven-man team, the position of quarterback, the scrimmage line, the calling of offensive signals, and the giving up of the ball after a designated number of downs. He is best remembered, however, for originating the idea of selecting "All-American" college teams. Included here is part of an address he gave to the NCAA's annual convention in 1921. It conveys a typical view of the uses of college athletics in the early twenties. Could Biff have fitted into the type of college team Camp describes?

FROM WALTER CAMP, "ADDRESS TO THE NCAA ANNUAL
CONVENTION"
(*Proceedings of the 16th Annual Convention of the NCAA*, 29
December 1921: 78–81)

Sometimes people rage against the tremendous organization of athletics. What happened before we had organized athletics? Then we had the town and gown riot. You can tell by the fines in college what we had. A man was fined two shillings and sixpence for going skating. He was fined two shillings and sixpence for having liquor in his room. He was fined three shillings and six for having people of dissolute character in his room. All that sort of thing has pretty well gone out with organized athletics, and that is one of the things for which it should have credit.

Now, let us take the teams. We have been preaching for twenty years "more athletics for everybody," and incidentally we have sometimes spoken against the teams, and said that they stop the athletic work of the rest of the men in college. But if this policy prevails, and the athletic teams are toned down, and everybody plays, and there are no organized teams, we shall lose organized athletics. . . .

But let me tell you what organized athletics do for the men on the bleachers who are not physically fitted to play football. The cardinal sin of youth—and it has become the cardinal sin of youth since we have organized athletics—is typified in the man who is "yellow"; and those men on the bleachers know when a man is yellow or a quitter, and that is the one thing that the boy cannot be in college today. He can do most anything else, but he cannot be yellow or a quitter. How did this work out for us when we needed men? These boys had been urged to go out on the team to show what they could do, and when the war came on and they were able to take a gun they showed what they could do for their country. The boy in our college today gets the fighting spirit, which, after all, is what we want our athletics to give. We were not trained in a military sense, but we had that bed-rock of fighting spirit, and that is the spirit you are getting from organized athletics into the bleachers.

People tell us that we ought not to make such a great stir about victory, we ought not to be so keen to win, we ought to go in and have a good game and like the other fellow and have a good time with him, and when it is all over, that is the end of it. You cannot get boys to love each other when they are playing on opposite sides. You cannot do it. The worst quarrels are always between two brothers when they fight with each other. That is human nature. What we want in the boys in college is *pluck*. That is the great thing we want. A man can go far on that. Look before you leap, if you like, but don't look long. That is the principle that boys ought to be brought up on. And then we will have the kind of men that we need in this country. They will be the leaders, and in these troublous times we need them.

• • •

Now, I don't know how far one can go in directing these sports of youth. You know what a man will say when you ask him frankly, "What do you want to make of your boy?" He wants him strong and well, but he does like to have him make the team. He hopes to have him get his letter. He would like to see him one of the boys that shall come up to the top. He wants to see him a "thoroughbred." You all know what I mean by that. He is not going to take any pride in the boy if he merely goes into the gymnasium and develops a wonderful muscular system, but does not play and get on any of the teams. He may be the best physical specimen in the world, and yet if you nail the father right down to what he wants, that is not all that he wants. He hopes that his boy will stand as a leader in his group of boys.

Now, what does the boy respect,—the boy himself,—and he is the one you have got to deal with? You cannot make him over again. You cannot start him anew. What does he respect?

Just as you and I respect money and power, he respects physical prowess. He wants to be the leader in his gang. He strives to be able to excel the other boys. He wants to be something that means the same thing to him that money and power will later in life mean to him, but if you talk to him about making himself a fine physical specimen, so that at forty he will be well and strong, he hopes to goodness he will be dead long before he is forty. A man of forty is a Methuselah to him. You cannot interest him that way. But you can interest him in his sport, in making his team, in doing things that will make him physically strong by using the attraction of making the team. That is the whole story.

And after all, it comes down to spirit, and spirit is what you want, and that is what you drill into your teams, and you drill it into athletics at the same time, and you drill it into everybody who comes in contact with it.

George Garrett's "locker room talk" describes his experiences as a young football player in the thirties and forties. His memories of the rough and dangerous conditions that prevailed in high school and pick-up football in the poverty-stricken South during the thirties give a good sense of how the game was played in the early days. Arthur Miller's experience was similar when he played for Abraham Lincoln High in Brooklyn as a 120-pound second-string end. His autobiography, *Timebends*, describes a teammate's grinding his cleats into Miller's neck during a scrimmage and Miller's receiving the torn ligament that eventually kept him out of the army during World War II.

FROM GEORGE GARRETT, "LOCKER ROOM TALK: NOTES ON THE SOCIAL HISTORY OF FOOTBALL" IN *SPORTS IN AMERICA*
(Peter Stine, ed. Detroit: Wayne State University Press, 1992, 115–22)

The locker room. Here where we are (suddenly?) the shy, soft, nude old guys who once did swagger and pop towels and stand and sing in the rosy steam of the showers, soaking our bruises away. You could do a history of American sports, the caste and class of it all, just from different kinds of locker rooms. The locker rooms I have seen lately would all serve for the model of the country club locker room in my youth. Of course, my youth was the Depression and ended with World War II. And my youth was almost entirely spent in the South. Which was uniformly poor and proud and fortunately ignorant of other places and their quality of life. We were always short of everything in our Southern locker rooms, from liniments to soap, from shoelaces to towels. Only years later in the dressing rooms (locker room was no longer really accurate) of Princeton University did I discover the luxuries of clean whites (jock and T-shirt) and towel every day.

In those Depression days Southerners played harder and hit harder and were meaner than other people. So it seemed.

Everything was in short supply. Not enough pads or jerseys or helmets even on the high school teams. Sometimes, routinely, we had to trade off stuff with somebody else to go in or to leave a game. And a team would have only two or three footballs, maybe one of those new enough to still have its shape. On a wet rainy day the slick, smooth, old footballs got wetter and wetter and heavier and heavier. Until passing one was like shot-putting. Catching a pass was like catching a cannonball.

Shoes were a huge problem, seldom fit or were comfortable. They were heavy, in any case, leather, high-topped and blessed with hard, pointed cleats, "male" cleats with a screw on them that fit in a hole on the sole of the shoe or "female" cleats, with the hole in the cleat and the pointed screw permanently fixed on the shoe sole. These latter worried you, at least if other people were wearing them; because if a cleat got loose and fell off you could be cut to pieces with that pointed metal screw. The cleats were bad enough. Once on the ground, knocked or fallen, you protected your hands and face (no face masks until the '50s) as best you could from cleats. When somebody else from another team went down, you went in stomping those cleats.

Absence of face masks caused many injuries. Broken noses were common. Also missing teeth. In high school, the guy with the locker next to mine, name of Carnahan unless I misremember, had no teeth at all. Had an upper and lower plate he would leave in his locker. He had blocked a punt and lost every tooth in his head.

Well, so what? Carnahan was tough. What else could they do to him? Tough was what we wanted to be. You might not possess or develop much skill, but you could take plenty of punishment and pass it on, dish it out, too.

Nobody wanted to play "dirty." But what that meant, what the limits were, is hard to recall. None of it had anything to do with the rules. You broke the rules when you had a chance, and when you got caught you got a penalty. Some of the forbidden things to do we actually practiced doing.

Nobody wanted to have a reputation, singly or as a team, for being dirty. We wanted to look dirty, though. We would not send our game uniforms to the laundry, so we could look all grass-stained and muddy. If there was precious blood on your jersey, you preserved it. If by some chance you ended up with a clean uniform, you rolled in the dirt during the warm-up.

Sometimes, for no particular reason except that we had seen it in newspaper photographs, we put burnt cork below our eyes. Once when the coaches were out of the locker room, the whole team painted our whole faces black with burnt cork. Ran onto the field with Al Jolson faces and the coaches responded with screaming, stamping, hat-throwing tantrums. Coaches of that era did not like jokes or joking around. And they hated not just the sound but the very idea of singing on the bus.

The bus? It was a yellow school bus. Greyhound was a luxury for college ballplayers.

Before there were school teams there was the public park, in my case Delaney Park, where we met every day after school and all day, except for church, on the weekends, and played tackle football until it was much too dark to see any more.

I owned the football, a good one my father had gotten for me. Contrary to the expectation and the figure of speech, owning the ball meant that I had no choice but to be there early and stay late. Day after day. Year after year.

You could learn a thing or two without really trying, without thinking about it much.

At Delaney Park I saw, and played with and against, the best, most gifted runner I have ever seen. I mention his name here and now to celebrate it, though I do not know if he is alive or dead. Name was Leroy Hoquist, and he had more moves, and more graceful ones, than any runner I have seen since then. And I have logged a lot of hours over the years watching football in the stadium or on TV. When I was playing, later, I have seen close up some pretty good ones. Have actually tackled a Heisman Trophy winner in the open field and have chased after and piled on some others, famous and unknown. But never a one who could run like Leroy Hoquist. He was all air and fire. Pure smoke when you went to grab him.

He was supposed to go to the University of Florida on a scholarship. But something happened—maybe a death in the family, some unanticipated hardship, who knows?—and he went to work for a local undertaker, driving a hearse, an ambulance, sometimes, in more recent times, a limousine. Last time I saw him he was driving a limo at a family funeral, in my family.

Watching that guy run with a football was like watching Baryshnikov at his best.

And what does all that mean? Nothing, I guess. Except that—do you see what I mean?—you didn't have to be a star to be a star. In the heart of the Depression good memory must have meant more than good publicity.

STUDY QUESTIONS

1. What is the significance of the artist from *St. Nicholas* making the two boys carrying the sport's hero older and bigger than the boy they carry?

2. How closely might this resemble a picture of Biff at Ebbets Field?

3. What virtues does Frank Merriwell embody? What makes the other boys recognize him as a leader? What is it that makes Leslie Gage so clearly a villain?

4. Has Biff Loman learned the same lessons from playing sports as Frank Merriwell? What does Arthur Miller suggest Biff has learned from being a football hero?

5. How does F. Scott Fitzgerald's use of language, particularly adjectives, contribute to the reader's imagining of Amory's high school football game? How does the passage cause you to think about football, and about the football player?

6. To whom does Amory compare himself in his mind, and why? Are his comparisons fair?

7. What are Walter Camp's arguments in favor of organized athletics? Are they convincing arguments? Do they apply to organized athletics now?

8. Has Biff Loman learned the things that Walter Camp says come from playing team sports—not to be a "quitter," and to have a "fighting spirit"? Is Biff's characterization realistic and believable?

9. Would you want to have Biff on your team? Why or why not?

10. Are Camp's comments that fathers want their sons to win at sports because they want them to be leaders in their groups an accurate description of Willy Loman's attitude? What does the play suggest are the consequences of this attitude? Does this attitude prevail in America today?

11. How do the equipment used for high school football during the Great Depression and the conditions under which it was played differ from those of today? Why does George Garrett mention the specific things he does?

12. What are the implied differences in Garrett's recollections between high school and college sports?

13. What qualities or characteristics does Carnahan represent for Garrett? What were the values that made him a hero?

14. Does Garrett's story about Leroy Hoquist have a point or moral? How does Garrett's attitude toward him compare with your attitude toward Biff Loman?

SPORTS AND AMERICAN VALUES

The documents in this section present four divergent points of view on the relationship between sports and American cultural values. Georges Lechartier offers a European's view of the pervasiveness of sports in Americans' way of thinking during the 1920s. Allan Harding uses an interview with a famous businessman–football coach to preach the application of the values learned in playing team sports to business and life in general. Stephen Hardy gives an example of an athlete who became tremendously successful in the sporting goods business. All of them should prod students to think about the relationships among sports, business, and American cultural values, and how these are reflected in *Death of a Salesman*. Finally, Michael Novak offers philosophical reflections on the meaning of team sports, and their ability, when at their best, to forge a bond of community among teammates and to bring out some of the best qualities in individual players.

Georges Lechartier, writing originally in *La Revue de Paris*, remarks on the extent to which the American "love of fair play" and passion for sports had permeated education, business, politics— in short, the entire American culture—by the early twenties. In the tradition of St. Jean de Crèvecoeur and Alexis de Tocqueville before him, he presents a French analysis of American character in the light of his observations. How far do his observations describe any of the characters in *Death of a Salesman*?

GEORGES LECHARTIER, "AMERICANS AND SPORT"
(*Living Age* 310 [10 September 1921]: 658–64)

The passionate interest with which Americans followed the Dempsey-Carpentier fight is but another illustration of the importance which they attach to sport. We shall never understand their national character fully until we comprehend this passion.

It is based upon love of "fair play," though the game may be killing a man—a sport governed by its own frontier code. The very stage-robber roughs, and the bullies who pioneered the Far West, obeyed certain laws of their trade, designed to give every man a fair chance. That once granted, individual initiative, courage, shrewdness, and daring had free rein. The dead were buried where they fell, and the sheriff's jurisdiction ceased.

Americans inherit from their heroic frontier traditions, which all admire and many still regret, both reverence for fair play and passion for sport.

Though this nation did enter the war in the service of a great ideal,— for the Yankees are incorrigible idealists,—another important motive, a controlling motive, was their love of sport.

I recall what a San Francisco journalist said to me in 1915, when I remarked upon the number of pro-Germans in the West: "When we see Germany, with all the world against her, holding her own and even driving back the Russians, we feel that she plays the game well and applaud her skill. If the man on the street is pro-German, it is because of his sporting instinct." It was sporting sentiment, again, that made the Americans almost unanimous for war as soon as they saw Germany breaking the rules of the game with her submarines.

An American street lad cannot insult another worse than by calling him no sport. A boy who will meekly tolerate almost any other charge will instantly resent this one with his fists.

So the taste for sport, acquired at a tender age, continues throughout life. Everywhere in America you see athletic fields, tennis courts, and golf links. They are attached to factories, and occupy public parks. Operatives flock to them as soon as their work is over, and generally spend Saturday afternoons at such games. About a quarter of the forty square miles of park around Chicago is used for baseball fields, golf links, tennis courts, and other athletic objects. Matches between towns, factories, schools, and cities, always draw great crowds, who follow them with passionate interest.

• • •

Sport is an element in the games of the United States. But it is found not only there. You discover it in education, in business, in politics, and in manners. It is everywhere.

In business as well as boxing and baseball, Americans figure chances. Instead of shirking risks, they seek them as a sport. They thus acquire quickness of conception, sureness in action, promptness in decision, a disciplined spirit of adventure, and great energy in execution. When the rules of a game are once agreed upon, rarely does either party violate them. If he does, then it is each one for himself, and any stratagem becomes fair play. The American's motive is not solely to make money, but also to win.

Allan Harding presents an application of the values of football to life in an article based on an interview with "Hurry-Up" Yost, a businessman who took ten weeks off from banking to coach the University of Michigan football team each season. Harding offered his 1922 magazine audience a description of "the kind of men who win out, not only on the football field but in the game of life," a typical example of the belief that the most important values and attitudes for success in business were taught on the athletic field, a belief it appears that Willy Loman accepted at face value.

FROM ALLAN HARDING, "HOW TO 'PLAY YOUR GAME'—
WHATEVER IT IS"
(*American Magazine* 94 [November 1922]: 84)

"A man who can make a consistently fine record as a quarterback is, to my thinking, just about as fine a type of man as can be found. The qualities he must have are rare. For he must not only be master of himself but he must command the confidence and loyalty of the men who work with him. He must also have good judgment, ability to think quickly and, sometimes, daringly. He must be a pretty good psychologist—whether he knows what psychology is or not. For he must be able to guess what his opponents are thinking; and he must know how to *make* them think what he wants them to.

"However, he may have judgment and coolness and all the rest; but if he doesn't inspire confidence and enthusiasm in his fellow players, he won't be a success. I have seen a team play magnificently under one quarterback—and go to pieces when another one was put in. The team was just the same as before. But the new man couldn't *lead* them. That's the rarest type of human being: the great general and leader.

"You've seen men like that in business. Their subordinates will work their heads off for them. Put another man in—and the subordinates don't seem to *have* any heads to work with!

"A lot of other folks might learn something from the attitude of a team toward a quarterback whom they respect. The plays he calls for don't always succeed. There are a hundred things that may happen, any one of which may defeat the play. His judgment itself may sometimes be at fault. He isn't infallible. Nobody on earth is. So the other members of the team might complain sometimes that he had 'made a bum choice' of plays. They might criticize him, and 'knock' him, either privately or publicly.

"But a good football team doesn't do that sort of thing. And neither does a good team of any other kind. It is disloyalty of the meanest sort; and it reacts on the very people that practice it. They undermine their own chances of achievement. So long as a man is your leader—whether he is your boss in business, or your captain, or your quarterback, or the president of your club, or the head of your family—give him your absolute loyalty; play his game to the limit, shut your mouth against making any criticism of him, and shut your ears against *listening* to any such criticism!"

Looking at athletics from the business side, Stephen Hardy's portrait of Albert Goodwill Spalding describes the strategy by which the most successful sporting goods maker in America developed the business in conjunction with the development of big-money sports and the college athletic associations in the first half of the century. This should help us to assess the credibility of the Loman brothers' business ideas and to see more readily the way in which sports are so closely tied to business in America. Assessing the enterprising Spalding's track to fame and fortune should lead us to ask how far Biff, given the type of person he is, could follow such a path.

FROM STEPHEN HARDY, "ALBERT GOODWILL SPALDING (1850–1915)," IN *ESSAYS ON SPORT HISTORY AND SPORT MYTHOLOGY*
(Donald G. Kyle and Gary D. Stark, eds. College Station: Texas A&M University Press, 1990, 59–63)

Born in 1850 in the rural village of Byron, Illinois, Spalding came of age in Rockford, a rail station about one hundred miles west of Chicago. Bitten by the infectious baseball bug of the day, he quickly developed a reputation as a crack pitcher, and in 1865 he was invited to join the "Forest City's," a team newly formed by local business boosters who hoped to promote their town through baseball. The Forest City's competed within the loosely organized National Association of Baseball Players, giving Spalding exposure to the big leagues. He caught the eye of Harry Wright, manager of the famous Cincinnati Red Stockings, and Wright convinced the young pitcher to join him in jumping in 1871 to the Boston team of the new National Association of Professional Baseball Players. Spalding pitched brilliantly for five seasons in Boston, helping the Red Stockings to four consecutive championships, 1872–75. In July of 1875, however, this industrious, sober professional—the type that

Chadwick worked so hard to promote—committed his second sin of "revolving," or team jumping. He signed a contract to be player-manager for 1876 with the Chicago White Stockings. Lured to Chicago by coal merchant William Hulbert, Spalding not only shored up the franchise with other defectors, but also helped Hulbert create the National League of Professional Baseball Clubs.

Spalding pressed a design of regimen on all players and teams that wanted to be a part of professional baseball. The National League was arguably America's first serious sports bureaucracy, with hard rules on player contracts, franchise locations, game management, and scheduling. For an old "revolver," Spalding became a hard-line critic of "overpaid players" who were only interested in "their own aggrandisement." He successfully led wars against several rival leagues, including one organized by the players' union. His work with the National League was essential to the creation of a model sports bureaucracy. Yet Spalding's venture into sporting goods had a much more profound effect on the development of an industry of providers, thanks to his promotion of expertise, standardization, and bureaucracy.

Spalding opened his sporting goods business in March of 1876, with his brother, J. Walter, as partner. It was a small retail operation but it grew quickly through sound financial and marketing strategies. These included backward integration into manufacturing, a decisive move in a time when most name-brand sporting goods were the products of contracts between retailers and silent manufacturers. The Spalding brothers, however, knew the economies that existed in integrated manufacture and distribution. Within two decades the firm of A. G. Spalding and Bros. dominated a strong field of rivals that included Rawlings, Reach, Wright and Ditson, Meacham Arms, McClean, and many others. Indeed Spalding had silently acquired several rivals, who continued to sell goods under their own brand names. The Spalding name itself, however, circulated widely, in many sports, with equipment produced in specialty factories around the country, and sold through Spalding or allied retail outlets or through the mail.

The Spaldings certainly sought market share for their own brand name, but in so doing they also promoted the larger industry of providers and experts. Advertisements sent a clear message that homemade games and handcrafted equipment would no longer do in an industrial age. For instance, in the spring of 1893, the firm ran a series of clever ads in the *Sporting News*. Each week the commentary supplemented cartoons illustrating the hazards of inferior equipment and the value of genuine Spalding balls, chest protectors, bats, and shoes. One notice describing Spalding bats began with a story about a pathetic "crank" who could not even hit a ball until his team captain insisted that he throw away the

"Jonah" bat that was fashioned by a "wheelwright up in the country." Likewise there was the hapless runner who staggered between bases in clodhoppers habitually bought "from some inexperienced cobbler." As the advertisement warned, a cobbler might be able to help with some things, but "not with Base Ball shoes." This was the fundamental message of all manufacturers and it echoed all of Chadwick's lines. Sports were a specialized product not to be entrusted to the hands of oldstyle crafts-men, whether they worked in leather, wood, or words.

The Spaldings did not wait for others to join this chorus. They aggres-sively led the field. One of their shrewdest practices was the publication of guidebooks edited by prominent experts like Henry Chadwick. The earliest guidebooks in baseball had been issued by general publishing houses like Beadle and DeWitt. This changed in 1876 when the Spaldings began to publish their own guide, filled with the National League rules, records, history, instruction, and lots of advertisements for Spalding products. By 1885 they were ready to launch their Library of American Sports, intended to educate the public in a variety of sports. This venture was so successful that the Spaldings created a subsidiary firm in 1892, the American Sports Publishing Company. With James E. Sullivan as pres-ident, this publishing house produced hundreds of guidebooks and publications on an impressive range of sports.

Making and selling guidebooks became standard practice in the sport-ing goods industry. Smart retailers advertised the availability of guide-books in their "depots." R. E. Dimick, a St. Louis dealer, noted in a February, 1889 issue of the *Sporting News* that "we make a specialty of sporting books of every description. They are very good to have when settling disputes." Sporting goods firms were selling inexpensive, stan-dardized packages of expert knowledge that linked sporting goods to game forms. One could buy booklets by experts who would convey the intricacies of tennis, football, skating, croquet, and baseball in their finest detail.

Involving scattered experts and scientists of sport could give products legitimacy. It would not, however, ensure the levels of authority that the Spaldings sought in the marketplace. For this they needed closer align-ment with young governing bodies like the National League or the In-tercollegiate Football Association. They found this through tie-ins as the manufacturer of "official" equipment. Their efforts began, as always, in baseball, where in the late 1870s they wrestled the official ball away from the L. H. Mahn Company of Boston. This began a long, aggressive cam-paign of negotiating the rights to produce both the official rules and guidebooks and the official equipment in a vast range of sports at all levels, from the playground league to the National League. Such tie-ins benefited both sides.

A good example is the Intercollegiate Football Association whose guiding spirit was Walter Camp. The early rules, from 1876 to the mid-1880s, were privately printed in Princeton. By 1887, however, they were published by Wright and Ditson, a sporting goods firm willing to try new markets such as tennis and football. In 1891 an interesting turn occurred. The Spaldings took over the publication of the rules in this, the first year of their silent partnership with Wright and Ditson. Wright and Ditson could continue to sell their name-brand goods, but they could not continue to publish an increasingly valuable guidebook.

A year later, the Spaldings captured the most valuable tie-in of all—official status for their name-brand football. Prior to this, the official ball had been a British import, hardly acceptable for a chauvinist like A. G. Spalding. In May, 1892, however, the association voted to make Spalding No. J Foot-ball an official ball with the further stipulation that "all matches of the Association must be played" with such a ball. The company wisely cemented its relationship to the IFA by retaining Walter Camp as editor of the annual guidebook and by selling Spalding equipment to Yale at a discount. All of this was helped by Julian Curtiss, a Spalding executive, who happened to be a Yale alumnus and friend of Camp's. When necessary, Curtiss had no qualms about asking Camp's predictions on rule changes that might affect Spalding equipment such as the "head harness."

Camp, the IFA, and the Spalding firm all enjoyed increased authority through this kind of relationship, represented in mutual endorsements. Just as an endorsement helped the tangible goods in the marketplace, so too did "official" goods provide legitimacy and authority for the distant endorsers. Walter Camp grasped this principle firmly. Describing football in his *Book of College Sports*, he cautioned that "it is best that players should never use anything but the regulation ball," either the British "J. Lillywhite" or the American "Spalding." He also insisted, however, that the regulation ball "should bear the stamp, '*Adopted by the Intercollegiate Foot-ball Association*' " (my emphasis). The sale of every Spalding ball paid interest to Camp's young association, for every person who bought an official IFA ball likely bought into Camp's basic version of the game.

A. G. Spalding suffered few setbacks in his business career. His dogged pursuit of standardized games, products, and leagues clearly lent force to a Sportgeist weighted toward regimen. At the same time, his practices in the sporting goods market set off other forces that frustrated his visions of a disciplined labor force. Part of his conception of the Sportgeist rested on an orderly community, managed by capitalists for private profit and public amusement. He became a champion of loyalty to contract and community. There was an underlying problem, however, in the ties between experts and sporting goods. Experts garner their own status and prestige, just as they produce market share for the products they endorse. Spalding aggressively sought star players as individual product endorsers. It was a distinct irony that his use of star endorsements nurtured individualism, which continued to haunt professional sports in the forms of contract jumping and contract holdouts. Further, players who recognized their value in the market for goods created their own collectives to fight the magnates for higher wages. Spalding's empire in sporting goods fuelled a part of the Sportgeist that ran headlong against his own peculiar vision of the compliant athlete.

Michael Novak, a celebrated American thinker, presents a philosophical view of the values of team sports and their relation to American culture. Moving beyond the clichés about team spirit and the work ethic that pervade popular writing about sport, Novak explores the origin and meaning of the "bond of brothers" that is, at the best of times, achieved in team sports, and its significance for lifting the human spirit. We should consider whether or not sports have ever uplifted any of the Lomans in such a way. Also, what happens to individuals like Biff, who must go from being active players to anonymity?

FROM MICHAEL NOVAK, "THE THIRD SEAL: BOND OF
BROTHERS," IN *THE JOY OF SPORTS*
(New York: Basic Books, 1976, 132–41)

Pulling on the uniform of a team one admires is a ritual of election. One has been accepted. More than that, it signifies an opportunity to act in a special kind of world: a world of record and legend and cherished significance.

Most of the actions of one's life go unnoticed. An ex-football player on a college campus, no longer recognized, no longer assisted and upheld by coaches and authorities, has resumed the anonymity in which nature places most of us. Being an active player is like living in the select circle of the gods, of the chosen ones who act out liturgically the anxieties of the human race and are sacrificed as ritual victims.

• • •

. . . [S]ports are a bond of brotherhood in an elemental sense. All the brothers die. Against death, we wrestle for at least the momentary victories of brilliant form, which live in memory. Immortal deeds.

Sports are celebrations of brotherhood in yet a second way. There are sports of solitude: hiking, swimming, running. And all sports drive one into one's resources of solitude: in the end, either the solitary individual heart has courage and stamina or it has not. Deep in the recesses of the solitary heart the most intense conflict of the agon is played out. The outward body is only this inner struggle's sacrament, its expression in fleshly acts.

But team sports introduce another factor altogether. At birth, while totally dependent upon a mother, incapable of sustaining life alone, the human infant is egocentric. What pleases or displeases, what warms or chills, pains or pleasures—these are the infantile preoccupations. Only with difficulty does a child learn to consider others. Often, indeed, such consideration is yielded only as a quid pro quo. In order to survive, one makes deals. Josiah Royce, the great Harvard philosopher, believed that not all human beings, even when they have attained physical maturity, attain moral maturity, or even its precondition, "a moral point of view." That point of view, he said, consists in displacing the self from the center of one's affections and concerns; in allowing other human beings to stand with the self at the center of one's perceptions and one's actions; to become many-centered rather than self-centered; to concede to other humans the same standing as one yields oneself. To be morally mature, the human being must learn to pivot his life upon community, not upon the solitary self. It is, Royce opined, a very difficult lesson, rarely learned.

For millions of youths in America, at least, this lesson is first lived out in sports. Even if its moral implications are not abstracted out from the experience, expressed in words, stated in propositions, and tested in laws of logic, the indispensable moral experience is offered to the reflective mind. Better to have the experience than to form the propositions. Better to have lived community than to know how to define it. On the other hand, to define it is not necessarily to injure it. Those who have known the experience can test the philosopher's words against what they have known; he may, or may not, be capable of grasping it. Philosophers are engaged in a game as well, a serious game, a game of putting experience into words, and many suffer defeat.

When a collection of individuals first jells as a team, truly begins to react as a five-headed or eleven-headed unit rather than as an aggregate of five or eleven individuals, you can almost hear the *click*: a new kind of reality comes into existence at a new level of human development. A basketball team, for example, can click into and out of this reality many times during the same game; and each player, as well as the coach and the fans, can detect the difference. "We were at the top of our profession," Dave DeBusschere wrote in his *The Open Man: A Championship*

Diary: "We had shown that, without the best individuals, we could be the best team. We were a unit, a beautiful, cohesive unit. . . ." Yet there were nights that 1970–1971 season—once, for example, when the Knicks played the Bucks in Milwaukee—when the Knicks fell back into playing individual basketball, each one doing his thing, using the others but not really playing with them, not one with them. Play would begin to be ragged. Brilliant individual efforts would flash out, but the magic of unity was gone. The spell the team could weave on its opponents and the beauty of five playing as one, as if with a single swift intelligence, a single generous heart, a single reflexive system in five sets of arms, legs, leaps, cuts, and shots, were dissipated. The human race itself is not merely an aggregate of individuals; thus, images of human unity excite some hidden longing in the heart, some long-forgotten memory or expectation. For those who have participated on a team that has known the click of communality, the experience is unforgettable, like that of having attained, for a while at least, a higher level of existence: existence as it ought to be.

• • •

In football, the feeling of community is a little different. Its critics talk about fascism, authoritarianism, lockstep discipline. Football is a series of set plays, and split-second execution is essential. Concentration must be extremely high, for even in practice, without opposition, the plays fail a high percentage of the time. For perfect execution in the game, intense concentration and extreme alertness to the unexpected are indispensable. Thus, even when players are standing on the sidelines, they must maintain a high level of attention. Indeed, concentration on the game begins on Tuesday and hits a high pitch the evening before the game is played. In the game itself, each individual has only a few opportunities to act; each act must be perfect. Lapses of attention, a reflex only an instant slow, a failure to anticipate a feint, a fake, or a sudden turn of events—these cause perfection to be lost. To play football well, one must school one's attention to the highest possible levels of awareness; to play football wholeheartedly is to live a higher form of life, beyond the ordinary, to drink deep of possibilities of consciousness heretofore neglected. What to the casual observer seems accidental, fortuitous, reflexive is more often than not the fruit of highly tutored consciousness, the eyes constantly taking in multitudes of signals concerning possibilities yet to be realized. Out of the corner of his eye, the defensive halfback spots an unfamiliar stride on the part of an opponent, sets his own body muscles in a new pattern without yet moving outwardly, leaves the receiver open enough to attract the pass, and then breaks in on it in time to knock it down or intercept it. It is a game of intense calculation—a difference of inches separates perfect offense from perfect defense.

In football, no one offensive player can execute a play, and no one defensive player can cover the entire field. In the rapidly changing patterns of play, each player must recognize instinctively what each of his teammates will do; were two of them to converge on the same spot in the same way, one would be leaving undone something else that needed to be done. Indeed, one of the great features of the game is the harmony between a runner and his blockers, as each shifts his angles so as to trap the defenders into futile movements; if either the blocker or the runner miscalculates, the attempted block drives the defenders into, instead of away from, the runner. No coach, no system of authority, can command the instinctive, instantaneous reactions of players on the field; but for a winning team a thorough system of tutoring the instincts (by devising practice sessions that make the fundamentals second nature) can eliminate habitual mistakes and alert the players to variations they are likely to face.

In football, as in politics or business, everything depends on execution. However superior the talent, however excellent the strategy and the preparation, football is fundamentally a game of intense exertion, intelligence, and rapid violent force. If one side hits harder and more swiftly than the other, the best-laid plans are disrupted. Here, too, a team depends on its every member. Each must accept the high intensity and the pain of hitting harder than the opposition. If only two or three do so, the opposition will take the game to the weak spots. Contrariwise, if a team can take the game to their opponents' most highly motivated players, and beat them, its feeling of invincibility—and the dismay of its opponents—is bound to spread. Confidence affects one's ability to dare, one's timing, one's poise, one's feints. Confidence—and here, indeed, is a mystical component— somehow flows like an electrical charge not only into one's own hands and legs but into the ball itself, and like an icy dagger into the heart of one's opponents. A pass thrown with conviction somehow finds the 8-inch hole in the fingers of the defense, and a pass totally desired by a receiver somehow sticks in his fingers no matter what the difficulties. Not always so, of course; but it does happen.

STUDY QUESTIONS

1. How does Georges Lechartier suggest that American reverence for fair play is related to the U.S. entry into World War I? Do you agree with him that the motives he describes are related to an American love of competitive sports?

2. Do you agree with Lechartier that Americans tend to play by the rules? How does Hap Loman's view of business relate to this?

3. How important is "winning," as opposed to making money, in the American view of success? Do you find incidents in *Death of a Salesman* that illustrate this?

4. Do you agree with "Hurry-Up" Yost's description of what it takes to be a successful quarterback? Does Biff Loman have these qualities? Why does he lose his ability to lead when he grows older?

5. Do you agree with the description of leadership that Yost gives at the end of his interview? How does this version of leadership fit with the values of a democratic society?

6. How does the contemporary business of professional team sports differ from the way it operated one hundred years ago, when Spalding was starting his sporting goods business? Are today's "free agents" different from the "revolvers" as they are described in Hardy's article? Are they considered overpaid? Do today's fans tend to think the money from professional teams should go to the players or the owners? What are the arguments on each side?

7. Spalding is credited with discovering clever and successful ways of marketing sporting goods, based not on the quality of the goods, but on brand-name recognition. Are these methods still used by the sporting goods industry? What effect does this have on the price and quality of sporting goods?

8. How did Spalding go about cornering the market for high school and college sporting goods? Are his strategies still practiced by big sporting goods manufacturers?

9. How does the plan that Hap and Biff hatch for their "Loman Brothers" sporting goods line compare with the methods employed by Spalding and the other big sporting goods manufacturers? Is the Lomans' view of the business different from that of the successful companies?

10. Hardy points out a conflict in the last paragraph of his article between Spalding's pursuit of individual star endorsements for his products and his desire to control sports and the sporting goods market

through his business practices. Why are these things in conflict? Does American individualism inevitably conflict with corporate interests in the sports world?

11. Do you agree with Michael Novak that participating in team sports helps to develop a "moral point of view"? Does playing sports make the individual player less selfish? Does Arthur Miller suggest that this is true of Biff Loman?

12. According to Michael Novak, what are the positive qualities that team sports help to bring out in the athletes? Can you think of examples of this process either in life or in the play?

13. What connections does Michael Novak make between the game of football and life? How does his view of this relationship compare with that of "Hurry-Up" Yost and Georges Lechartier?

14. Novak suggests that team sports provide access to a level of being that is not available to the individual alone, "a form of life ablaze with communal possibility." What does he suggest are the elements of this higher community? Do you agree with him? Is there evidence of this community in *Death of a Salesman*?

TOPICS FOR WRITTEN OR ORAL EXPLORATION

1. Write a description of a contemporary high school football hero, trying to capture the characteristics that you consider typical.

2. Write a paragraph like the one from *This Side of Paradise*, describing the experience of a player in a contemporary high school or college football game. Think about what is universal about the experience and what is particular to a time and place.

3. Write a sketch of the ideal athlete of the 1920s and 1930s, based on your reading of the first section of this chapter, and compare and contrast Biff Loman with this ideal.

4. Write a speech like Walter Camp's in which you defend the role that football currently plays in American high schools or colleges.

5. Write a critique of Walter Camp's speech in which you analyze and evaluate his arguments. Or, taking on the character of Willy Loman, write a letter to Biff in which you describe Walter Camp's speech. How would Willy respond to Camp?

6. Write a newspaper editorial for or against maintaining football at your school.

7. Taking on the role of a tourist from another country, discuss the importance of sports in the American character today.

194 Understanding *Death of a Salesman*

8. Discuss the impact of athletic brand names on American culture.

9. Write a sketch of a contemporary high school or college football coach, comparing the values he espouses and lives out with those of "Hurry-Up" Yost and those of either Willy Loman or Charley.

10. Outline the arguments for both sides of the proposition that "sports are a preparation for life," and explain why you agree or disagree with the proposition. Then take on the role of either Willy or Charley and explain why you agree or disagree with the proposition.

11. As Hap Loman, write up a proposal to A. G. Spalding to back Loman Brothers Sporting Goods, in which you explain how your ideas for marketing agree with his.

12. Discuss the relationship among good sports equipment, athletic clothing, and athletic prowess as it is articulated by one of the contemporary manufacturers of sporting goods.

13. Based on your reading of Hardy's essay on Spalding and your own knowledge of the current situation, write an essay about the concept of "amateur athletics" in high school and college.

14. Write a code of conduct for the amateur athlete of 1920 and another for the amateur athlete of today.

15. Write an essay about the meaning Michael Novak gives to the phrase "bond of brothers" in the context of team sports.

16. Write an essay about the relationship of the two brothers, Hap and Biff Loman. What are its positive and negative characteristics? Is this a realistic depiction of the relationship between brothers?

17. Michael Novak places great importance on the "ritual" nature of sport. From your own experience or observation, describe one or more rituals that help to create a sense of community among the players on a team.

18. Michael Novak sees the potential of sport to "lift the human spirit" as its most valuable function for the human community. Write an essay explaining your agreement or disagreement with this idea, considering the effect of sports on the Loman family.

SUGGESTED READINGS

Crepeau, Richard C. "Where Have You Gone, Frank Merriwell? Decline of the American Sports Hero." In *American Sport Culture*. Ed. Wiley Lee Umphlett. Lewisburg, PA: Bucknell University Press, 1985.
Day, Frank Parker. "The Challenge of the Carnegie Report." *Proceedings*

of the 24th Annual Convention of the NCAA (1 January 1930): 96–100.

Mrozek, Donald J. *Sport and American Mentality, 1880–1910*. Knoxville: University of Tennessee Press, 1983.

Sage, George Harvey. *Sport and American Society: Selected Readings*. Reading, MA: Addison-Wesley, 1970.

Simon, Robert L. *Fair Play: Sports, Values, and Society*. Boulder, CO: Westview Press, 1991.

Spears, Betty, and Richard L. Swanson. *History of Sport and Physical Activity in the United States*. Dubuque: Wm. C. Brown, 1978.

Spivey, Donald. *Sport in America: New Historical Perspectives*. Westport, CT: Greenwood Press, 1985.

Talamini, John T., and Charles H. Page. *Sport and Society: An Anthology*. Boston: Little, Brown, 1973.

Umphlett, Wiley Lee. *American Sport Culture: The Humanistic Dimensions*. Lewisburg, PA: Bucknell University Press, 1985.

7

Death of a Salesman's Impact on American Culture

In February 1950, as the original production approached its first anniversary, Luke P. Carroll marveled that *Death of a Salesman* had already become a legend in many parts of the world, commenting that "why this play has approached the stature of an American legend in these distant lands defies analysis." In a single year, Arthur Miller had received more than a thousand letters explaining the personal way in which the play had related to their writers' lives. A number claimed to be the model for Willy or suggested that Miller record their lives too, because they were so much like Willy. Sermons, both spiritual and secular, had been preached on the text of the play; ministers, rabbis, and priests explained its exposure of the emptiness of Willy's dreams of material success, while sales managers used Willy as an object lesson on how not to be a salesman.

In the years following the original production, Willy Loman entered the world's consciousness as the very image of the American traveling salesman, an identity with which the business world was uncomfortable. Writing in the garment industry's own *Women's Wear Daily* shortly after the play's premiere, Thomas R. Dash articulated the conflict between identification with Willy and resistance to him that characterized the typical relationship that people in business were to have with the play. Noting that Willy's was an "individualized tragedy," and that "it does not follow that all salesmen necessarily are discarded to the ashcan after 35 years of service for one firm, that they crack mentally and that they dash themselves to pieces on a mad and suicidal ride to the hereafter," he nonetheless had to concede that "if you have traveled the road and are honest with yourself, you may recognize certain traits of Willy's in your own behavior pattern, both professional and personal" (p. 51).

In *Timebends*, Miller relates how, before the release of the 1951 film version of *Death of a Salesman*, Columbia Pictures executives showed him a twenty-five-minute short subject, shot on the campus of the Business School of New York's City College, which they intended to run as a preface to the film to deflate anti-Communist fears over its impact. This short "consisted mainly of interviews with professors who blithely explained that Willy Loman was entirely atypical, a throwback to the past when salesmen did indeed have some hard problems. But nowadays selling was a fine profession with limitless spiritual compensations as well as financial ones" (p. 315). Miller responded angrily, asking them why they made the film of his play if they were so ashamed of it, and pointed out that anyone offended by the play could easily walk out. The short was withdrawn.

By the 1960s, businessmen were nearly desperate to divorce the salesman's identity from that of Willy Loman. Only one in seventeen college students was willing to try selling as a career in 1964. Many business executives blamed this on Arthur Miller. "To many novelists, playwrights, sociologists, college students, and many others," wrote Carl Reiser in *Fortune* magazine, the salesman "is aggressively forcing on people goods that they don't want. He is the drummer, with a dubious set of social values—Willy Loman in the Arthur Miller play" (p. 124).

When plans were announced for the CBS television production of *Salesman* in 1966, the Sales Executives Club of New York mobilized itself to prevent further erosion of the salesman's image. Complaining that Willy Loman had been plaguing their "selling as a career" efforts for years, the club suggested changes in the script to improve the image of the salesman depicted in the drama.

Throughout the seventies, the effort to dissociate the image of Willy Loman from the public's concept of the salesman continued, without much success, despite the ever-improving material circumstances of the typical salesman and the greater security that came from an ever-higher ratio of salary to commission throughout the sales profession. Willy and the play had become an almost unconscious part of the businessman's vision and vocabulary, as is evident from just the titles of articles in business publications. "The Salesman Isn't Dead—He's Different" and "New Breed of Salesman—Not Like Willy" were succeeded by titles like "Deaths of a Salesman," "The Rebirth of a Salesman," and "The New Life of a Salesman."

With the worsening economy of the eighties, the cultural reality of Willy Loman was as powerful as ever, with a new meaning for a generation that had not been born when the play was first produced. Young people could not find jobs, and middle-aged workers were down-sized to boost profits in keeping with an increasingly "lean and mean" business strategy. Business executives were moving salesmen off salary and back onto commission—just as Howard Wagner had done to Willy—and calling it "Motivating Willy Loman." As John A. Byrne put it, "You really should get the carrot as big as possible without making the guy die to reach it. . . . Give him salary for the essentials, to help pay the rent and put food on the table, but not much else. Hell, he's supposed to be a salesman" (p. 91).

By the late eighties and nineties, Willy had taken on a life of his own, with little or no reference to the play. Evidence of the extent to which the culture at large saw Willy and the American salesman as identical was everywhere, in the most casual of references. A 1993 *Wall Street Journal* article on the certification, and thus professionalization, of salesmen is entitled "Willy Loman Might Have Had a Better Self-Image." One on the introduction of portable computers to the sales force is called "What Would Willy Loman Have Done with This?" Neither has any reference to Miller's play. An article on the faltering U.S. balance of trade in *U.S. News and World Report*, called "The Yankee Trader: Death of a Salesman," makes no reference to the play, but prints on each page the familiar image of Willy with his sample cases from the Joseph Hirsch drawing on the Viking Compass paperback, which had sold a million copies by 1968. An article opposing advertising by law firms is entitled "Willy Loman Joins the Bar: Death of a Profession?" An

article on producer Fred Friendly's efforts to use television to pop-
ularize the U.S. Constitution is called "TV's 'Willy Loman' of the
Law." And so on. By the end of the twentieth century, Willy Loman
had become everyone's image of the salesman as well as the salesman as Everyman.

Death of a Salesman has found its way into university and secondary school curricula throughout the world, and the responses
of succeeding generations of students have not diminished in immediacy or intensity. The experience of one high school student
who took the part of Biff in a reading of *Death of a Salesman*
staged by his class will serve for many. Meredith Kopald reported
his response:

> I see many parallels between myself and my father and the Loman
> family. My father is a salesman. He, too, is much happier with a
> batch of cement. I feel a strong "can't get near him" feeling with
> my father. The only way I can get and hold his attention is to tell
> him of all my accomplishments. We are not close as Willy and Biff
> are not. I dislike Willy a great deal and this dislike stems from my
> anger and disappointment in not being close to my father. At the
> end of this play I was made acutely aware of this anger and disap-
> pointment.

The student was so affected by the play that he confronted his
father in much the way Biff confronts Willy:

> We talked and talked. For almost half an hour my anger poured
> from my body into his. When I finished and we had both broken
> down in tears, I told him everything I had ever wanted to tell him.
> After my anger had all spewed out, for the first time in my entire
> life I felt love toward him. *For the first time!!* I feel I have grown
> up in a very big way. I think I have done in 17 years what took Biff
> thirty-four.
>
> All of this because of a play, a bunch of words printed on paper.
> How can a play do this? Genius, I say!! *Death of a Salesman* is the
> greatest piece of literature I've ever read. (p. 59)

In many countries, in many languages, in all kinds of productions, from the most sophisticated efforts of London, Broadway,
and Hollywood to a high school classroom reading, *Death of a*

Salesman has had the power to move audiences profoundly. In this play, Arthur Miller has captured something that is essential in the human experience of the twentieth century. Willy Loman, it seems, will live in our consciousness for some time to come.

FIGHTING WILLY'S IMAGE

The selections in this section are examples of the recognition on the part of the American business community that Willy Loman has defined the salesman for the American public and of the strategies they have used to try to change the image. A consideration of these various reactions to the play should help students to determine their own reactions, and to begin to analyze what it is in their experience and culture that is causing those reactions. It should also give them a sense of just how influential good drama can be on a society and its value systems. By 1962 the public's attitude toward the life of the salesman was at one of its lowest points. The article from *Newsweek*, included here, "New Breed of Salesman, Not Like Willy," describes typical efforts by American business organizations in the early sixties to professionalize the salesman and to make his occupation a career of choice for college graduates. In direct opposition to Willy's image, American business was trying to define a "new salesman" in the sixties, "a man with a softer touch and greater breadth, a new kind of man to do a new—much more significant—kind of job." "To be sure," suggests *Newsweek*, "the old-style drummer is no longer in the mainstream. But he's still paddling around out there with his smile and shoeshine, his costume a bit more subdued and his supply of jokes, sad to relate, a bit low." The point of the article was to show the extent to which the Willy Lomans had been displaced by a younger generation of better educated, more scientific salesman whose emphasis was on providing information and service to their customers rather than on their sales pitch or their personal relationship with the buyer.

In 1967 David R. Hayes made an inspirational film for salesmen called *Second Chance*. It featured the Green Bay Packers' football coach, Vince Lombardi, in a narrative that allowed him to use his "break-'em up football coaching technique on a fictionalized typical salesman." In the article from the show business trade paper *Variety* by Morry Roth included here, Hayes explained the reason for his scripting the film as a play rather than an inspirational talk: "We had to undo for the art, science and business of selling . . . what Arthur Miller had done in damage to the field in his stageplay, 'Death of a Salesman.' " Hayes says that he decided to do it with

"Miller's own tools—that is, drama," using the popular football coach's ability to sell players on winning as the central dramatic focus of a film that was meant to sell salesmen on selling. Within two years, the trade film had been sold to 7,000 companies and had made the fortune of Hayes' industrial film company, Take Ten, Inc. The introduction of dramatic conflict into trade films wrought a major change in the industry, one of Willy Loman's many influences on American business.

Martha Farnesworth Riche's "Willy Loman Rides Again" shows the extent to which Willy has become not only the symbol of the salesman for Americans, but a real person. Edward Spar, the president of a marketing statistics firm, used Willy's route as an example of sensible county-based marketing for the Association of Public Data Users in 1987: "Loman's territory was simply a matter of convenience and logic. 'If that company existed in reality, Willy's territory wouldn't have changed,' Spar wagers." The route that Spar gives Willy is completely imaginary: "Up to Westchester, through Putnam—all the way to Albany, Route 23 over to Pittsfield in Berkshire County, then down to Hartford and back to New York." Although Willy does mention having seen a hammock in Albany, the only indications of his route in the play are his turning back from Yonkers on the night the play begins and his description of his route when he returns from his trip in the first daydream scene: Providence, where he met the Mayor, Waterbury, Boston, "a couple of other towns in Mass., and on to Portland and Bangor and straight home," a not very logical and rather improbable route. To Spar and the writer of the article, Willy was not a character in a play but the prototypical salesman with the "New England territory." If only he had had more modern techniques and better data, the thinking goes, he would have been a better salesman.

"NEW BREED OF SALESMAN, NOT LIKE WILLY"
(*Newsweek* 64 [5 October 1964]: 94–97)

"You don't understand. Willy was a salesman. And for a salesman, there is no rock bottom to the life. He don't put a bolt to a nut, he don't tell you the law or give you medicine. He's a man way out there in the blue, riding on a smile and a shoeshine. And when they start not smiling back—that's an earthquake. And then you get yourself a couple of spots

on your hat, and you're finished. Nobody dast blame this man. A sales-
man is got to dream, boy. It comes with the territory."

Shortly after Charley speaks these lines in the shattering final scene of
Arthur Miller's "Death of a Salesman"—at the grave of Willy Loman—
Willy's widow utters two agonizing cries and leaves the audience literally
in tears and full of compassion for the dead salesman. Then the applause
dies, the people leave the theater, and, out in the night air, they divorce
art from reality. The image of a salesman replaces the death of a salesman,
and it is not always prepossessing.

Almost anyone can quickly conjure up distasteful stories of foot-in-the-
door peddlers, of oily bunko artists and grating street hawkers, of back-
slapping, fanny-pinching traveling men. The American salesman, it
sometimes seems, has been able to sell everything but himself.

Indeed, reports Sales Management magazine, "selling is a dirty word."
In a poll of nearly 1,000 students, from 123 universities, the magazine
could find only one out of seventeen willing to try selling. "I would
infinitely prefer to return to shoveling manure than to be a salesman,"
replied a Johns Hopkins student who had grown up on a farm. "I never
met a salesman I didn't loathe," commented a Pennsylvania collegian. To
a Yaleman, selling was "too frustrating and too prostituting." And a student from Buffalo saw salesmen as "boorish, uneducated brutes."

But this is hardly the real truth about the American salesman. Today
there are some 1.6 million salesmen* in the U.S., peddling everything
from buttons to rocket boosters, and their art has progressed as much
as any other. To be sure, the old-style drummer is no longer in the mainstream. But he's still paddling around out there with his smile and shoeshine, his costume a bit more subdued and his supply of jokes, sad to
relate, a bit low.

Nomads: In Atlanta early this month, a rumpled and obviously soul-
weary middle-aged salesman parked his battered station wagon in front
of Buckhead Hardware in the fashionable north side and tried to sell
partner George Murray some umbrellas. "Well, actually," said Murray,
"we don't carry umbrellas." Then, looking at some samples: "These look
a little shopworn."

"Why sure," replied the rack jobber (a drummer who sells anything he
can carry), "these are my samples. Been showing them for several years.
Bound to get a little beat up. But these are fine handmade items, made
in Italy. Can't get this around here."

---

*The last census listed 4.8 million "sales workers." Well over half, though, were
retail clerks, and the census also counted such classifications as newsboys
(200,000) and real-estate agents (200,000).

"Where have you been storing them?" asked Murray, sniffing. "They smell sort of musty."

"No siree," came the answer. "That's just me. I always smell like that."

After the drummer had gone, without an order, Murray told *Newsweek*'s Joseph Cumming: "We get a lot like that, still. They're working their way to Florida, usually . . . Maybe they'll hit Atlanta selling umbrellas and go into Miami selling shirts and socks. All he's got is himself, his personality, and his salesmanship."

In Chicago one morning last week, another old-timer, but a solidly based one, set out at 8:15 to make his round of calls. Louis Schneider, 62, a tanned, 5-foot–7-inch dynamo, slid into his white '64 Chevrolet and headed for the South Side to peddle his line of men's hosiery, underwear, and specialty items. First stop was Fuller's Department Store, and Schneider walked in with a sample box tucked under his arm. "You must have an item under your arm," he confided to *Newsweek*'s Steve Saler. "Never enter empty-handed. Show the buyer that you're working." As he waited for a buyer, he described his selling tactics: "I try to get my branded items [which include Fruit of the Loom and Health-knit] into the store, my main lines . . . The hardest thing is to get brand items in. Then they work for themselves."

Ten Cases: After some small talk and banter with the buyer, Schneider pulled a black jacket from his box and lowered his voice to a confidential whisper: "Take a look at these. I sold ten cases Monday . . . If you want to be conservative, buy two cases."

"My heart's not in it," the buyer came back. "Give me a case. If it was anybody else but you, I wouldn't take any."

"You should take more," Schneider insisted. "I wouldn't kid you, boy. You're not a customer, you're a friend. I may not have any more left." The order stayed at one case.

In all, Schneider made six calls that day and sold about $1,000 worth of merchandise. "When you get through the day, you're really knocked out," he says. But he has "always liked selling." Besides the good income (in excess of $15,000 a year), "it gives you a broad education. You meet all types of people and know how the other part of the world lives." Still, Schneider wouldn't be a salesman if he had it to do over again—"I'd be a lawyer or a doctor or an accountant" (he never went beyond grammar school). "My generation is the last of the old-school salesmen, and old salesmen are drying up, even me."

Taking the place of the Schneiders is a new breed of salesmen, bred for today's vast industrial complexity.

As a group, they are less colorful, less fun than the old-timers. But they are far better trained and far more responsive to their customers' needs.

The whole concept of "service" has been expanded far beyond the layman's idea of installing a machine and fixing it when it wheezes. International Minerals & Chemicals Corp. of Skokie, Ill., has one of the finest service programs going. Two-thirds of the firm's $225 million in sales are in fertilizers and plant foods. "This was a product which was essentially the same as competitors' products," admits Anthony E. Cascino, vice president of the agricultural products marketing group. "We had to convince the customer to buy our product even though the price was higher. To do this, you have to make yourself of indispensable value to your customers."

New Milieu: Thus, in 1958, with mankind still buzzing over the sputniks, Cascino introduced his hard-sell, "Full Orbit" sales program. A 47-year-old, pint-size whirlwind, Cascino kicked it off at a razzle-dazzle sales meeting featuring smoking rockets and slogans like "Out-of-this-world service for down-to-earth results and sales." It included a package of 42 marketing, technical, financial, and management services for customers—all free. Did a customer want help in training his own salesmen? IMC would send an expert. Need some assistance with his accounting? Call on IMC. Anything from public relations to collecting bills—call on IMC. With all this, IMC grinds out brochures, sales aids, film strips, and the like in quantities to warm a printer's heart.

In this new selling milieu, the salesman's responsibilities burgeon far beyond such traditional ones as supplying price lists and expediting delivery. "He becomes," says Cascino, "a management consultant"—not necessarily an expert in all these fields, but capable of recognizing a need and where to go to satisfy it. The salesman is no longer a peddler but, in the words of John J. McCarthy, GE's consultant in sales training and marketing, "the manager of a long-lasting, favorable relationship" between customer and supplier.

Sold Out: Even to the new breed, there are still distasteful elements to selling. For those who travel a lot—and many are on the road 50 per cent of the time or more—moving around can become a lonely bore. There's constant pressure to make quota, and keep take-home pay up. No one ever gets used to a door slammed in his face. The turnover among newly hired salesmen, both experienced and raw recruits, can be high. Companies polled in one survey hired 16,000 salesmen in 1963; by December, fully 5,000 had left, or nearly a third. What's worse, the companies expected that another 8,000 would turn in their sample cases before 1964 rang out—for an awesome 81 per cent turnover in two years.

But there's money to compensate for that, and that old "dream" of the Willy Lomans. The highest-paid man in his company, reports senior vice president James S. Bingay of Mutual Life Insurance Co. of New York, is not the president but a salesman. How much commission does an agent earn from selling $1 million worth of coverage? "It depends on the mix [or kinds of policies]," says Bingay, "but probably over $30,000, minimum."

A salesman's time is his own, to use fruitfully or squander, as he wishes—and many like it that way. Challenge—that's another lure. "I love the satisfaction of beating the hell out of a competitor," says ex-quarterback Milstead. "Getting orders is like scoring touchdowns in a game. There can't be but one winner."

MORRY ROTH, "UN-DO *DEATH OF A SALESMAN*: VINCE
LOMBARDI VS. WILLY LOMAN"
(Variety, 16 April 1969: 7)

For 20 years, executives in all sorts of corporations dependent upon high morale among their salesmen have deplored the damage done psychologically by Arthur Miller's stageplay of 1948, "Death of a Salesman" and its Columbia Pictures' screen version of 1952. Their regret relates to a film made here two years ago by Take Ten Inc. under the title "Second Chance," copies of which have now been sold to some 7,000 U.S. companies, with 10,000 prints expected eventually to be sold. This is American business using dramatic technique to offset a sales-derogating drama.

• • •

. . . [B]ack to "Second Chance" and the boomish effect it has had upon the industrial film firm headed by David R. Hayes which is this year expecting to double its 1969 gross of $500,000, thereby becoming a leader in the industrial screen production competition of Chicago.

Hayes' big break came a year ago when he hesitantly submitted a film on sales motivation to Vince Lombardi, then coach of the Green Bay Packers pro football club. To Hayes' considerable surprise, Lombardi not only liked the deal being offered, but was wildly enthusiastic about the script, which echoed Lombardi's favorite theme—the ability of men to surpass themselves.

The dramatized script had Lombardi demonstrating his break-'em-up football coaching technique on a fictionalized typical salesman. This "Second Chance," as it's titled, became a smash hit in industrial film circles, serviced via Dartnell Corp.

"We had to undo for the art, science and business of selling," Hayes says, "what Arthur Miller had done in damage to the field in his stageplay, 'Death of a Salesman.' I decided that we would have to do it with Miller's own tools—that is, drama. The days when you can just lecture salesmen or give them some sort of an elaborate pep talk are over."

On the basis of his success with "Second Chance," Hayes two weeks ago completed filming a new dramatized sales motivation film called "The Professional" with Van Johnson and Forrest Tucker. It was shot in nine days and the stars received per day what they would get for making a major film, according to Hayes.

Hayes' films are not the first trade films to use Hollywood scripting techniques, but they probably have been the most successful. Prior to "Second Chance," few in the field had used dramatic conflict in their script and what visual photographic experimentation had been used was in the nature of gimmickry. Hayes is a close observer of the young film-makers, a preoccupation that evidences itself in "The Professional" by way of shooting half the picture with hand-held cameras.

Hayes is now looking for bigger film game. He is cautious about disclosing his projected features until he gets them fully scripted and cast. "Somebody announces new feature film projects every Monday and Thursday," Hayes said, "and nothing comes of them. I've got the screen rights to Jerry Kramer's 'Instant Replay' and I've got two other properties ready to shoot. But I'm not going to announce any of them until I can give a firm starting date."

MARTHA FARNESWORTH RICHE, "WILLY LOMAN RIDES AGAIN"
(*American Demographics* 10 [March 1988]: 8)

Despite the flashy attractions of client-created polygons or zip codes tagged with evocative names, public and private firms continue to update and even create new databases and statistical series organized along county boundaries. But aren't counties old-fashioned?

Remember Willy Loman's sales territory from *Death of a Salesman*? Up to Westchester, through Putnam—all the way to Albany, Route 23 over to Pittsfield in Berkshire County, then down to Hartford and back to New York. As Edward Spar, president of Market Statistics, told the Association of Public Data Users last fall, Loman's territory was simply a matter of convenience and geographic logic. "If that company existed in reality, Willy's territory wouldn't have changed," Spar wagers.

History is one reason it wouldn't change. Older companies used the county as the basic building block for their territories because it was the easiest, if not the only way to define geographic areas within states. Though computers now make it easy to rearrange areas according to new criteria, it isn't easy to rearrange sales people who have invested in a particular territory.

But an even more compelling reason to stay with counties is the wealth of data available for them. When the 1970 census came out in machine-readable form, businesses began to rank, sort, and analyze county-based geography by demographic characteristics. Just a few years later, the government's revenue-sharing program directed the Census Bureau to provide annual population estimates for counties to make sure the federal government distributed its funds fairly. Add in business data like the Commerce Department's annual County Business Patterns, and a rich database is born. Now it is easy to measure county-based markets by comparing the percentage distribution of sales by territory with the percentage distribution of the population that might buy the product.

What's new in county data? Probably faster, more compact delivery systems containing more information, predicts Spar. His firm already provides county-level data on compact disks. But the basic data will be the same, and the techniques probably will not change much either. So when you come down to it, Spar says, "Willy will still have to get into the jalopy and cover Albany to Pittsfield to Hartford and back to New York."

STUDY QUESTIONS

1. According to the *Newsweek* article, why did college students in the early 1960s object to selling as a profession? Are these attitudes still current today?

2. Which of the salesmen described in the *Newsweek* article is most like Willy Loman? What is your emotional response to this description? How does the writer use language, particularly adjectives, to manipulate your attitude toward him?

3. What are the characteristics of the "old-style" salesman, Louis Schneider, that make him successful? What cultural attitude toward selling as a profession does he reflect?

4. According to the *Newsweek* article, what were the most important "new" ideas about salesmanship in the early 1960s? How was the old-style salesman expected to change in order to function in this "new selling milieu"?

5. According to the *Newsweek* article, what were the chief enticements for a selling career in the early sixties? Had these changed since Willy Loman's day? Have they changed now?

6. Do you agree with David Hayes that *Death of a Salesman* is a "sales-derogating drama"? Is Arthur Miller attacking salesmen or the sales profession?

7. Why does Hayes think drama must replace the "pep talk" as a means of motivating salesmen? Do you agree with him?

8. Why does Edward Spar make up a fictional sales route for Willy Loman? What makes Willy, a character in a play, a useful example for a speech to the Association of Public Data Users?

9. Trace on a map the route Edward Spar gives Willy Loman from his home in Brooklyn and back again. Then trace the route Willy describes for the boys in the first daydream scene. How do you account for the differences between the two? Which is more likely to have been the normal route for a salesman from Brooklyn?

THE SALESMAN AS CULTURAL PHENOMENON

The following articles represent attempts to delve beneath the surface identification of Willy Loman's name with the profession of salesman to look at the cultural and moral issues that reverberate from the dramatized life and death of this character to the real lives of contemporary Americans. The obituary of Jerry Rubin comments ironically on the life of the Yippie revolutionary turned stockbroker at the same time that it shows the universality of Willy Loman's values. In America, everyone is a salesman, whether he sells shoes or stocks or revolutionary ideas.

Keith Mano's "Deaths of a Salesman," published in 1977 in the politically conservative magazine *National Review*, looks with sympathy and compassion at the life of a typical salesman. But it also exposes the emptiness and the bleakness of his life in a way that is in keeping with the vision of Miller's play, which some observers found fault with as dangerously critical of American values in 1949. Jeff Faux's "What Now, Willy Loman?" appeared in the left-wing magazine *Mother Jones* in 1983. Speaking of "underemployed 30-year-olds" who were being forced to "bring their families home to live with bewildered and resentful parents," and middle-aged people "with kids and mortgages who have been out of work for three months," Jeff Faux suggested that "Willy Loman could again symbolize a widespread middle-class tragedy—people trapped by rising expectations that no longer fit the cruel realities of the labor market." While coming at the issues from very different political points of view, these writers agree that the existential condition of the typical American salesman has not improved much since 1949. Thus, we see that *Death of a Salesman* has lasted well; its themes and messages are still as relevant today as they were when it was first written. *Death of a Salesman* should not be viewed purely as a historical piece, and students should be encouraged to uncover its current relevance to their own lives in the light of this discovery.

FROM JEFF FAUX, "WHAT NOW, WILLY LOMAN?"
(Mother Jones 8 [November 1983]: 52–54)

On warm days I see them on park benches—clean-shaven men in suits or neat working clothes, staring vacantly into space. They sit in hotel lobbies and coffee shops—women dressed for interviews, their eyelids half closed, exhausted by their futile search for work. The shame of unemployment shows on their faces. "It's as if I have a disease," one tells me. "No one wants to talk to me anymore." I hear about underemployed 30-year-olds who expected by now to be moving into their first house. Instead, they bring their families home to live with bewildered and resentful parents. I talk to old friends with kids and mortgages who have been out of work for three months. They are beginning to panic. And I cannot help thinking of Willy Loman, the tragic hero of Arthur Miller's great play *Death of a Salesman.*

Pursuing the dream of middle-class status and success, Willy does everything he thinks a good salesman is supposed to do. He smiles, he tells jokes, he hustles women receptionists. But Willy's talents are ordinary at best, and his value in the market is marginal. "Pop!" cries his elder son, "I'm a dime a dozen, and so are you!" So when the company has used him up, it throws him into the street.

The play was written in the 1940s, and the economic boom years that followed seemed to date Willy Loman. Sure, there were white, middle-class Americans who didn't make it, but the good times that lasted for the next three decades made them exceptions. Americans of average talent and drive entered the middle class through the tremendous expansion of white- and blue-collar jobs that allowed them to buy a house, send the kids to college and look forward to a secure retirement. They came to believe that what they had was a result of their own talents and hard work. They were living proof that anyone who really tried could make it in America. Accordingly, their politics became conservative.

But things are changing. Willy Loman could again symbolize a widespread middle-class tragedy—people trapped by expectations of status that no longer fit the cruel realities of the labor market. Confronting that reality, the middle class might even move to the left in the 1980s.

The roughly 50 percent of families in the middle of the income distribution is a *working* class. It includes blue-collar workers in unionized jobs, civil servants, technicians, clerical workers, lower and middle managers and, of course, salespeople. The bulk of this group's income is from wages and salaries: the group depends, therefore, on the existence of large numbers of steady middle-income jobs. These jobs are becoming harder to find, however. For example, a graph of the typical distribution

of wages and salaries in a corporation used to resemble a barrel, with
the bulk of the jobs in the middle. Now it is beginning to look more like
a wine carafe, with some jobs on the top, a lot of jobs on the bottom
and a squeeze in between.

One reason is the ongoing deindustrialization of America, the shift of
employment away from relatively high-paying unionized jobs in the manufacturing and construction industries and toward unorganized lower-
wage services. Deindustrialization has many causes: the most important
are increased competition from foreign firms and the building of factories
overseas by American corporations in search of cheap labor. Between
mid-1979 and late 1982, some three million manufacturing jobs were
eliminated in the U.S., most of them in heavily unionized industries such
as steel, autos, electronics and machinery. At the same time, more than
two million jobs were added to the largely unorganized service sector.

• • •

. . . [O]nly three percent of the New England workers laid off from the
shoe, textile and similar old industries were rehired by the high-tech companies that blossomed in Massachusetts between 1957 and 1975. Furthermore, in the fast-growing industries of New England, the distribution
of wages and salaries are much more polarized—squeezed in the middle—than they were in the old declining industries.

The conservative assault on the public sector is also taking its toll on
the middle class. Jobs in the government and the government-supported
nonprofit sector tend to be even more concentrated in the middle than
jobs in the private sector, and they have provided the major opportunities
for minorities and women to enter middle-income brackets. They have
now largely dried up.

• • •

Not to worry, say the free marketeers. So what if there are fewer
middle-level jobs. Just send the missus to work! Well, most families *already* have both adults out working, and an increasing number of people
are in families headed by one adult, or are not in families at all. Society
now gives Willy Loman's wife permission to go out on her own, but it's
a limited liberation if she can't make enough money to support herself.

• • •

With the Right still occupying the White House, it may seem like pie
in the sky to be contemplating a middle-class shift to the left. After all,
Willy Loman did not become politicized. He killed himself so that his kids
could collect his life insurance. The tendency to internalize failure, to
accept the market's decision as the true assessment of your worth, is

always strong in America. It is reinforced by a culture that glorifies material success. Not a success? What's wrong with you? You should learn more about computers. Or take a course in assertiveness. ("I gotta overcome it," says Willy. "I know I gotta overcome it. I'm not dressing to advantage, maybe.")

But it could be different this time around. The middle-class family is no longer dependent on the lone male breadwinner. Popular culture creates fewer of the awful pressures of bourgeois machismo that destroyed Willy. Men and women seem able to look at themselves and the world around them more realistically than they could in the 1940s. Willy Loman never knew who he was.

And in terms of the politics of it all, Kevin Phillips may be right. The conventional experts and the press that slavishly follows them invariably look at the future as a simple extension of the recent past. "American politics works like the stock market," he says: "when all the experts agree it's time to buy, it's usually time to sell." As disappointments mount and it becomes less credible and satisfying for the middle class to blame its troubles on the poor, this generation of Willy Lomans might begin to question the religion of the marketplace that treats all working people with such profound contempt.

KEITH D. MANO, "DEATHS OF A SALESMAN"
(National Review 29, no. 1 [7 January 1977]: 35)

"Sir," I say, "if you'll just give me one moment. I have . . ." He's a purchasing agent, a seneschal of commerce: favor-granter, commission-builder, lord, oh. "X-Pando Pipe Joint Compound expands while . . . see . . . the test tube . . ." His head is anywhere else. It'd be easier to make eye contact with a mole. "Two thousand degrees Fahrenheit . . . 10,000 psi for all . . . it can withstand . . ." He will listen as children listen on their way out-of-doors: uh-huh, uh-huh, sure, okay. Slam. "Freon and ammonia . . . even dilute acid . . ." He moves. My voice is higher; I entreat. I sound like an innocent man being booked for murder in some foreign police station. "Use on broken . . . hard to reach . . . even where . . ." Glass is blown up/around me. We are in the same place, yet a trick of time-warping has altered our relationship: I speak from five minutes hence or ago. "Price . . . just let me show you . . . an introductory . . ." Once, about 15 years back, I all but drowned. Mid-lake, my calf muscles went into torrid cramp, sewn briskly stiff with hot wire. Children dug sand on shore, women were basted with Solarcaine, and, for them, I was the two legs of Breughel's *Icarus*. Gone; no, not gone: never there. Ahhhhmmmm, water sang a long sleep to me, going down, pearls that were my eyes. I remember it now: this is my tenth death today. I'm a salesman.

• • •

Salesmen get euphemized, too. Arrid is their friend. Also Aqua-Velva, Supphose, Head and Shoulders. They knock back Scope as an aperitif to the morning. Appearance mustn't distract from your product line. Ties are an emblem of their vassalage: the short choke chain by which they are held. And yet I find them intelligent; literate even. Not people who think Joyce Kilmer is a rest stop on the New Jersey Turnpike. They run to wait in outer offices and, waiting, often read. My own Mid-Atlantic sales rep, Marvin Mort, is a professional nature photographer of surpassing grace and wit. He can invest tree stumps with the titan stature that New Mexican mesas have. And, God, they earn their living. They have taught themselves a pragmatic schizophrenia: push enough to reach some arrogant purchasing agent; humility enough when he will grant them no more polite attention than I'd grant heat mirages on asphalt. Gelusil and Maalox and Rolaids; Valium and Tranxene. All together now: you can hear—it's felt underfoot, it's tidal—the buzzsaw gush of ulcers across Pennsauken. They return a commission on their stomach lining: more than 10 per cent.

The vice president of a solder firm laughs. He isn't happy. "What's going on here? I wanted to make a deal with this p.a. from a big Philadelphia jobber. You know what my sales rep told me? He told me, 'I never talk to that SOB, he played a dirty trick on me once.' Some rep, huh? A salesman is supposed to eat dirt. He should have a bowl of dirt for breakfast every day. What else is he good for?"

I, too, am a vice president. I've been on both sides of the desk. I've made men invisible. The story that follows is some kind of confession: absolve me if you can. One day an unspeakably maimed Vietnam veteran came to my office. The staircase is 15 high steps up. He was selling magazine subscriptions: they didn't interest me. Things like *Snowmobile Maintenance*. No, I told him, I won't buy. Let me give you a check instead. No, he insisted, I don't accept charity, just subscriptions. Yeah, I said, let's cut the bull: for me a subscription to *Snowmobile Maintenance* is charity. Take the check. He wouldn't. He had spent three years in a VA hospital and, I guess, he'd had enough of small deaths. He started, hung between crutches, to fill out an order form. It made me blind with anger. Perhaps there was fear as well: crumpled legs torment the self-assurance. I told him to leave. He left; he cursed me. It's 15 high steps down from my office. I heard every step. That's what the sales transaction can bring out in men. But, no: forget it. You can't absolve me.

There are no territories in the Soviet Union. Salesmen personify what is right/what is wrong with capitalism: initiative, energy; humiliation, stress. Yet, despite all those small deaths, many salesmen live very well indeed. A rep told me: "People think we're the lowest of the low. But they can't do without us." It's true. They carry the marketplace on their persons. Salesmen are heralds between one sovereign state of commerce and another. They should be honored, immune as Montjoy was before Henry V on St. Crispin's day. They seldom are. Yet, at large expense of spirit, they make human the blind, instinctive thing that free enterprise is.

"DEATH OF A SALESMAN"
(Obituary for Jerry Rubin, *Hartford Courant*,
30 November 1994: A18)

Jerry Rubin's death at 56 on Monday is a sobering milestone for "The Big Chill" generation. The long-haired founder of the radical Yippie movement of the 1960s, a member of the infamous Chicago Seven, seemed invincible when he sneered at the establishment and led the nation's youth in rebellion. His followers thought they, too, were invincible.

His death two weeks after being hit by a car in a jaywalking accident brings a rather ordinary end to a colorful life, and a reminder that a memorable season has passed.

The antics of the man who had the chutzpah to appear before the House Un-American Activities Committee dressed as Thomas Jefferson, the man who romped through demonstrations wearing an Uncle Sam hat and brandishing a toy M-16 rifle, the brazen jester who urged his peers to "kill your parents" and decried capitalism by sprinkling dollars onto the floor of the New York Stock Exchange made him a cult hero to some and a crazy or a traitor to others.

To the counterculture, Mr. Rubin later came to stand for hypocrisy when he committed the mortal sin—selling out. He announced in 1980 that he had grown up and would join the dreaded establishment and become a venture capitalist. His followers felt betrayed and his critics vindicated.

But Mr. Rubin was always a good salesman who knew how to market a message. Like many others of his generation, he realized that idealism alone doesn't put bread on the table.

Few adults don't regret some excesses of their youth. But Mr. Rubin's generation considered itself revolutionary. Jerry Rubin once wanted to change the world. The world did change, indeed. And so did Mr. Rubin.

STUDY QUESTIONS

1. What is the chief character trait that the salesman must possess, according to Keith Mano? Does he make this trait look attractive?

2. Why does Mano tell the story of the magazine salesman? Does it have a moral? What is your response to Mano as a character in this story? To the salesman?

3. What does Mano mean to convey in the closing sentence of his article? Do you agree with him about the relationship between free enterprise and the salesman?

4. What similarities does Jeff Faux see between the situation of Willy Loman in the 1940s and the unemployed people of the 1980s?

5. What are the causes that Faux suggests for the widespread unemployment of the middle class in the 1980s?

6. Where did Faux think the middle class would lay the blame for its predicament in the eighties? How did he see them as differing from Willy Loman? Do you agree with him?

7. Do you see a relationship between Jerry Rubin's death and Willy Loman's? Why does the writer of Rubin's obituary tie them together? Do you think this is appropriate?

TOPICS FOR WRITTEN OR ORAL EXPLORATION

1. The *Newsweek* article introduces two examples of the "old-style" salesman, the umbrella salesman and Louis Schneider—an unsuccessful salesman and a successful one. Analyze the characteristics the writer associates with success and failure in this profession. What does he imply is necessary to succeed in the old-time selling world of Willy Loman? How does this relate to what Miller implies in *Death of a Salesman*?

2. Either in a group or on your own, analyze the "new image" that the *Newsweek* article was suggesting for the salesman. What kinds of language and imagery are used? What is the purpose of associating salesmanship with the space program? What is the purpose of this image campaign? Then write an essay comparing the changing image with the real changes that were taking place in the profession. How, according to the article, would the job of the salesman really change, and how would it affect his life? Does this live up to the new image?

3. The *Newsweek* article emphasizes the large amount of turnover in the selling profession and the negative attitude toward it among

young people who were choosing their careers in the early 1960s. Write an essay in which you describe the attitude toward selling in your own generation, and offer explanations for it. Has *Death of a Salesman* influenced your own view of the selling profession?

4. David Hayes used as the theme of his motivational film for salesmen "the ability of men to surpass themselves," a theme that he and Vince Lombardi saw as directly opposing Miller's message in *Death of a Salesman*. Individually or as a group, discuss the elements in Miller's portrayal of the salesman's life that would be most discouraging to contemporary sales people. Then write a dialogue between a football coach and a young sales person that counters the young person's discouragement.

5. Compare Willy's description of his New England trip in the first day-dream scene to Edward Spar's description of his trip. Pay particular attention to the language that is used and the details Willy mentions to the boys when he talks about his trip. Write an essay comparing Willy's view of the road experience with Spar's. Which one finds the sales profession more interesting and rewarding? Which one places more value on the salesman?

6. Keith Mano's article opens with a fantasy of what it would be like to be a salesman trying to make a sale to a reluctant buyer. Write a fantasy of your own in which you imagine yourself as Willy Loman trying to make a sale to a reluctant buyer. First describe the situation, the prospective buyer, and the product being sold. Be as imaginative as you can in suggesting to the reader just what the experience is like.

7. Write an essay in which you compare and contrast Keith Mano's defense of the salesman in his final paragraph to Charley's speech about Willy in the Requiem scene of *Death of a Salesman*. What qualities does each of them ask us to admire? What do they ask us to excuse? What value to society do they see in the salesman? Which of them do you find to be more effective?

8. Jeff Faux contrasts Willy Loman's tendency to blame himself for his failure with the possibility of becoming "politicized," of taking political action to change the system he feels is victimizing the middle class. Write an essay explaining your agreement or disagreement with his statement that "the tendency to internalize failure, to accept the market's decision as the true assessment of your worth, is always strong in America. It is reinforced by a culture that glorifies material success."

9. Both Keith Mano and Jeff Faux suggest that contemporary sales peo-

ple have to contend with pretty much the same economic problems and social attitudes that Willy Loman did, despite the obvious impact of Miller's play. Write an essay in which you explain the impact of the play on your own view of sales people and the American business world. Do you think Arthur Miller's play can really affect the way these things are perceived?

10. Write an obituary for Willy Loman in which you make clear the strengths and weaknesses of his character and the significance of his life.

SUGGESTED READINGS

The following list includes articles referred to in the introductory material in this chapter as well as items that shed further light on *Death of a Salesman*'s cultural life.

Byrne, John A. "Motivating Willy Loman." *Forbes* 133 (30 January 1984): 91.

Carroll, Luke P. "Birth of a Legend: First Year of 'Salesman.' " *New York Tribune*, 5 February 1950, section 5: 1.

Dash, Thomas R. " 'Life' of a Salesman." *Women's Wear Daily*, 24 February 1949: 51.

Kopald, Meredith. "Arthur Miller Wins a Peace Prize: Teaching, Literature, and Therapy." *English Journal* 81 (March 1992): 57–60.

Reiser, Carl. "The Salesman Isn't Dead, He's Different." *Fortune* 66 (November 1962): 124–27.

Schaars, Mary Jo, and Norma Greco. "Arthur Miller, Willy Loman, and Jason: Responses to Meredith Kopald." *English Journal* 81 (March 1992): 61–62.

Shockley, John S. "*Death of a Salesman* and American Leadership: Life Imitates Art." *Journal of American Culture* 17 (Summer 1994): 49–56.

Zorn, Theodore. "Willy Loman's Lesson: Teaching Identity Management with *Death of a Salesman*." *Communication Education* 40 (April 1991): 219–24.

Index

ABOUT THE AUTHORS

BRENDA MURPHY is Professor of English at the University of Connecticut and the author of *Miller: Death of a Salesman* (1995), *Tennessee Williams and Elia Kazan: A Collaboration in the Theatre* (1992), *A Realist in the American Theatre: Selected Drama Criticism of William Dean Howells* (1992), *American Realism and American Drama, 1880–1940* (1987), and, forthcoming, *Cambridge Companion to American Women Playwrights* and *Congressional Theatre: Dramatizing McCarthyism on Stage, Film, and Television*.

SUSAN C. W. ABBOTSON has taught English for fifteen years, first in secondary school and more recently at the University of Connecticut. She currently teaches in the Freshman Studies department at Johnson and Wales University. A recent Ph.D., she wrote her dissertation on Arthur Miller and August Wilson. She is also author of the Drama section in *Resources for Teaching: Literature and Its Writers* (1997) and of a number of entries in the forthcoming *Cambridge Guide for Children's Books*. She has published essays in *Charles Lamb Bulletin, English Studies, South Atlantic Review, Journal of American Drama and Theater*, and *Modern Drama*.

The Greenwood Press "Literature in Context" Series
Student Casebooks to Issues, Sources, and Historical Documents